GLOBAL BUSINESS STRATEGY

Asian Perspective

Hwy-Chang Moon
Seoul National University, Korea

World Scientific

NEW JERSEY • LONDON • SINGAPORE • BEIJING • SHANGHAI • HONG KONG • TAIPEI • CHENNAI

Published by

World Scientific Publishing Co. Pte. Ltd.
5 Toh Tuck Link, Singapore 596224
USA office: 27 Warren Street, Suite 401-402, Hackensack, NJ 07601
UK office: 57 Shelton Street, Covent Garden, London WC2H 9HE

Library of Congress Cataloging-in-Publication Data
Mun, Hwi-ch'ang.
Global business strategy : Asian perspective / by Hwy-Chang Moon.
p. cm.
Includes bibliographical references and index.
ISBN-13: 978-9814273190 (hardcover)
ISBN-10: 9814273198 (hardcover)
1. International business enterprises--Asia. 2. International business enterprises--Management. 3. Business planning--Asia. I. Title.
HD62.4.M846 2009
658.4'012--dc22
2009034160

British Library Cataloguing-in-Publication Data
A catalogue record for this book is available from the British Library.

Typeset by Stallion Press
Email: enquiries@stallionpress.com

Printed in Singapore.

Preface

This book discusses how a firm can formulate a successful global business strategy by incorporating the Asian perspective. There are substantial differences between Western and Asian businesses that multinational corporations cannot ignore. Without a proper understanding of Asian business practices and environments, even the most successful multinationals, such as Wal-Mart, could fail in the Asian market. However, this does not mean that the differences outweigh the similarities. Many of the key success formulas may work equally well in both sides of the world. The point here is that either overemphasizing or underestimating the differences could lead to undesirable outcomes. Today, a firm's competitiveness is often determined more by its disadvantages, such as lack of understanding of a new market, than by its advantages. Thus, this book aims to bridge the Western and Asian business practices, rather than to overemphasize the unique features of Asian business practices.

For this purpose, each chapter is organized into three sections. The first section explains strategy models developed by eminent scholars. These are fundamentals that all strategists, whether practitioners or scholars, should be familiar with. The second section presents analyses, criticisms, modifications and extensions of these models in order to better explain various cases in the real world, particularly in Asia. The final section shows how the strategy models, both original and extended, described in the first two sections can be applied to explain strategies in Asian cases, including non-Asian firms in Asia and Asian firms in non-Asian countries.

This book is written from a practical viewpoint and incorporates many important strategy models that practitioners will find useful in formulating effective strategies. People working outside the pure strategy field will also find these strategy tools useful if they understand that the core value of strategy is not in the creation of new ideas, but in the advancement of analytical skills. For the purpose of academic curriculum, this book is suitable for Business Strategy and International Business courses, with a special focus on Asia, at both the graduate and undergraduate levels.

This book could not have been completed within a reasonable time frame without the high talent and dedication of my assistants. Special thanks go to Jin Uk Kim, who summarized articles and incorporated my analyses while attending my lectures. He has made extraordinary contributions to this project from start to finish. Special thanks also go to Lorna Geddis, who conducted extensive research in collecting appropriate case studies. In addition, I would like to thank Jimmyn Parc, Wenyen Yin, Ted Moon, Inhyoung Lee and Euijae Kim for their insights and critiques. I am also grateful to the brilliant minds who attended my Global Business Strategy class. Their stimulating discussions and ideas, many of which have been incorporated into this book, were a constant source of inspiration. Finally, I would like to thank World Scientific Publishing Co. for their valuable help in publishing this book.

Hwy-Chang Moon
Seoul National University

Contents

CHAPTER 1

The Basics of Strategy

Chapter Guideline

Although many business strategy books deal with Michael Porter's strategy models, few successfully present Porter's key points and their true implications in an easily digestible manner. This chapter serves to this end. We will first explain the different units of strategy analysis, followed by Porter's strategy models for their appropriate levels of analyses. These strategy models will then be applied to Asian cases in order to demonstrate how they function in different business environments.

1.1 Competitiveness of Product, Firm, Industry and Nation[1]

Competitiveness is often confused with productivity. While productivity refers to the internal capability of an organization, competitiveness refers to the relative position of an organization against its competitors. These two important concepts are often confused and used interchangeably. In his seminal work, *The Competitive Advantage of Nations*, Porter (1990, p. 6) clearly states that the only meaningful concept of competitiveness at the national level is productivity.

For example, a firm may enhance its competitiveness by simply changing its strategies (e.g., new marketing strategy), while maintaining the same level of productivity. Likewise, a nation can enhance its

[1] This section is extended from Moon and Peery (1995).

competitiveness by changing national policies (e.g., currency devaluation, protectionism), without increasing its domestic productivity. Therefore, we need to distinguish competitiveness from productivity and highlight the relevant strategies at various levels of analyses. Some important strategy models can then be integrated and suggested for further development.

Competitiveness of a Product

A product is competitive if it has a lower price and/or superior differentiation than those of comparable products. Porter's generic strategies are thus relevant to the competitiveness of a product, but not always to that of a firm. This is why Porter's generic strategies are criticized when they are applied to a firm-level analysis. For example, critics state that the generic model focuses only on the last few hundred yards of what may be a skill-building marathon (Hamel 1991).

Another criticism is that the generic strategies of low cost and differentiation are useful for categorizing competitive strategies, but in themselves do not suggest where costs should be cut or how products should be differentiated (Kogut 1985). In addition, as the generic strategies model was primarily designed to explain domestic business strategies, it does not adequately describe the complexity of global business strategies. This is mainly because few firms pursue solely a cost or differentiation strategy in global competition; in fact, major competitors frequently adopt both cost and differentiation strategies (Moon 1993).

Competitiveness of a Firm

Another criticism regarding Porter's generic strategies is that it neglects the core competence in formulating firm-level strategies (Prahalad and Hamel 1990). The most important perspective in explaining the competitiveness of a firm is the resource-based view of the firm. This theory views the firm as a bundle of resources and capabilities that strategically focuses on (a) factor market imperfections,

(b) the heterogeneity of firms, (c) varying degrees of specialization, and (d) the limited transferability of corporate resources. According to this view, the competitiveness of a firm depends on the ability to identify and deploy its core competence. However, this concept is not entirely new as core competence, or unique resource, is closely related to ownership advantage and the capability to deploy the advantage, which is explained extensively by the internalization theory discussed in the foreign direct investment literature. Thus, theories related to foreign direct investment can provide important insights into firm-level global competitiveness that are not available in other approaches.

When going abroad, a firm has to choose between standardization and customization. In order to analyze these two international strategies, the integration-responsiveness (I-R) framework should be used. The two imperatives of this framework are pressures for global integration on the production side and pressures for local responsiveness on the marketing side. In reality, many businesses find it necessary to pursue multifocal strategies or transnational solutions, responding simultaneously to pressures for global integration and local responsiveness.

Competitiveness of an Industry

Most of the existing theories in strategic management are related to the competitiveness of a product or firm. On the other hand, Porter (1990, p. 18) raises an important question regarding the international competitiveness of a nation's industry by asking why firms based in particular nations achieve international success in distinct segments and industries. He defines international success of a nation's industry as "possessing advantage relative to the best worldwide competitors" (Porter 1990, p. 25). Porter then introduces the diamond model, an analytical model composed of four determinants — factor conditions, demand conditions, related and supporting industries, and business context. These four determinants are very similar to, yet more refined than, the variables included in his five-forces industry model (Porter 1980, 1985, 1990).

Despite the far-reaching explanatory power of Porter's diamond model, it is still quite limited when applied to global business. The original single-diamond model has thus been extended to the double-diamond model and other models to explain the multidimensional nature of global businesses.[2]

Competitiveness of a Nation

A nation's competitiveness is different from a firm's competitiveness. For example, competition between the USA and Japan is not like the zero-sum game between Coca-Cola and Pepsi. If you buy a can of Coke, it is Pepsi's loss; but the USA and Japan can both be winners through competition and cooperation, using different but often complementary sources of comparative advantages. However, when nations endowed with similar comparative advantages compete in a particular industry, the competition becomes largely a zero-sum situation.[3] Modeling competitiveness at the national level is thus not an easy task.

Popular models for national competitiveness are international trade theories and foreign exchange theories. More recent theories include the diamond model and its extended models. On the other hand, some scholars argue that if we hope to revitalize the competitive performance of a nation's economy, we must invest in people, not in nationally defined corporations. In the 21st century, the education and skills of the workforce may be the dominant competitive weapon.[4]

Where to Start?

We have briefly reviewed competitiveness at different levels of analyses and the relevant strategy models for each level. The conceptual clarity

---

[2] See Rugman and D'Cruz (1993); Moon, Rugman and Verbeke (1995, 1998); Cho (1994); Cho and Moon (2000); and Cho, Moon and Kim (2008, 2009) for the evolution of the diamond model.

[3] There is an interesting debate on this by Krugman, Prestowitz and Thurow. See Cho and Moon (2000).

[4] For example, see Reich (1990) and Thurow (1992).

will help portray the vivid institutional reality. Theories for each level are somewhat overlapping and sometimes misused. Among the four different levels of analyses, firm-level competitiveness is probably the most important unit in understanding our globalized economies because it is not nations, but firms, that compete in the real world. For the purpose of analyzing industry or product competitiveness, the basis of understanding must be at the firm level. We will thus start with the firm's competitive strategy and, when necessary, appropriately incorporate strategy models at other levels.

1.2 Porter's Competitive Strategy

Michael Porter is well known as the guru of strategic management, so we will first review Porter's key points (1980, 1985). We will then discuss some issues associated with Porter's model and suggest extensions in the later chapters.

Porter raises two central questions underlying competitive strategy. First is the attractiveness of industries for long-term profitability and the factors that determine it. Not all industries offer equal opportunities for success and it is important to choose an attractive industry. Second are the determinants of relative competitive positions within an industry. In most industries, some firms are much more profitable than others, regardless of what the average profitability of the industry may be. A firm can improve or erode its position within an industry through its choice of strategy.

The First Question: Industry Attractiveness (Five-Forces Model)

According to Porter, competition and profitability are driven by industry structure, not by whether an industry is emerging or mature, high- or low-tech, regulated or unregulated. The key determinant of industry profitability is its structure. Some industries such as postage meters and grain trading are extremely profitable, while some high-technology industries such as personal computers and cable television are not profitable for many participants.

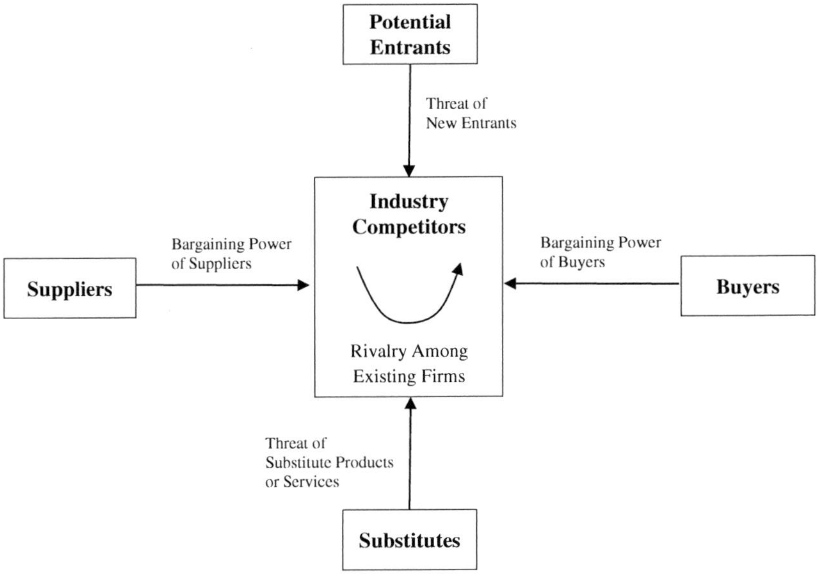

Fig. 1. The five competitive forces that determine industry profitability.[5]

In any industry, whether it is domestic or international or whether it produces a product or a service, the rules of competition are embodied in five competitive forces: the entry of new competitors, the threat of substitutes, the bargaining power of buyers, the bargaining power of suppliers, and the rivalry among existing competitors (see Fig. 1).

The collective strength of these five competitive forces determines the ability of firms in an industry to earn, on average, rates of return on investment in excess of the cost of capital. The strength of the five forces varies from industry to industry and can change as an industry evolves. Here, Porter forwards an important argument that a firm is not a prisoner of its industry's structure. Firms, through their strategic choices, are capable of influencing the five forces to their advantage. If a firm can shape the industry structure, it can fundamentally change an industry's attractiveness for better or worse.

[5] Porter (1980), p. 4.

Many successful strategies have shifted the rules of competition in this way. Contrary to the critics' assertions, Porter's conception of firm strategy is not that of a passive recipient of immutable industry forces, but a proactive entity which has the power to change the very business environment in which it operates.

In a recent update, Porter (2008) notes that understanding the five forces is important not only for individual firms, but also for investors. The five forces can be a powerful tool for investors to distinguish between structural changes and short-term "bubbles". Commonly used investment decision tools such as financial projections and trend extrapolations can be misleading, as they tend to overemphasize transient factors and industry profitability. From a macro perspective, this leads to misallocation of resources to unprofitable segments and unnecessary volatility. If managers and investors both focus on industry structure, the capital market would not exhibit such inefficiencies that we commonly witness.

The Second Question: Firm Competitiveness (Generic Strategies)

The second question in competitive strategy deals with a firm's relative position within its industry. There are two basic types of competitive advantage a firm can possess: cost advantage or differentiation advantage. Cost and differentiation advantages in turn stem from industry structure. They result from a firm's ability to cope with the five forces better than its rivals. Here, again, Porter argues that industry structure and firm strategy are not insulated, but are interconnected with each other.

The two basic types of competitive advantage combined with the scope of activities lead to three generic strategies for achieving above-average performance in an industry: cost leadership, differentiation, and focus. This is explained in Porter's early work (Porter 1980; Fig. 2) and later he divides the focus strategy further into two variants (Porter 1985; Fig. 3). In *cost focus*, a firm seeks a cost advantage; while in *differentiation focus*, a firm seeks differentiation in its target segment.

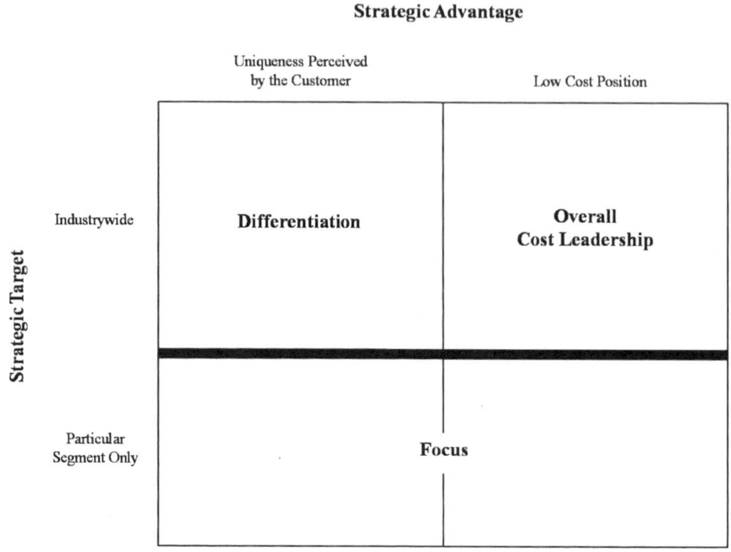

Fig. 2. Three generic strategies.[6]

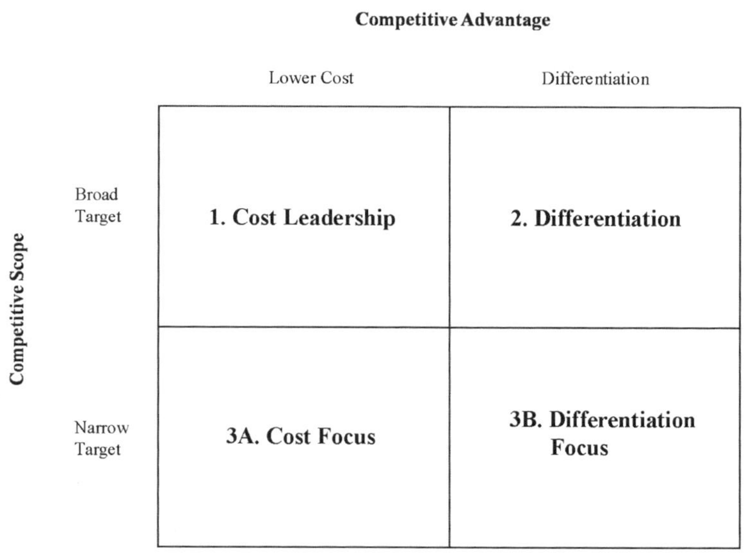

Fig. 3. Four generic strategies.[7]

[6] *Ibid.*, p. 39.

[7] Porter (1985), p. 12.

Stuck-in-the-Middle

Each generic strategy takes a fundamentally different approach to creating, sustaining and combining a firm's competitive advantage and deciding the scope of its strategic target. Usually, a firm must make a choice among the four strategies, or it will be "stuck-in-the-middle" which leads to a competitive disadvantage on all fronts. In most industries, quite a few competitors are stuck-in-the-middle. These firms will earn attractive profits only if the structure of its industry is highly favorable, or if the firms' competitors are also stuck-in-the-middle.

Stuck-in-the-middle is a very controversial concept that many scholars criticize.[8] However, Porter is more cautious than his critics may think. Porter asserts that a cost leader cannot ignore the basis of differentiation. If its product is not perceived as comparable or acceptable by buyers, a cost leader will be forced to discount prices well below competitors' to gain sales. Therefore, a cost leader must achieve parity or proximity in the basis of differentiation relative to its competitors to be an above-average performer, even though it relies on cost leadership for its competitive advantage. Similarly, a differentiator thus aims at cost *parity* or *proximity* relative to its competitors, by reducing cost in all areas that do not affect differentiation.

The Real Value of Porter's Generic Strategies

Porter's critics say that his generic strategies focus too much on competition and therefore his strategic vision is too narrow.[9] However, in many cases, this criticism is unfounded because Porter actually broadens the strategic options since generic strategies provide alternate routes to superior performance. While other strategic planning concepts have been narrowly based on only one route to competitive advantage (most notably, cost), generic strategies allow more leeway in selecting the appropriate generic strategy which allows firms to survive and prosper without being locked in a constant state of competition with each other.

---

[8] Critics of stuck-in-the-middle will be analyzed further in Chap. 5.

[9] Various critics of Porter will be explored extensively throughout later chapters.

Evolution of Generic Strategies

The generic strategies remain useful to characterize strategic positions at the simplest and broadest level. In his later work, Porter (1996) introduces the three basics of positioning — varieties, needs and access — in order to enhance the understanding of generic strategies to a greater level of specificity (see Fig. 4). For example, according to Porter, Ikea and Southwest are both focused on cost, but Ikea's focus is based on all the home furnishing *needs* of its target customer group (e.g., a price-sensitive young family) while Southwest's is based on offering a particular service *variety*. This is an interesting extension to the original generic strategy, but there is room for debate and further development. This will be further discussed in a later chapter.

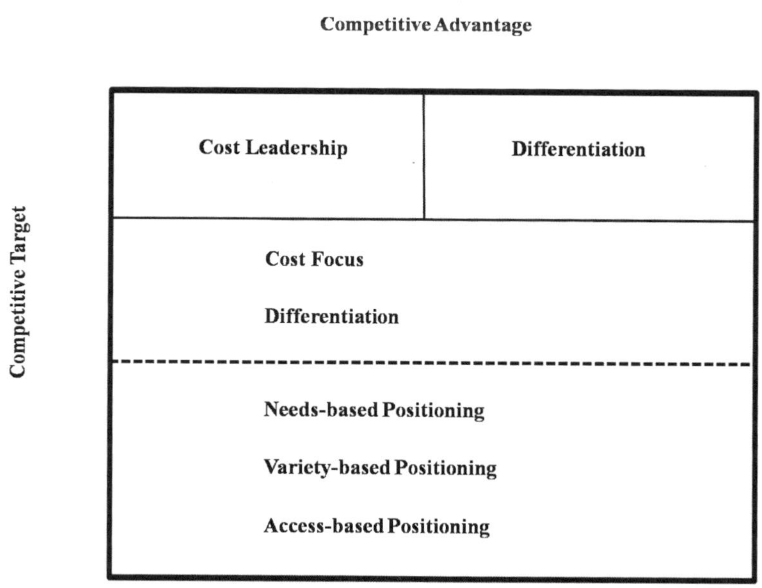

Fig. 4. Four plus three generic strategies.[10]

[10] This figure is a modified version of Porter (1996).

1.3 The Value Chain and Competitive Advantage

A firm's competitive advantage stems from the many discrete activities of designing, producing, marketing, delivering and supporting its product. Each of these activities can contribute to a firm's relative cost position or be the basis of differentiation. Competitive advantage (Porter 1985) is about how a firm actually puts the generic strategies (Porter 1980) into practice. How does a firm gain a sustainable cost advantage? How can it differentiate itself from competitors? Competitive advantage grows fundamentally out of the value a firm is able to create for its buyers. So, Porter introduces a very useful tool — the value chain — to disaggregate buyers, suppliers and a firm into the discrete but interrelated activities from which value stems. Potential sources of competitive advantage are everywhere in a firm. Every department, facility, branch office and other organizational units have a role that must be defined and understood.

The Generic Value Chain

The value chain displays total value, and consists of *value activities* and *margin*. Value activities are the physically and technologically distinct activities of a firm. Margin is the difference between total value and the collective cost of performing the value activities. Value activities can be divided into two broad types: *primary* activities and *support* activities. Primary activities are those involved in the physical creation of the product, its sales, and its transfer to the buyer as well as after-sales assistance. In any firm, primary activities can be divided into the five generic categories shown in Fig. 5. Support activities assist the primary activities by providing purchased inputs, technology, human resources and firm-wide functions. The dotted lines in Fig. 5 reflect the fact that procurement, technology development and human resource management can be associated with specific primary activities as well as support the entire chain. Firm infrastructure is not associated with a particular primary activity, but supports the entire chain.

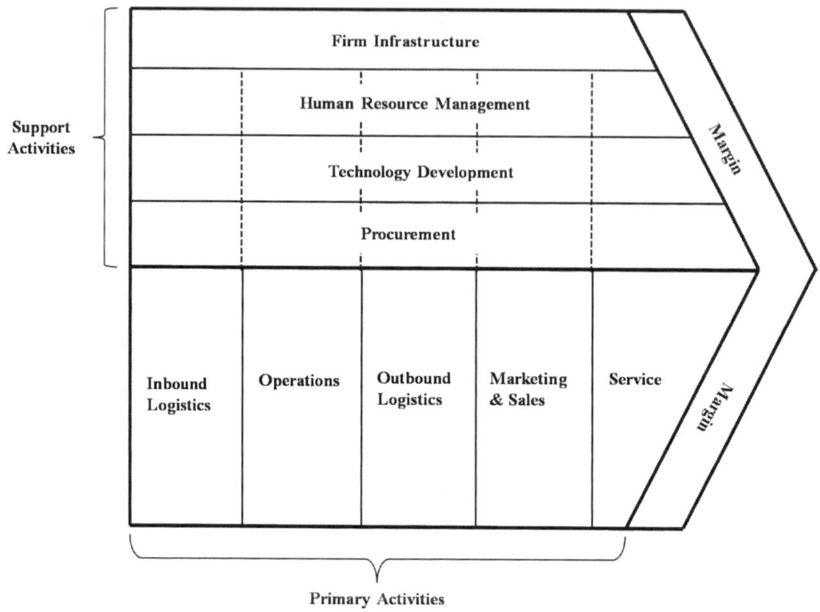

Fig. 5. The generic value chain.[11]

Primary Activities: Five Generic Categories

- *Inbound Logistics* — Activities associated with receiving, storing and disseminating inputs to the product, such as material handling, inventory controlling, vehicle scheduling and returns to suppliers.
- *Operations* — Activities associated with transforming inputs into the final product form, such as machining, packaging, assembly, equipment maintenance, testing, printing and facility operations.
- *Outbound Logistics* — Activities associated with collecting, storing and distributing the product to buyers, such as finished goods warehousing, order processing and scheduling.
- *Marketing and Sales* — Activities associated with providing a means by which buyers can purchase the product, such as

[11] Porter (1985), p. 37.

advertisement, promotion, sales force, channel selection, channel relations and pricing.

- *Service* — Activities associated with providing service to enhance or maintain the value of the product, such as installation, repair, training, parts supply and product adjustment.

The relative importance of each category depends on the industry. For a distributor, inbound and outbound logistics are the most critical. For a service firm such as a restaurant or retailer, outbound logistics may be largely nonexistent and operations is the vital category. For a bank, marketing and sales are critical to competitive advantage. For a high-speed copier manufacturer, service represents a key source of competitive advantage. In any firm, all five categories play some role in its competitive advantage.

Support Activities: Four Generic Categories

- *Procurement* — This is the *function* of purchased inputs used in the firm's value chain, not the purchased inputs themselves. Purchased inputs include raw materials, supplies, and other consumable items as well as assets such as machinery, laboratory equipment, office equipment and buildings. Improved purchasing practices can strongly affect the cost and quality of purchased inputs, and other activities associated with receiving and using the inputs and interacting with suppliers.
- *Technology Development* — This refers to how every value activity embodies technology, be it know-how, procedures or the technology embodied in the process equipment. Porter terms this category of activities as "technology development" instead of "research and development" (R&D) because R&D has too narrow a connotation to most managers. Technology development does not solely apply to technologies directly linked to the end product. It also takes many other forms, from basic research and product design to media research, process equipment design and servicing procedures.

- *Human Resource Management* — A firm performs myriads of activities related to recruiting, hiring, training, developing and compensating all types of personnel. Human resource management supports both primary and support activities (e.g., the hiring of engineers) and the entire value chain (e.g., labor negotiations). This management affects competitive advantage in any firm, through its role in determining the skills and motivation of employees and the cost of hiring and training.
- *Firm Infrastructure* — This refers to activities including general management, planning, finance, accounting, legal affairs, government affairs and quality management. Unlike other support activities, infrastructure usually supports the entire chain and not individual activities. In diversified firms, infrastructure activities are typically split between the business unit and corporate levels (e.g., financing is often done at the corporate level while quality management is done at the business unit level). However, many infrastructure activities occur at both the business unit and corporate levels.

Subdividing the Value Chain

Everything a firm does should be captured in a primary or support activity. Therefore, each generic category of the value chain can be further divided into discrete activities, as illustrated for one generic category in Fig. 6. The appropriate degree of disaggregation depends on the economics of the activities and the purposes for which the value chain is being analyzed. The basic principle is that activities that (a) have different economics, (b) have a high potential impact of differentiation, or (c) represent a significant or growing proportion of cost should be separated.

Linkages within the Value Chain

Although value activities are the building blocks of competitive advantage, the value chain is not a collection of independent activities, but a system of interdependent activities. Value activities are related through linkages within the value chain. Linkages are relationships

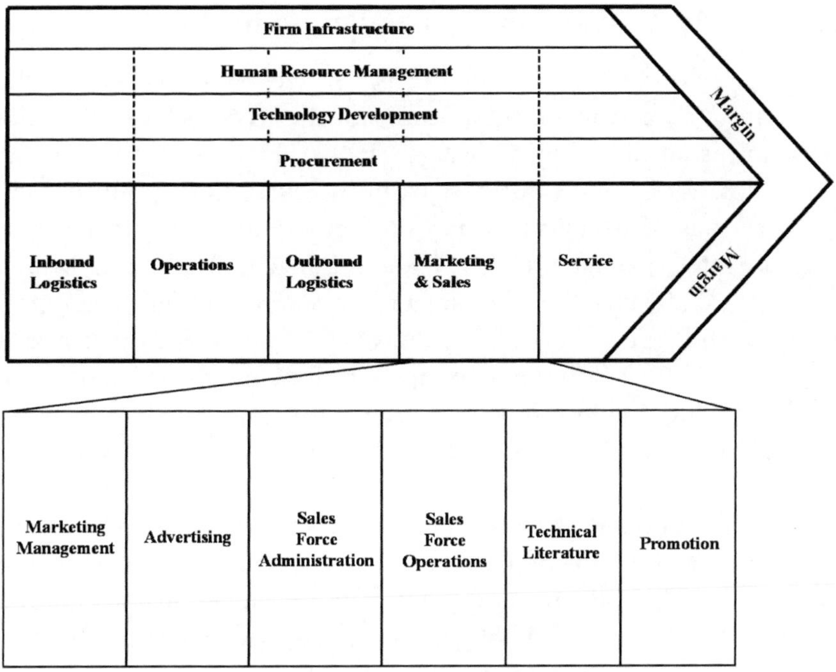

Fig. 6. Subdividing a generic value chain.[12]

between the performance of one value activity and that of another. Linkages can lead to competitive advantage in two ways: optimization and coordination. Examples of optimization include a more costly product design, more stringent materials specifications and greater in-process inspection, which may reduce service costs. A firm must optimize such linkages in order to achieve a competitive advantage. Linkages may also reflect the need to coordinate activities. The ability to coordinate linkages often reduces cost or enhances differentiation. Better coordination, for example, can reduce inventory throughout the firm. Linkages imply that a firm's cost or differentiation is not merely the result of efforts to reduce costs or improve performance in each value activity individually. Much of the achievement is the result of linkages.

[12] *Ibid.*, p. 46.

Case Study 1: Wal-Mart's Challenge in Asia[13]

"The secret of successful retailing is to give your customers what they want," Sam Walton, the founder of the world's largest retailer, wrote in his autobiography (Walton 1992). He also noted that one must think about one's business from the customer's point of view. Wal-Mart has continued to thrive in many countries outside of the United States, particularly in Mexico, Canada, Brazil and Britain. However, Wal-Mart failed in Japan, Korea and India because the company did not understand its Asian customers and, just like its French rival, Carrefour, ended up withdrawing from these countries. Wal-Mart's failure in these three countries provides important lessons for Western multinationals that aspire to garner success in these markets.

On the contrary, British retailer Tesco has achieved remarkable success in the Korean market. The British retail giant owns 89% of Samsung Tesco, but has relied heavily on local managers from Samsung. Tesco reported that its overseas growth has been driven by Asia, where profits grew by 30% in 2006. Consequently, this was the same year it became the second-largest retailer in South Korea, making South Korea one of Tesco's biggest overseas success stories (Center for Management Research 2006). If one overseas retailer prospered in Korea, why couldn't Wal-Mart do the same? What went wrong with Wal-Mart? The following illustrate the reasons behind Wal-Mart's failure in Korea, Japan and India:

- *Cheap Real Estate* — Large stores, vast parking lots and huge distribution centers have been an integral part of Wal-Mart's success. So, it is understandable how Wal-Mart could easily expand to places with cheap real estate (Latin America), but have a hard time expanding to places where real estate is expensive (South Korea and Japan).

[13] Information for this case study is abstracted from *The New York Times* (2006a, 2006b), the Wal-Mart website (www.walmart.com) and *The Economist* (2008a).

- *Price* — Wal-Mart's focus has always been on low prices. It provides merchandise in bulk for prices below its competitors'. However, Koreans prefer high quality over price and often equate low price with low quality. Wal-Mart focused on maintaining low prices and selling in bulk, while its local competitors, E-Mart and Lotte Mart, focused on selling the product's quality by building eye-catching displays and hiring employees who hawked their goods with megaphones.
- *Frequent Visits* — Wal-Mart is an ideal store for consumers to visit once a week. Most American consumers visit Wal-Mart once a week and buy in bulk because American shoppers rarely shop without their automobiles. However, in Japan, most consumers visit stores almost every day, by bicycle, and do not purchase in bulk. With such a stark difference in consumer behavior between Japanese and American consumers, Wal-Mart was unable to succeed in Japan.
- *Government Protection* — Wal-Mart was unsuccessful in entering India, where the government is adamant about protecting the country's retail sector. Over 90% of Indian retailers are very small, traditional and unorganized, and there was fear that Wal-Mart could eventually undermine the small retailers dominating the Indian market.

Wal-Mart's experience in India implies that the company should have planned to buy more local goods, which could help Indian farmers and small manufacturers. More importantly, Wal-Mart should have changed its cost leadership strategy when entering certain Asian countries. The company's "Everyday Low Price" approach backfired in Korea and Japan, where consumers tend to equate low prices with low quality. The one-size-fits-all approach should have been changed from standardization to localization and from a cost to a differentiation strategy.

Although Wal-Mart is successful in the United States, the same competitive advantage may not translate into success in foreign markets. Asian consumers shop at large retailers, not for cheap

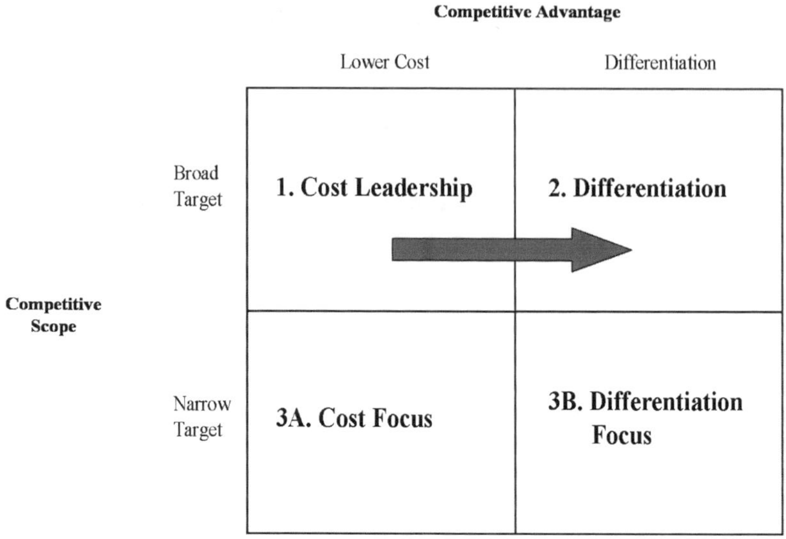

Fig. 7. Wal-Mart's international strategy.

and bulky items, but for the convenience of a variety of smaller-sized quality products. Using the generic strategies model, Wal-Mart's cost leadership strategy in the United States should have been changed to a differentiation strategy in Asia. The optimal strategic prescriptions are outlined in Fig. 7.

Case Study 2: *Sogo Shosha*'s Changing Competence[14]

A *sogo shosha* is a form of industrial organization and a kind of vertically integrated trading company that originated from Japan. The term *sogo shosha* is Japanese for "general trading company", but is often confused with *zaibatzu* or *keiretsu*. The *zaibatsu* commonly consists of a primary enterprise — usually a *sogo shosha* — surrounded by subsidiaries engaged in a wide range of operations such as

[14] Information for this case study is abstracted from the Mitsubishi Corporation website (www.mitsubishicorp.com), Mitsubishi's INNOVATION 2007 management plan (www.mitsubishicorp.com) and others.

banking, insurance, shipping, mining, real estate, food processing and manufacturing.

The seven largest *sogo shosha* in Japan are Mitsubishi Corporation, Mitsui & Co., Itochu, Sumitomo Corporation, Marubeni, Toyota Tsusho and Sojitz. These *sogo shosha* supply large volumes of raw materials and distribute goods from large manufacturers to smaller distributors and to numerous retailers. What make them unique are their size, scope, information-gathering capabilities as well as their functional diversity. They are the Japanese traders that operate at the center of Japan's global economic foray, and serve as intermediaries for half of their country's exports and two-thirds of their country's imports.

Other nations have tried to emulate this system to promote a similar kind of economic success. South Korea's large conglomerates (e.g., LG, Samsung and Hyundai) all have their version of the *sogo shosha* (*jonghap sangsa* in Korean), while Chinese firms have started to implement the *sogo shosha*-type companies with assistance from Japanese firms. The United States tried to replicate the *sogo shosha* in the early 1980s with the signing of the Export Trading Company Act of 1982. Such export companies, however, never developed as the American tendency to reject government-sponsored programs and the lack of publicity derailed this effort.

In the 1990s and 2000s, the *sogo shosha* found itself at a crossroads, adapting to new market conditions and opportunities. These opportunities included new business fields of high technology, such as biotechnology, computer technology, information technology and telecommunications. The *sogo shosha* also had to prepare for the increasing globalization of the world. There are both new opportunities as well as threats with this new environment.

Facing these new challenges, the *sogo shosha* is now changing its business models as follows:

- The activities of *sogo shosha* encompass not just trading, but also investments and other activities. The essence of *sogo shosha* is to provide any needed service to propel the businesses forward.

- The *sogo shosha* is engaged in business with customers around the world in virtually every industry, including energy, metals, machinery, chemicals, food and general merchandise.
- The *sogo shosha* actively studies market trends and takes initiatives to develop new business. Finding a new growing industry and industry segments is critically important for *sogo shosha*'s sustainable growth.
- The uniqueness of *sogo shosha* is the ability to ***link and coordinate*** functions such as logistics, financing and marketing. The *sogo shosha* thus shares risk with business partners and adds value to the business.

Therefore, the real value or core competence of *sogo shosha* is to find a problem or ***imbalance*** within the value chain and fix it. The *sogo shosha* can thus make the value chain more efficient and enhance its productivity. As shown in Fig. 8, this will contribute to the enrichment of society as well as its business partners in the linking activities of the value chain. As the industry structure becomes more sophisticated and as new industries emerge, *sogo shosha*'s role and scope of business will become greater. When the *sogo shosha* leverages its organizational strengths and networks of its affiliated companies, its power and thus potential benefits to its business partners will become even greater, as depicted in Fig. 9. Leveraging these organizational strengths and linking them to other activities of the industry value chain are unique advantages of *sogo shosha* that are clearly differentiated from other organizations.

Case Study 3: Playing into Asia[15]

In a recent article titled "Asian invasion," *The Economist* (2008b) reported that "for millions of East Asians, online gaming is not so

[15] Information for this case study is abstracted from *The Economist* (2008b), *The New York Times* (2006c), Runckel (2005) and the Blizzard Entertainment website (www.blizzard.com).

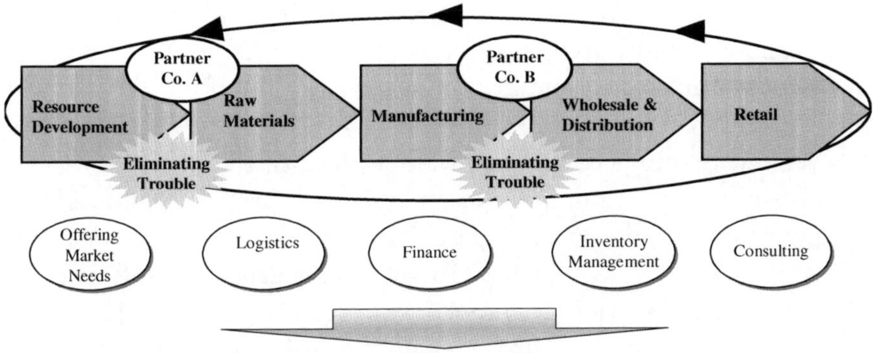

- Find any imbalances in the value chain, then overcome the obstacles to minimize the transactions cost.
- Optimize the entire value chain through win-win strategy with partners.

Fig. 8. Industry value chain and the *sogo shosha*.

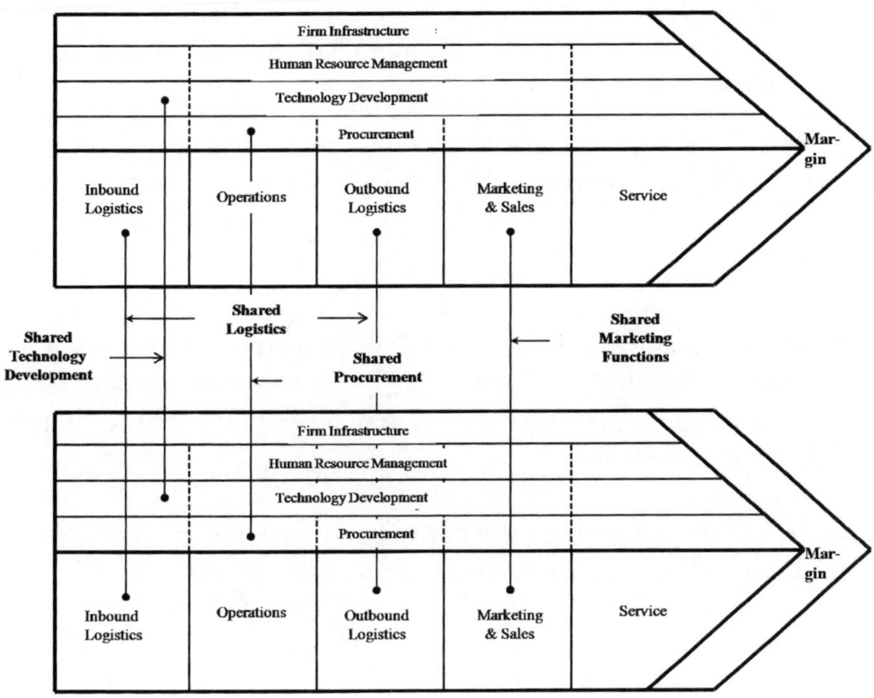

Fig. 9. Leveraging *sogo shosha's* strengths.

much a hobby as a way of life." In Korea, China and Japan, Internet cafés can be found on virtually every street corner, where legions of devoted gaming fans spend a considerable amount of time and money. Online gaming is big business, particularly in East Asia, and the Western gaming companies want a piece of the action.

However, the gaming industry in East Asia uses a decidedly unique business model compared to more traditional methods utilized by Western companies. In the West, games or software are sold off the shelf as packaged goods which can be installed and played on PCs or game consoles. In Asia, games or software are usually given away for free as a download and users can play for nothing. Revenue is generated by small payments made by avid customers to buy add-ons for their in-game characters.

Western gaming companies also face a number of barriers in entering the Asian market:

- *Language Barrier* — Games require language translation in addition to software rewrites to accommodate different alphabets and characters.
- *Piracy* — Most Asian countries do not have stringent enforcement of copyright protection. Asian programmers are adept at replicating and disbursing software, which compounds the problem for Western companies.
- *Gamer Culture* — Online game rooms and Internet gaming cafés provide a major social venue for most East Asian teens and young adults. Therefore, the online components of games are more important in Asia than the stunning graphics that entertain Western audiences.

The Asian model has benefits that are lacking in the Western model or can help overcome the barriers faced by Western firms:

- *Lowering the Entry Barrier* — This can be achieved by allowing new users to play for free. This will ultimately lead to a wider customer base, since more people are likely to try the product.

- *Overcoming Piracy* — Ironically, making the games free of charge will automatically mitigate this problem. If the games are free, firms need not worry about piracy. The company can then generate profit through advertisements or extra services (e.g., special weapons, new characters, extra events) to the gamer.

One Western company which altered its business strategy and became successful in Asia is Blizzard Entertainment, based in Irvine, California, USA. With its "World of Warcraft" online game, which has over 10 million subscribers worldwide, it seems to have found a strong foothold in Asia.

Blizzard has customized its servers for six different languages, thus overcoming the language barrier that many companies face when selling a product abroad. Blizzard has also circumvented the piracy problem by giving away World of Warcraft software for free and then charging for the game service, either hourly or monthly. Furthermore, Blizzard has expanded and opened subsidiaries around Asia in order to overcome cultural differences.

This model is becoming so successful that it is now being applied outside of Asia. Electronic Arts (EA) is preparing to release "Battlefield Heroes," which will be free to download but will hopefully generate revenue from in-game advertising and the sale of character upgrades. Thus, what began as a distinctively Asian model may now be developing into a global standard.

If the larger and more powerful Western gaming firms wish to enter the Asian market, they should follow Blizzard's lead and move away from spending money on highly sophisticated graphics and fancy packaging aimed only at young teenage males. Games in Asia need to be free to download and easily accessible by a wide range of people. Applying the generic strategies model, we see that although a differentiation focus strategy is effective in Western markets, a cost leadership strategy may be more effective in Asian markets (Fig. 10).

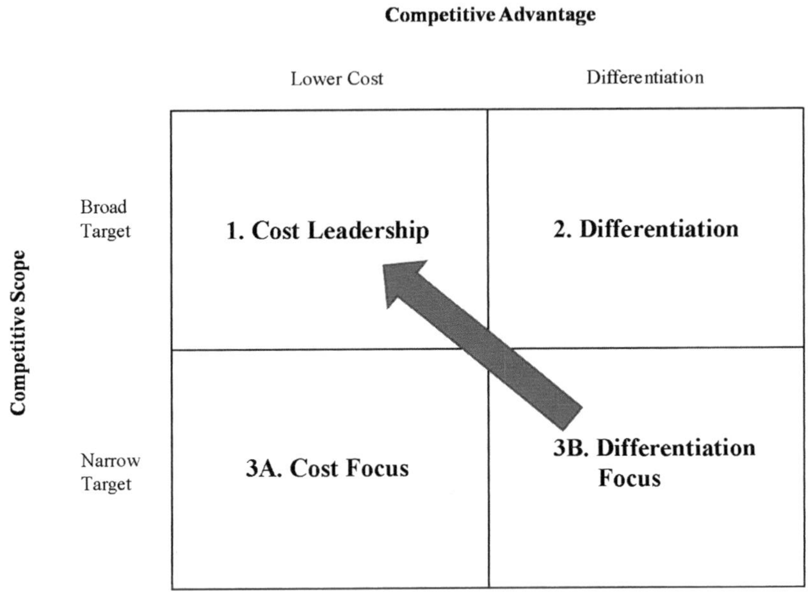

Fig. 10. Asian gaming strategy.

Case Study 4: Starbucks in China[16]

Starbucks, perhaps one of the most successful global companies in the world, has had its fair share of problems in China. The company views China as a must-have market, and is making it a clear priority for growth outside of the United States. Starbucks is well known for the standardization of its stores and whether one enters a store in New York in the United States, London in the United Kingdom or Paris in France, it is almost impossible to tell which city's Starbucks one may be in. However, the company's formula has not been as well received in China and other Asian countries as it has been in the West.

There are a number of cultural differences that have played a strong role in redefining Starbucks' Asian strategy: (a) Asia is traditionally a continent known for having a tea-drinking culture rather than a

[16] Information for this case study is abstracted from *The New York Times* (2005a), *Seattle Post-Intelligencer* (2005) and *The Economist* (2007a).

coffee-drinking culture; (b) Asians tend to view coffee or tea shops as a place to socialize; and (c) Asians tend to eat while drinking.

Starbucks is a coffee shop and, for the most part, keeps its tea menu to a minimum. However, after entering the Chinese market, the company discovered that many customers, while enjoying the Starbucks atmosphere, preferred a cup of tea to a cup of coffee. The company, therefore, was forced to expand its standardized menu to include a wider variety of tea.

In the West, Starbucks' revenue is driven by the speed and frequency of its transactions. Customers tend to grab their coffee and a quick pastry before scurrying out the door to their next appointment. However, coffee or tea is more of a social event than a daily necessity in the East. Customers come to meet and chat with their friends and thus Asian customers spend more time in the stores, on average, than their Western counterparts. Starbucks has had to increase the size of its stores to an average of 2,000 square feet (185.806 m^2) to accommodate all of the dalliers.

Another change came due to the company's realization that Asians tend to eat and drink simultaneously. Starbucks was forced to expand its menu once again to include more food. For example, Starbucks catered to local tastes by providing snacks such as mooncakes. Although Starbucks has made numerous efforts to adjust its formula to suit the Chinese market, the efforts may not be enough.

On July 13, 2007, Starbucks was forced to close the doors of its branch in the Forbidden City in Beijing, China. It was argued that the image of the coffee shop "trampled over Chinese culture" and the outlet was described as "a symbol of low-end US food culture." As a result, Starbucks may have to rethink its branding and marketing strategy if it wishes to be fully accepted by China. Traditionally, Starbucks has relied upon a differentiation focus strategy. However, with its problems in China, the company may have to move to a broad differentiation strategy in order to please Chinese customers — for instance, by including more Chinese menus and so enlarging its competitive scope — as shown in Fig. 11.

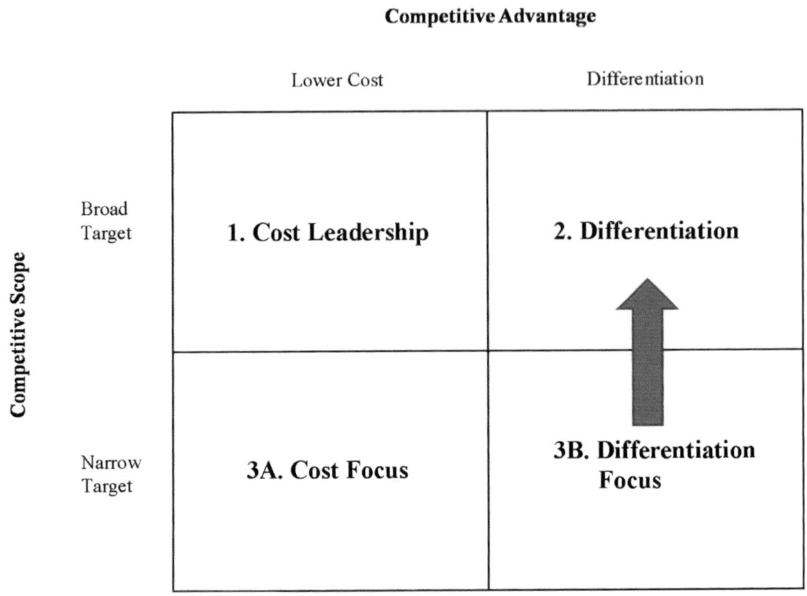

Fig. 11. Starbucks' strategy shift.

Discussion Questions

1. Why are the ideas of competitiveness and productivity so often confused? What do competitiveness and productivity mean to you? Are they entirely different or interchangeable?

2. Do you agree that there is a need to differentiate among product, firm, industry and nation when applying frameworks or models of competitiveness?

3. Are there any weaknesses in the five-forces model? Would you add, subtract or alter it in any way in order to improve it?

4. What do you think of the terminology used in the three generic strategies? Is it clear? How would you improve the three generic strategies?

5. Do you agree that being "stuck-in-the-middle" is always disadvantageous? Can you think of any examples where this is not so?

6. What do you think of the extension to the three generic strategies? Is the extension effective?
7. Do you agree with the division of the value chain into primary and support activities? Can you think of any other activities that are omitted?

CHAPTER 2

Alternative Business Models

Chapter Guideline

Porter's models laid the foundation for gaining an overarching view of business strategy. Now, it is time to look at alternative models which provide us with outlooks both complementary and contrary to Porter's views. This chapter will provide a summary of three alternative models from a producer, a customer and an all-inclusive viewpoint. The three alternative models are applied to Asian case studies in order to help readers gain a better understanding of the models' application in the Asian business context.

2.1 Knowledge Creating Strategy

When Michael Polanyi first formalized the concept of "tacit knowledge" in 1966, it had profound influences throughout all branches of academia. Rather than regarding knowledge creation as a value-free and objective process, Polanyi opened up the possibility of viewing knowledge as something that can be derived from a "pre-logical phase of knowing", or tacit knowledge (Smith 2003). Business management is no exception to this influence and many business scholars have used Polanyi's concept, especially in refining the concept of "knowledge economy".

Ikujiro Nonaka (2007) is a good example of a business scholar who integrated Polanyi's insights into the discipline of business management. Nonaka claims that in an unpredictable economic environment, knowledge is the only true consistent source of competitive advantage for an organization. Those organizations that can create, disperse and embody "new knowledge" will be the ones that achieve true success because they have the proper framework necessary for continuous innovation. This idea is not entirely novel, of course, as it was first introduced by Peter Drucker's articulation of the knowledge economy (Drucker 1969). Nonaka advances Drucker's concept and fuses it with Polanyi's tacit knowledge.

According to Nonaka, Western companies view the company as a machine whose responsibility is to generate quantifiable data and information. On the other hand, some Asian companies (mostly Japanese, in Nonaka's analysis) tend to view the company as a living organism which is constantly in flux. Nonaka goes on to explain that within this organism, there are two types of knowledge: explicit and tacit.

- *Explicit Knowledge* — Formal and systematic and, therefore, easily communicated and shared.
- *Tacit Knowledge* — Highly personal, hard to formalize and difficult to communicate.

The implication behind distinguishing the two types of knowledge is to underscore the fact that merely processing explicit knowledge does not provide a fertile ground for innovation. Rather, a firm must learn how to tap the tacit knowledge base that exists within the firm and transform it into explicit knowledge, which can then be shared and learned by others.

Nonaka identifies four patterns of knowledge that exist within the firm:

- *From Tacit to Tacit* — This process is similar to socialization or the cultural adaptation process. For example, it is only through years of carefully observing the master that an apprentice will finally begin to learn the tacit side of the art of creation. Tacit knowledge cannot be communicated easily, as the possessor of the tacit knowledge is usually unaware of this knowledge or cannot systematically convey it to others.

- *From Explicit to Explicit* — This refers to using explicit knowledge to create a new form of explicit knowledge (e.g., utilizing company data to compile a new report). This type of knowledge creation is highly common and crucial for a firm's basic operation. However, it neither extends the knowledge base of a firm nor provides a fertile plain for groundbreaking innovations.
- *From Explicit to Tacit* — This process internalizes explicit knowledge and transforms it into tacit knowledge. A company worker may acquire explicit information through reports and meetings, and then internalize that knowledge, thus transforming it into tacit knowledge.
- *From Tacit to Explicit* — The final stage is to organize and externalize the internalized knowledge in a manner that can be applicable and understood by others within the organization. For example, a highly experienced staff member reads a report and internalizes it (explicit → tacit). The staff member can then organize this internalized knowledge into a format which can be applied to an innovative new product (tacit → explicit). This new information then becomes systemized and distributed to other employees within the firm to foster further innovation.

The patterns are not mutually exclusive, but rather act in unison to form a "spiral of knowledge" (see Fig. 1).

Understanding the knowledge spiral is only the first step. One also needs to know how to jumpstart the process of developing new knowledge. Nonaka identifies three stages in the process: (a) metaphor, (b) analogy, and (c) model. Using this process allows firms to draw from symbolism rather than from concrete fixed ideas. The process should begin with the metaphor, which is based on intuitive understanding. The next step is analogy, which provides a structure for the metaphor and connects two disparate concepts together. The final stage is the model. Here, contradictions are resolved and concepts are transferred in a systematic manner, and the transfer of tacit knowledge to explicit knowledge is complete.

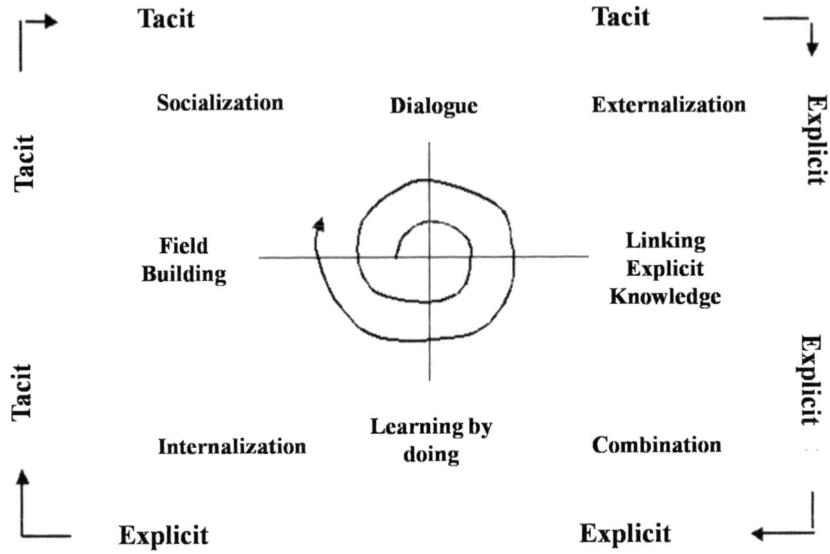

Fig. 1. Knowledge spiral.[1]

This abstract concept is easier to understand through actual cases in which this process crystallized tangible results. In 1978, Honda's top manager first came up with the slogan, "Let's Gamble", which expressed the top management's desire for a completely new car. The taskforce then refined this slogan and came up with an even more ambiguous slogan, "The Theory of Automobile Evolution". This metaphor, which to a Western manager would seem rather baffling, united the Honda employees in the task of creating a revolutionary new concept car. This metaphor was further structured into what Nonaka calls an analogy, which reconciles two seemingly irreconcilable elements.

In the Honda case, the question boiled down to: "If the automobile was an organism, how should it evolve?" This attempt to imagine an inorganic machine as an organism gave Honda employees a fulcrum for innovation and ultimately led to the birth of the Honda

[1] Nonaka and Takeuchi (1995), p. 71.

City, a car which defied many of the conventions of automobile design. After this achievement, Honda systemized this knowledge and spurred a whole series of new cars based on the Honda City that share the basic concept of "automobile evolution" embodied in the initial model. The final step demonstrates the model phase of Nonaka's spiral of knowledge, as Honda successfully transformed what was initially a highly tacit knowledge into a tangible and reproducible explicit knowledge (see Fig. 2).

Nonaka does, however, caution that in real life it is difficult to clearly distinguish between these stages and often the lines become blurred. Throughout Nonaka's analysis are references that can be construed as being related to Japanese cultural elements, which give Japanese firms a distinct advantage in facilitating this kind of process. The Japanese values of harmony (和) and collectivism, noted by eminent Japan specialists such as Ruth Benedict (1946), facilitate a collaborative environment in which this knowledge creation process can be disseminated and integrated as a part of the firm's core competency. Thus, Japanese companies are able to build a knowledge-creating company culture, which requires a high level of teamwork, trust and emphasis on harmony.

On the other hand, the West is characterized by individualism which, when applied to a company setting, encourages personnel to work alone and build their own personal stores of knowledge in order to develop only themselves. Furthermore, the knowledge creation process in Western firms is more competitive, which means that the high level of collaboration and teamwork required for Nonaka's model to work would be relatively harder to achieve.

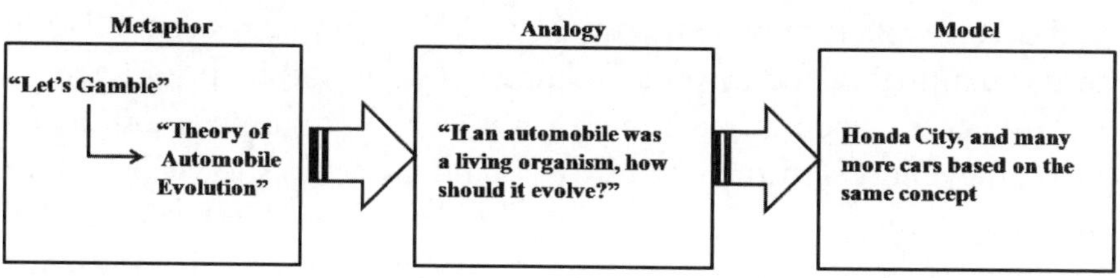

Fig. 2. Honda's spiral of knowledge.

Analysis

In a recent publication, *Managing Flow: A Process Theory of the Knowledge-Based Firm* (Nonaka *et al.* 2008), Nonaka extends his spiral of knowledge concept and explores how Japanese companies have continued to develop innovative products based on tacit knowledge management. It is undeniable that Nonaka's insights have shed light onto the inner mechanisms of innovation.

However, Nonaka's analysis is static as it does not account for the prior process required to reach this highly evolved phase of knowledge management. Managing tacit knowledge and transferring it to explicit knowledge may be an important source of added value for advanced firms such as Honda and Canon. However, for less advanced companies, especially those from developing countries, this kind of activity may be too complicated to manage. One can easily imagine that if a firm without extensive industry presence and know-how attempted to manage tacit knowledge, it could lead to organizational chaos and inefficiency. Therefore, one can extend Nonaka's static model into a dynamic one and clarify the potential mishaps that Nonaka's model can lead to.

As illustrated in Fig. 3, in the initial, factor-driven stage of economic development, explicit-to-explicit knowledge management should be the first important focus. An appropriate example for this kind of activity would be engineering technology transfers from developed countries' multinational corporations (MNCs) to firms in developing countries. In this phase, if firms of a developing country focus overly on tacit knowledge, it could backfire and create organizational chaos and inefficiency. Therefore, in the initial stage of development, the weight should be placed more on managing explicit-to-explicit knowledge transfer. Replicating and accumulating hard, quantifiable and systematic knowledge should be prioritized.

However, when firms move towards a more innovation-driven phase, they must shift their focus to tapping into tacit knowledge. Since an innovation-driven economy requires constant high-value-added activities for firms to stay competitive, managing the tacit knowledge creation process is highly important. As illustrated in Fig. 4, a solid base

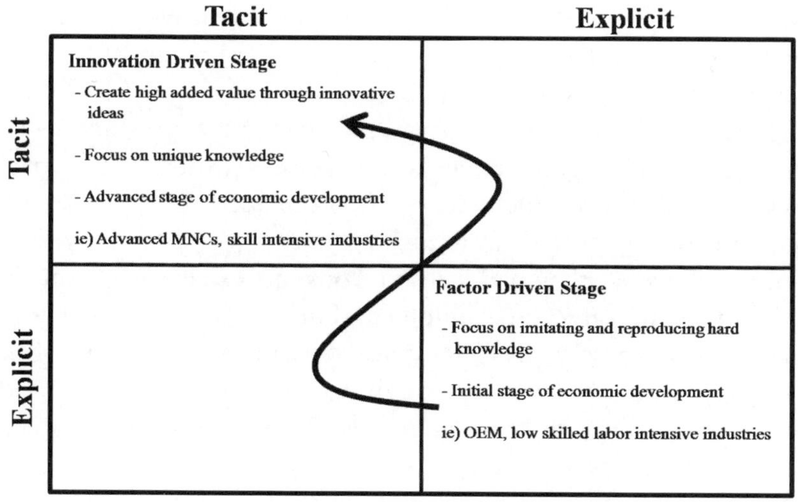

Fig. 3. Evolution of the spiral of knowledge according to stages of economic development.

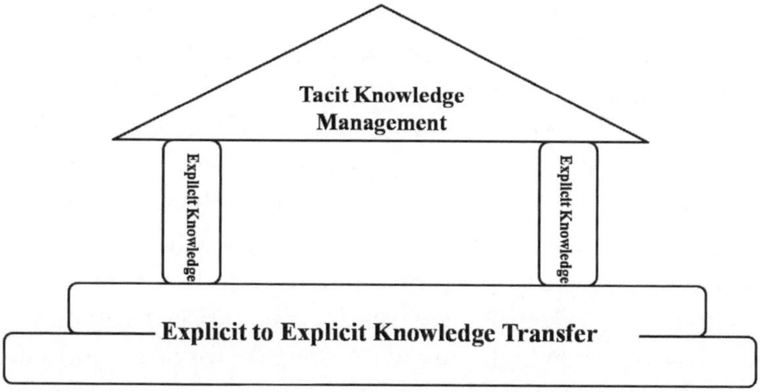

Fig. 4. Explicit-to-explicit knowledge transfer as a basis for tacit knowledge management.

of explicit knowledge must support Nonaka's prescription of harnessing the innovative power of tacit knowledge creation.

Therefore, the key is not to take Nonaka's point to the extreme. Of course, managing tacit knowledge is important, but it must rest on a solid foundation of prior explicit knowledge. Even the various

Japanese companies Nonaka discusses focused heavily on explicit-to-explicit knowledge transfer during the initial stage of economic development. It is well known that in the post-war era, Japanese companies started out by imitating American and European products and selling their products at lower prices (explicit to explicit). However, after the Japanese economy progressed through the initial stage and moved on to the innovation stage, Japanese firms began to internalize what they had learned from this experience (explicit to tacit) and then created their unique and innovative products (tacit to explicit). If Japanese firms did not accumulate this prior base of hard knowledge over the years through explicit-to-explicit knowledge transfer, managing tacit knowledge would not have been possible.

Furthermore, even for advanced firms, excessive focus on managing tacit knowledge could lead to organizational inefficiency. This point is very well illustrated by the case of Microsoft, which is at the forefront of innovation and creativity. Microsoft's corporate culture is well known to have a very high degree of individuality and organizational flexibility to facilitate an innovative knowledge creation process. However, the organization was too flexible and overly focused on creativity, so much so that it severely lacked organizational discipline. As Herbold, chief operating officer of Microsoft from 1994 to 2001, noted, the loose organizational structure — which was one of the core strengths of Microsoft's innovations — was also one of its biggest problems. Therefore, Herbold instituted various measures to standardize Microsoft's operational practices and enhanced discipline in this chaotic organization. The result was a more efficient and profitable Microsoft, which saved US$190 million annually on procurement alone (Herbold 2002).

For firms, the key message in this story is that every innovative practice needs to be founded on more traditional elements. A simple analogy to this story would be the process of learning martial arts. Regardless of one's natural athletic ability or reflex, everyone must start with repeatedly practicing basic kicks and punches to learn advanced moves such as combos and spin kicks. The same is true for knowledge creation and management processes. Without a solid foundation of explicit-to-explicit knowledge transfer, an excessive emphasis on tacit knowledge will lead to unnecessary organizational chaos and increased operational costs.

2.2 Customer Co-opting Strategy

Traditional economic and business theories took it for granted that the supply and demand sides were strictly segregated. However, this traditional boundary started to change when Toffler (1980) introduced the concept of "prosumer", a portmanteau word between producer and consumer. Following this breakthrough, many scholars adopted this idea in their analyses. Kotler (1986), for example, used the prosumer idea to present the benefits and challenges which marketers face with the rise of prosumerism. Many experts, especially in the computer programming arena, also commented on this exciting development as a novel way to enhance their product value. This concept of consumers and producers engaging in a collaborative production process has intrigued many scholars.

Along similar lines, Prahalad and Ramaswamy (2000) argue that in the new economy, companies must incorporate customer experience into their business models and deal with the many challenges that are involved. As John F. Kennedy famously told the American people in his 1961 inaugural address, "Ask not what your country can do for you — ask what you can do for your country", Prahalad and Ramaswamy assert, "Ask not what firms can do for the customers — ask what customers can do for the firm".

Previously, businesses and customers have had clearly defined roles, but over time those roles have shifted and the lines between the two have been blurred. The main reasons behind the shift are deregulation, globalization, technological convergence and the high-speed evolution of the Internet. The Internet has allowed consumers to conveniently access almost unlimited information regarding a firm's goods and services. When consumers visit corporate websites, they can not only read up on general company information, but also purchase standardized and customized goods, read shareholder information, check stock prices, access annual reports, and learn about new process and manufacturing techniques. As a result, customers are no longer merely passive recipients, but are rapidly becoming co-creators. The current market can be likened to a forum where customers assist in creating and competing for value. In short, the customer is a new source of competence, which in turn can be a new source of competitive advantage.

However, it is difficult to tap into this new source of competitive advantage, as even accessing internal competence can be challenging, let alone external competence. Furthermore, within a company there may be a limited number of staff, but the customers or potential customers of a firm can reach far larger numbers. Therefore, Prahalad and Ramaswamy (2000) provide several steps a company can take in order to ensure leverage in co-opting customer competence:

- *Encouraging Active Dialogs* — Companies currently have no monopoly or advantage over customers when it comes to information access. Thus, firms must treat customers as equal participants and be prepared to learn from the customers in order to allow dialogs to progress and evolve, lest the customer becomes uninterested. Nobody wants to have a one-sided conversation where they feel their thoughts and opinions are being ignored or disregarded. In the current economic climate, if one firm does not listen to its customers, another firm will.
- *Mobilizing Customer Communities* — Online customer communities can be tightly knit and remarkably sophisticated. Internet chat rooms, for example, are easy to start up and participate in, yet chat rooms should not be entirely unstructured and strict rules must be imposed. The benefit of customer communities is the speed with which they transfer information, which is known as "viral marketing". Product positioning can often depend on these online communities and their collective personalized experiences.
- *Managing Customer Diversity* — Companies can easily neglect the varying needs of their potential customers. Customers' experiences and consequent judgments of a product will vary according to their range of skills and knowledge or their level of

sophistication. Based on the customers' level of sophistication, their tolerance of problems or their concerns over privacy and security may vary and thus cannot be ignored.

- *Co-creating Personalized Experiences* — Customization refers to the manufacturer designing products to suit the customer's needs, whereas personalization has the customer involved in the actual creation process. This can be easily understood when one compares picking a meal out of a menu (customization) versus cooking together with the chef in the kitchen (personalization). Many firms have realized that personalization is highly desirable and thus offer opportunities on websites for customers to choose the style, material, size and so on, of their products.

However, managing the personalized experience can be even more challenging than developing it. Prahalad and Ramaswamy (2000) identify some useful ways by which a company can create opportunities for the customers to experiment and select their level of involvement in the process.

Firstly, the firm must be able to manage multiple channels of experience. The Internet is, of course, a very adaptable and accessible channel for customers; however, it may not be a suitable means for everyone. The firm must take into consideration all types of customers and which channels they would find the most convenient. This means that while a firm's website might be fun and user-friendly, there will still be customers who prefer face-to-face contact or even those who prefer to use the telephone rather than a computer as their main means of contact. Allowing for maximum satisfaction in only one channel of experience alienates a variety of customers from the firm.

Secondly, the firm must be able to manage variety and evolution. This is different from managing the variety of products available to the customer, and it is the variety of customers' experiences that must be managed effectively. Essentially, the range of customers' experiences will transcend the product itself. Thus, the firm needs products that can shape themselves to customers' needs and evolve alongside those needs. Products which are static or limited in any way will have a short selling life, and customers will easily lose interest in the firm.

Lastly, the firm should be skilled in shaping customers' expectations. Consumers are sensitive to "what is next", so companies should play a role in shaping those expectations. It is important to educate the customers as well as be educated by the customer in order to develop future product lines. This refers to encouraging active dialogs and mobilizing customer communities. With that kind of customer input, a firm can learn what the customer expects while simultaneously shaping their next move in the market.

After following the above guidelines, the firm should be in a better position to co-opt customers' competencies. However, the firm must remain vigilant as one of its best assets, the customer, can also become one of its biggest competitors. A shift in power is occurring due to information availability. No longer are companies mere price-setters, but they are also price-takers as customers are able to negotiate terms and prices with increased access to information. Companies that do not accommodate these new changes may find themselves pushed out of the market completely as their customers' preferences or loyalties change to suit their needs.

In order to access all competencies, the firm must be highly flexible and no fixed role should exist within the company. This can only be achieved through constant reconfiguration to optimize the firm towards co-opting customers. Prahalad and Ramaswamy (2000) acknowledge that this can be traumatic for employees within the firm, but this is where management should step in. It is the manager's responsibility to deal with the traumas that occur and to hire self-motivated staff members who are more responsive to change. The manager is required to maintain a stable center within the firm using organizational values as an anchor so as not to set the firm adrift on a sea of endless competitive possibilities.

Analysis

When Alvin Toffler introduced the term "prosumer" in his book, *The Third Wave*, in 1980, it signaled a fundamental shift in the linkage between consumers and producers. Toffler contended that the distinction between the two sides would become increasingly blurred and that value can be created from an active consumer who takes part in the production process. Toffler traced his ideas back to Gary Becker (1976), an American economist who first noted the importance of the "non-money economy". Becker's prediction that the nonworking sector (consumers) may generate significant added value for companies was the foundation for Toffler's ideas.

Prahalad and Ramaswamy's (2000) true contribution to this long train of thought is that they have presented a practical and focused way in which firms can utilize this concept into their everyday operations. By doing so, the two authors have concretely presented how to manage the prosumer's value-creating activity to the firm's best advantage. This is not to criticize Prahalad and Ramaswamy's lack of originality, but rather to highlight their true contribution. It is important for readers to understand that most, if not all, new ideas are based on a pre-established model or concept, which provides the basic framework for a new idea — Prahalad and Ramaswamy are no exceptions to this general truth.

Prahalad and Krishnan (2008) have further refined the idea of co-opting customer competence in a recently published book, *The New Age of Innovation*. They assert that co-opting customer competence has assumed increasing importance because of increased globalization and ubiquitous connectivity, which are forcing companies to re-examine how they deliver value to customers. The ability to reach out and touch customers anywhere, anytime means that companies must deliver not just competitive products, but also unique, real-time customer experiences shaped by the customer "context".

2.3 A More Comprehensive Strategy?

Many scholars have discussed and contributed to certain aspects or subvariables of strategic management, but not many have been able to actually provide an overarching framework. This is because such a sweeping contribution takes an exceptionally brilliant and committed mind. Only a select few have been able to present a timeless and overarching framework for business scholars.

Hambrick and Fredrickson (2005) attempt to achieve such an ambitious feat. The two start off by lamenting the sheer multitude of analytical tools that are in existence. This is directly related to the fact that the term "strategy" is thrown around without a precise definition or proper framework. They claim that the frameworks and tools available are too narrow and offer only pieces of a strategy. Strategy has become a "catch-all" term used to mean whatever one wants it to mean.

A strategy consists of an integrated set of choices, but it is not a "catch-all" for every important choice. In Fig. 5, for example, the company's mission and objectives stand apart from strategy. A company's objective of being number one in its industry drives its strategy, but is not strategy itself. Similarly, choices about internal

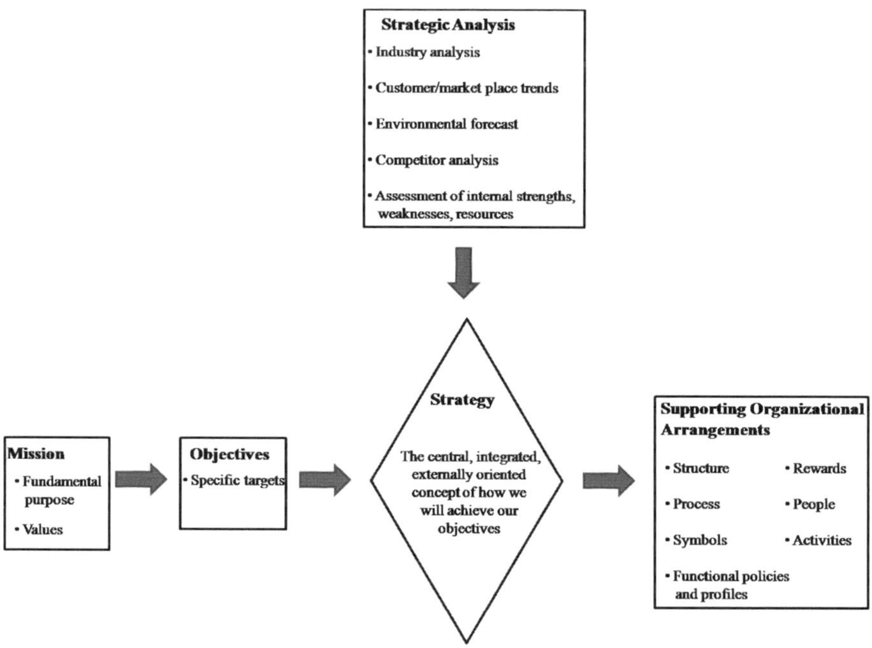

Fig. 5. Putting strategy in its place.[2]

[2] Hambrick and Fredrickson (2005).

organizational arrangements are not part of strategy. So, we should not speak of compensation policies and training programs as being strategy.

Hambrick and Fredrickson (2005) then present a framework for strategy design, arguing that a strategy has five elements — providing answers to five questions — which are arenas, vehicles, differentiators, staging and economic logic.

- *Arenas* — This simply refers to where a firm should be active. Within arenas, it should be considered which product categories, market segments, geographic areas, core technologies and value-creation stages a firm is going to be active in. The key is to be as specific as possible and to further detail how much emphasis will be placed on each particular aspect of an arena. For example, if a firm has two product categories, it may wish to designate one as its primary product and the other as its secondary product.
- *Vehicles* — This refers to the most suitable entry mode such as joint ventures, licensing and acquisitions. This must be considered carefully as entry is rife with uncertainty, but uncertainty can be reduced depending on the entry mode. The incorrect choice of vehicle could cause delays or even higher unforeseen costs.
- *Differentiators* — Differentiating the firm's product is important, as it is the primary source of the product's competitive advantage against other competing products. Differentiators can be based on image, customization, price, styling and product reliability, to name a few. While there is a need to create differentiators, the authors emphasize that firms must be careful not to overexpand themselves since this may dilute their core competencies.
- *Staging* — This is the speed and sequence of moves made by the firm. In particular, the speed of expansion coupled with the sequence of initiatives should be considered. Staging can be likened to the building of a house: first you need a foundation, followed by the walls and then lastly the roof. However, in business there is no absolute sequence and judgment should be

applied when considering other aspects such as resources, urgency and credibility. Staging has not been previously touched upon in other literature, and therefore it would be worthwhile to develop this aspect more fully.

- *Economic Logic* — This refers to the final and most crucial question of any profit-maximizing enterprise: how will the company generate revenue above the cost of capital? There are a number of ways in which this can be answered, such as providing lower costs through scale and scope advantages, or obtaining premium prices due to unmatchable quality and services. Although this is the last element, it is certainly not the least as the economics is usually the underlying fundamental reason for doing business in the first place. This economic logic should be rooted in the firm's fundamental capabilities.

Figure 6 visualizes the five elements. While not all of the above five aspects are new in strategic thought and competitiveness literature, together they do indeed provide a highly comprehensive model. The authors claim that all five of the above aspects are equally important to

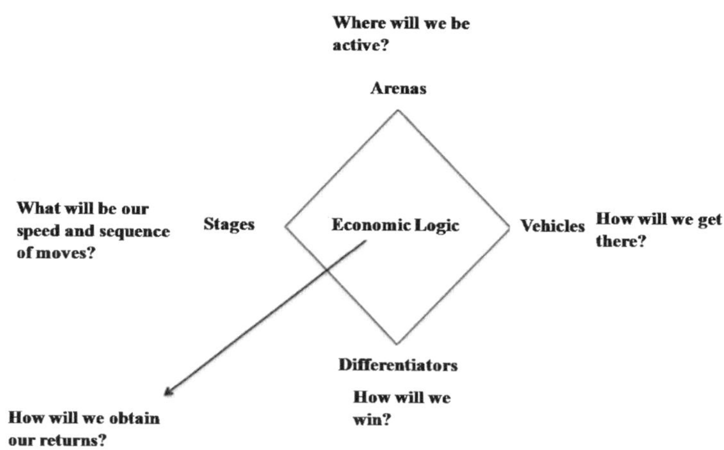

Fig. 6. The five elements of strategy.[3]

[3] *Ibid.*

strategy, yet most frameworks or tools only encompass one or two of the above elements. The five elements ultimately need to align with and self-reinforce each other. Once the strategy is in place, supporting activities can be arranged in order to reinforce the strategy.

Analysis

Hambrick and Fredrickson's (2005) article is a useful reminder for managers, consultants and scholars that using the word "strategy" without understanding its true implications can be dangerous. Strategy must be an overarching concept which encompasses multiple units on multiple fronts and multiple battles over time. Understanding the vast scope and comprehensive nature of this word is crucial for anyone who wishes to formulate or study strategy.

However, despite their highly valid analyses, their prescription is slightly redundant. The model (see Figs. 5 and 6), which attempts to encompass all the elements needed to constitute a strategy, seems rather cumbersome. Most critically, the majority of the elements that Hambrick and Fredrickson present overlap a great deal with Porter's five-forces model and generic strategies. For example, arenas can be likened to the five-forces model in Chap. 1, as both are used to determine the profitability and success factor of entering a particular industry. Furthermore, differentiators and economic logic are very similar to Porter's generic strategies, but Porter's model is perhaps more encompassing in that it is more focused and detailed. As a matter of fact, the generic strategies present a clearer and more readily applicable framework, while Hambrick and Fredrickson's description of differentiators and economic logic is rather elusive. Lastly, vehicles can be likened to entry modes, which are covered extensively in foreign direct investment literature. Various theoretical and empirical works on the efficacy of wholly owned subsidiaries, joint ventures and strategic alliances have been done previously.

Therefore, Hambrick and Fredrickson's true contribution is their attempt to fuse all the pre-existing models into one comprehensive framework in order to visually present what a strategy should consist of. This is highly valid and useful because it clearly defines the boundaries that separate an element and the strategy itself. However, the applicability and uniqueness of the framework is slightly questionable because of more practical and applicable models (e.g., Porter's five forces and generic strategies) that already exist. By trying to be too encompassing, it has reduced the coherence of each element and thus reduced the applicability of the model.

2.4 Which Model?

Chapters 1 and 2 have provided an overview of a range of business models, which can serve managers, consultants and scholars to help firms achieve their goals. The business models that have been reviewed offer a wide perspective of viewpoints and ways in which one can analyze the firm.

All of the models reviewed have their own unique strengths and weaknesses when compared with one another, and all are relevant in their own ways. Chapters 1 and 2 also offer practical real-life applications of the reviewed models, thus providing a clearer understanding of how they really work in the real world, particularly from Asian perspectives.

Our case studies will highlight the fact that there exists a need for firms to develop strategies which are suitable for certain regions. Firms should be flexible enough to realize that one all-encompassing strategy is no longer applicable in the world of global business strategy. A firm must be able to fine-tune certain aspects of its strategy in order to find the best fit, according to the area in which it wishes to operate and the customer that it wants to do business with.

Case Study 1: Toyota's IMV Project[4]

Toyota is one of the most successful Japanese companies and is often cited in case studies or its operations benchmarked, but not without

---

[4] Information for this case study is abstracted from the Toyota website (www.toyota.co.jp/en), *The Economist* (2007b), Ichijo and Kohlbacher (2007) and the Toyota Supplier website (www.toyotasupplier.com).

good reason. In the beginning, Toyota developed and produced cars in Japan and exported cars abroad. As its popularity and success grew, Toyota started to produce where its markets were located, such as in North America and Western Europe. Later, the company identified major business opportunities in newly industrialized economies (Korea, Taiwan, Hong Kong and Singapore) and then developing regions, most notably the BRIC countries (Brazil, Russia, India and China). However, Toyota quickly realized that its model could not adapt to developing countries' tastes and needs due to its lack of local knowledge.

To solve this problem, Toyota moved onto its next stage of development. The company developed a global production and supply network to solve the problems of local production. In particular, it launched the "Innovative International Multi-purpose Vehicle" project (hereby known as the "IMV" project), which was designed to learn about how to understand and pay attention to local needs.

As part of the project, Toyota upgraded and expanded its Thailand, Indonesia, South Africa and Argentina plants to extend its outreach in Asia, Oceania, Africa and Latin America. The success of the IMV project was very much dependent on local engineers working together with the Japanese engineers, along with close collaborations between headquarters, subsidiaries and affiliates. To further ensure success, Toyota set up joint training centers where Japanese and foreign personnel were trained together.

Instead of performing simple manufacturing operations in the target countries, Toyota started planning and developing with local engineers and designers. By doing so, Toyota has fundamentally changed how knowledge is created and disseminated within its organization. Previously, new knowledge was created in the Japan HQ and unilaterally transferred to subsidiaries, as illustrated on the left-hand side of Fig. 7. However, after the structural changes, new knowledge is also created in foreign markets and transferred to Japan. Joint training centers for all employees offer opportunities for knowledge transfer between employees and instructors, regardless of one's nationality and base of operation, as well as tacit-to-explicit knowledge transfers

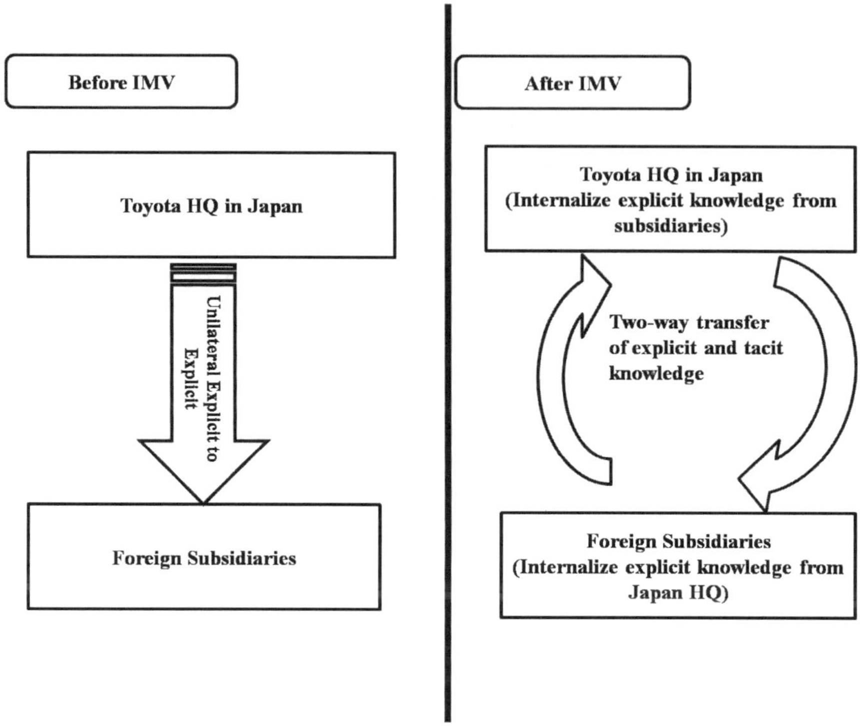

Fig. 7. Comparison of knowledge flow before and after IMV.

regarding new technologies and designs, as represented on the right-hand side of Fig. 7.

This kind of knowledge creation process also occurs within the domestic sphere. Toyota is well known for cultivating strong, long-term relationships with affiliated companies, subcontractors and suppliers. In particular, Toyota's support system provides high-level access to tacit knowledge, which can then be transferred into explicit knowledge. If any of Toyota's affiliates experiences problems in generating new knowledge, the company sends in teams of experts to work together with the affiliated company's personnel. Working together allows transfers of knowledge, which in turn improves the affiliates' competitiveness. Such cooperative and collaborative activities lead to positive results such as lower production costs, creation of appropriate technologies and better understanding of consumer needs. The transfer of knowledge also allows the firms to cultivate long-term relationships as they learn to understand and respect each other's operational methods. As the relationship continues, these feelings will grow and the transfer of knowledge becomes more significant as trust between the two parties increases.

This case shows the operational effectiveness of the collaborative knowledge-creating process between various parties. In Toyota, knowledge is created through cooperation between foreign branches and the Japanese home base, and also among Toyota's affiliates and subsidiaries. Furthermore, this case illustrates cultural aspects, which Nonaka (2007) touched upon. As we can see from Toyota's case, collaboration and cooperation among the different parties involved are crucial for this knowledge creation process to work. Particularly, Japanese cultural values, which place a high level of emphasis on collectivism and harmony, explain why this kind of knowledge creation process is better developed in Japanese firms than in Western firms.

Case Study 2: Renault Aims in Asia[5]

While the main focus of Nonaka's (2007) article is on Japanese firms, Western firms such as Renault have taken a similar approach. Renault is a French automaker that produces cars, vans, buses, tractors and trucks. As of 2007, the company was the ninth largest automaker in the world, in terms of motor vehicle production (Organization of Motor Vehicle Manufacturers 2007). The company is well known for numerous revolutionary designs, security technologies and motor racing. Renault, while wildly popular across Europe, has not made much headway in Asia until recently.

Renault has historically maintained all of its R&D, production and manufacturing facilities within or around France. This has

[5] Information for this case study is abstracted from the Renault website (www.renault.com), *The Economist* (2008c) and *The New York Times* (2002).

enabled it to become an expert regarding its European customers' needs and desires. However, upon going global, Renault has had difficulty in gauging the needs and desires of the Asian consumer, mainly due to a lack of tacit knowledge about this new market.

Therefore, when entering the Japanese market, Renault made a move to form an alliance with Nissan, the Japanese automaker. The two auto giants combined their production facilities, allowing Renault and Nissan engineers to work side by side. Thus, Renault was able to integrate many of Nissan's manufacturing operations and technologies into its other production sites. Not only did the two firms work together in the production side, but they also put their heads together in the design department. From this aspect, the alliance was mutually beneficial. As the design teams worked together, there was a two-way transfer of knowledge. Nissan started to build cars which were more suited to the European market, and thus it improved its market share in Europe; while Renault started to build cars which were suited to the Asian market.

The two companies were able to transfer a high level of tacit knowledge between each other. Renault then decided to form a joint venture with the Korean automaker, Samsung Motors, in order to continue its successful foray into East Asia. The two started actively producing cars together and have managed to maintain a fairly large market share within Korea (third in the market with a 9.3% share in 2007). Renault has successfully introduced the French brand into Korea and now tries to extend this success to other Asian countries.

As a result of its successes in Asia, the Renault group has come to realize the benefits of knowledge creation and transfer. Renault's R&D centers were traditionally maintained in France and operated by French designers and engineers. However, since its experiences in Asia, the firm has opened up international design centers — employing 20 different nationalities — which are aimed at (a) developing creativity, (b) stimulating innovation, and (c) supporting Renault's international operation.

One of these international design centers is based just outside of Seoul, South Korea. Besides the main activities mentioned above, this design center is also expected to work with other design centers in the

Asian region and track design trends within Asia. Merely having the different nationalities working together creates an environment suitable to the transfer of explicit knowledge, but by working so closely together and through observation of each other's methods, tacit knowledge is also more efficiently transferred.

Renault's experience with knowledge creation and transfer has been very successful, partly because of a suitable choice of partner. Partners must be willing to transfer the knowledge and a high level of trust should be involved, particularly when the partners are not only collaborators but also competitors. Renault's case illustrates how a non-Asian company can be engaged in a highly collaborative process with Asian firms to facilitate a two-way transfer of tacit and explicit knowledge. Renault could potentially be a model for other Western firms to follow in terms of engaging in a highly cooperative alliance with Asian firms for mutual gain.

Case Study 3: The Singtel Experience[6]

Singtel is one of Asia's leading telecommunications groups, with operations and investments in more than 20 countries around the world. The group provides a comprehensive portfolio of services and has leveraged customer competence in several different aspects. Using Prahalad and Ramaswamy's (2000) stepping stones, we can explain how Singtel has co-opted the customer.

- *Encouraging Active Dialogs* — Singtel operates numerous online venues known as Teleshops. These are interactive stores where customers can visit to discuss new services and issues regarding software design and usability, or talk about service problems, with Singtel technicians or in-store experts. Customers can also physically go to the stores and mingle with other Singtel users. Singtel utilizes this concept by adjusting its services and designs to meet the expectations and needs of its customers.

---

[6] Information for this case study is abstracted from the Singtel website (www. singtel.com).

- *Mobilizing Customer Communities* — Singtel has not been particularly successful in this category, although it does provide a comprehensive website as well as contact points for customers. Singtel could benefit from offering a blogging service to customers, as generating customer communities can often result in forms of "viral marketing" where the customer helps position products and services within the industry.
- *Managing Customer Diversity* — Singtel not only offers online support through its website, but also provides call centers which are available for more non-Internet-savvy customers. Walk-in centers are available and numerous, offering speedy and reliable services. Singtel also provides global center services, both online and in the form of call centers for its global customers. In addition, customers can choose from a range of billing choices — online or traditional paper. Moreover, online shopping is available, whereby the customer can purchase not only a provider service but also a cellular phone, as one can in the walk-in centers. Offering a wide range of customer contact points allows the customers to create their own experience of the product, thus increasing their satisfaction.
- *Co-creating Personalized Experiences* — The company understands that a 15-year-old girl may have different service needs than a 45-year-old businessman who travels regularly, and thus adjusts its services to suit individual needs. Therefore, Singtel offers a range of services, which can be highly personalized to suit different wants and needs. Furthermore, customers can actually adjust the software provided on their cellular phones and select only the services that they want. Personalizing experiences is important as consumers receive exactly what they desire. Their feelings of satisfaction increase and they are more likely to maintain a regular relationship with the firm.

In sum, Singtel offers its customers not only unique, but rather integral, opportunities to enhance their participation; as a result, both the customer and the firm benefit. Singtel has been successful in its efforts by encouraging active dialogs, managing customer diversity and co-creating personalized experiences. Singtel, however, would benefit more from focusing on mobilizing customer communities. Viral marketing, in particular, is becoming an increasingly essential aspect of marketing as communication technology continuously progresses. As we shall see in the following case study, Apple has managed to achieve significant leverage in terms of viral marketing.

Case Study 4: An Apple in Asia Tastes Just as Sweet[7]

Apple is a leading American multinational corporation which focuses on designing and manufacturing consumer electronics and software products. Apple has established a unique reputation in the consumer electronics industry that is based on its devoted customers. Although this customer base exists largely in the United States, Apple is beginning to make headway in Asia, in particular with its range of portable media players, iPods, and the highly desirable iPhone. One way that Apple is improving its market share in Asia is through leveraging customer competence.

- *Encouraging Active Dialogs* — Apple operates Apple Stores throughout Asia, which allow customers to try and test out a variety of new Apple products while trained staff members stand on the sidelines waiting to assist those with questions or problems. Furthermore, in-store technicians are normally available to deal with queries and technical problems. Customers, therefore, have an interactive space that they can readily access in order to discuss the products on sale with trained representatives and other customers. A further step could be to open the Apple cafés, which are beginning to appear in the United States. With the café

[7] Information for this case study is abstracted from the Apple Asia website (www.apple.com/asia), *The New York Times* (2008a) and The Mac Observer website (www.macobservor.com).

culture that already exists in Asia, the Apple café will surely be popular with the Asian consumers.

- *Mobilizing Customer Communities* — Online communities are particularly important in Asia, where the Internet is far-reaching and social barriers prevent people from having open conversations with strangers offline. Therefore, Apple offers discussion forums on all of its Asian websites in local languages. The discussion forums exist for users of Apple products as well as technicians and computer experts. One of the most well-known Apple forums, www.macrumors.com, is owned and operated by a former Korean doctor, Dr. Kim. Dr. Kim famously gave up his career in medicine to blog full-time on the widely successful website. Large varieties of sites exist throughout Asia and are creating a cult similar to that in the United States.
- *Managing Customer Diversity* — Apple manages customer diversity in two ways. The first is by providing a wide range of products within a particular product range. This allows the company to offer something to everyone within one product range. Second, Apple offers a number of channels through which the customer is able to communicate with the company. The most impressive and speedy channel is the Apple website, which can be accessed in almost any language and country where Apple is present. Manuals and downloads are available online, as is technical support. Apple also offers call center services that customers can access for any reason, ranging from reporting technical problems or complaints to ordering new products. Products can be purchased through any of the channels available.
- *Co-creating Personalized Experiences* — Apple now accepts software developments from users, which can be distributed among other users and downloaded for free. In this way, customers can personalize their Apple products to suit their own needs. However, Apple is often criticized for being too protective of new designs and concepts until they are launched. Were Apple to become more open during the design process, customer feedback

could benefit the company greatly and increase general customer satisfaction.

Overall, Apple has made significant achievements in terms of co-opting customer competence. Particularly in the areas of managing customer diversity and mobilizing customer communities, it has excelled. However, Apple would benefit more from further encouragement of active dialogs and co-creation of personalized experiences. Both of these aspects require development for a closer customer relationship, which Apple has avoided until now due to its secretive product development process. Opening up this aspect to its devoted customers and co-opting their competence will bring significant added value to the firm.

Case Study 5: Sharp's Five-Element Strategy[8]

Sharp, a Japanese electronics firm, started out as a simple metal-working business that went on to develop the hugely successful "ever sharp" pencil. Since then, its business has expanded to include audio and visual equipment, home appliances and information equipment. However, as Sharp looks to the future, its business focus and strategy are evolving once again. Using Hambrick and Fredrickson's (2005) five elements provides an understanding of its new focused business strategy.

Looking at Fig. 8, it can be seen that Sharp's current business strategy is very much future-focused, and the company is preparing for an alteration in its product line. As its product line (arena) changes, so too do the other aspects of its strategy. With the five elements of its strategy organized, the firm is now able to focus on supporting activities in order to reinforce its strategy.

In particular, Sharp has made a dramatic change in its arenas and also in the focus of its product ranges. As mentioned previously, Sharp began as a creator of the "ever sharp" pencil and then moved into the

---

[8] Information for this case study is abstracted from the Sharp website (www.sharp-world.com) and *The New York Times* (2006d).

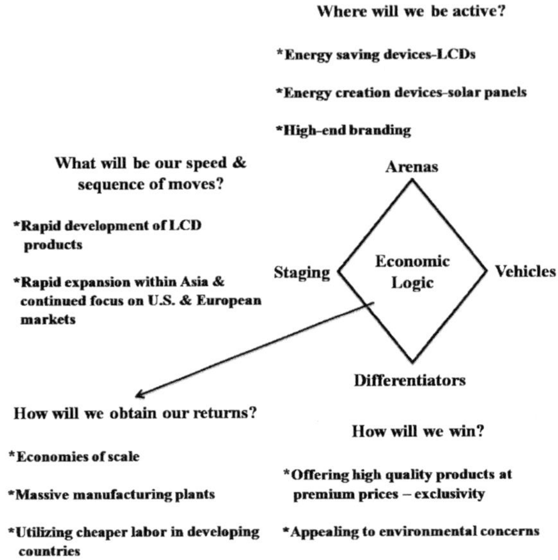

Fig. 8. Sharp's five-element strategy.

audio and visual equipment segment. However, due to intense competition in that field, Sharp has shifted to a more future-centric arena. Thus, its vehicle has changed to a focus on technological developments and intense R&D. The company's differentiator is that it is appealing to an entirely new customer base, while its staging must be rapid development and expansion in a relatively new arena in order to stay ahead of its competitors.

Case Study 6: Nokia's Five-Element Strategy in Asia[9]

Nokia is a Finnish multinational communications corporation, and is the world's largest manufacturer of mobile telephones and has maintained the market lead in this industry. Although Nokia originated in Europe, it has become determined to corner the market in Asia as well. Nokia has R&D centers in China and Japan, and

[9] Information for this case study is abstracted from the Nokia Asia Pacific website (www.nokia-asia.com).

production facilities throughout China and in Korea. As of 2009, the firm became the number one digital brand in Asia in terms of brand recognition (World Advertising Research Center 2009). Analyzing Nokia's Asian strategy, from the aspect of the five-element strategy, should offer an insight into how Nokia has achieved these successes and a competitive edge in the Asian market. Figure 9 illustrates an all-encompassing look at Nokia's Asian strategy, thus allowing the strategy itself to be benchmarked.

Nokia's arena has shifted from a mostly European focus to a more global one, with an aim to converge the Internet and telecommunications, in order to effectively deal with stiff Asian competition. As a result of not being accustomed to the Asian market, the company has chosen its chief vehicle for expansion to be alliances and acquisitions. This plan was devised to reduce the risks of entering unfamiliar territory. Its differentiator is to be affordable in Asia, rather than exclusive, and to continuously expand its services. Staging is to

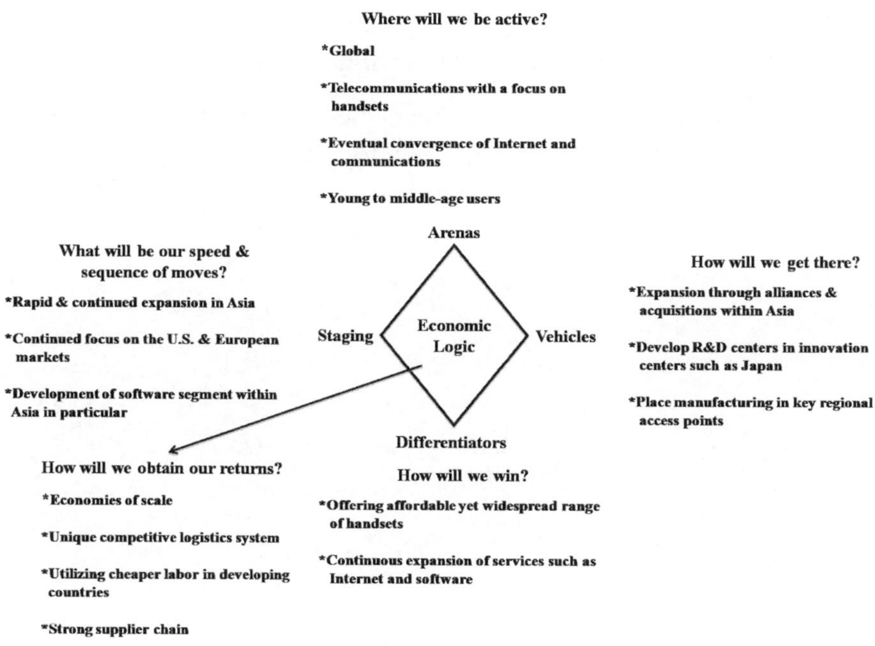

Fig. 9. Nokia's five-element strategy.

expand throughout Asia, while maintaining a focus on its stable European and American markets.

Discussion Questions

1. Do you agree that Japanese companies are more innovative than others, in particular Western companies? Why or why not?
2. Is one type of knowledge ever better than another? When is explicit knowledge better than tacit knowledge or vice versa?
3. Do you believe that firms are really co-opting customer competence? What are your experiences as a consumer?
4. Do you agree with the steps recommended for co-opting customer competence? Would you add anything?
5. How would you define strategy? Which elements are important in creating a strategy?
6. Do you agree with the five elements by Hambrick and Fredrickson (2005)? Would you change anything?
7. Do you believe that a firm can really become more competitive by following any of these models? Will following these models always have positive effects on the outcomes?

CHAPTER 3

Applications of Business Models to Non-Business Areas

Chapter Guideline

This chapter will revisit Porter's model, but under a different context. In each section, Porter analyzes the most recent developments in society, business and technology through the lens of his analytical frameworks. The first section discusses the impact of the Internet on the business environment and proposes several guidelines in using this technology to the firm's fullest advantage. The next section explains how philanthropic institutions can enhance their performance through a more strategic approach. The last section introduces the concept of strategic corporate social responsibility (CSR), and proposes a framework for firms to maximize societal and firm benefits simultaneously.

Summary of Previous Models

In the previous chapter, we looked at three alternative views and business models presented by leading scholars. Nonaka's (2007) article presented us with a new framework for knowledge management, and Prahalad and Ramaswamy (2000) discussed very practical ways in which firms can utilize their customers to increase their value. Hambrick and Fredrickson (2005) proposed a framework that succinctly distinguishes between strategy and other elements. We have also identified several problems and possible extensions that could enhance the efficiency of each model. Now, we come back to Porter and analyze three emerging hot topics through the lens of Porter's analytical framework.

3.1 Strategy and the Internet

The Internet was (and still is) regarded as one of the most powerful forces shaping business strategy, along with globalization. Yip (2000) asserted that the Internet is a globalization driver which will expand the opportunities for a wide geographic scope of operations because of the transformative effect this technology will have on the business landscape. This observation still holds true, but many investors misinterpreted or took these insights to the extreme and recklessly invested in many unproductive ventures related to the Internet.

When the "dot-com bubble" burst in 2001, many came to the realization that the Internet is not a miracle invention that would somehow propel business strategy into a completely new world. As Warren Buffett shrewdly noted in an interview with the BBC (2001), the dot-com bubble was largely a result of irrational exuberance. Re-evaluation of the relationship between the Internet and business strategy poured forward after the irrational exuberance popped and left many investors wondering how this madness had occurred. Rangan and Adner (2001), for example, analyzed the relationship between the Internet and business strategy, and debunked the seven common myths surrounding the Internet. Their conclusion was that, rather than regarding the Internet as a completely revolutionary technology, it should be regarded as an additional tool that can be utilized for a firm's benefit. Rangan and Adner's analysis is largely correct, but leaves us without a clear prescription.

Porter (2001) offers a comprehensive diagnosis and prescription to the irrational exuberance generated by the advent of the Internet. He starts off by describing the recent focus on the Internet as a general fervor. Many businesses overestimated and misunderstood this new technology, and assumed that the Internet would bring a sea-change to the business environment. Companies rushed to embrace this new technological innovation and hastily claimed that the world of business had entered a completely new phase in history.

New concepts and terminologies such as "e-business strategies" and "new economy", which have been increasingly thrown around by many business leaders and scholars, reflected the overall mood around the turn of the year 2000. However, Porter debunks this myth and claims that the Internet is simply an enabling technology, albeit a powerful one. Most people focused on what the Internet can do for their business. They pointed to features such as high switching costs and the network effect, which can provide huge advantages to those who move first. It is true that most businesses must embrace the new technology; indeed, it would be quite difficult to sustain a competitive edge without incorporating the Internet into the overall scheme of things. Yet, this does not mean that the Internet should be adopted at the cost of existing competitive advantages.

The most successful companies are not those that rush into fully integrating themselves with the Internet, but those that use the Internet as a tool to complement and bolster their previous sources of competitive advantage. What most of these optimists forgot is that sustainable profitability does not come from simply adopting a technology that everyone else can easily replicate. A standardized technology such as the Internet cannot be a source of uniqueness. Rather, what is truly important is how to differentiate, specialize and provide unique services to the customers, utilizing the Internet as a means to an end. A standardized technology such as the Internet can be utilized by everyone and anywhere, which quickly diminishes the potential for early movers to continuously exploit it as a source of sustainable competitive advantage. Simply put, if you can do it, soon everyone else can too. So how can you be more profitable than others just by using the Internet?

The practices of many companies in the early 2000s amply supported Porter's concerns on the overblown emphasis on the Internet. First, many companies subsidized the use of the Internet and provided the service virtually free of charge. Companies hoped to make up for their loss of revenue through advertising and other non-sales means. Furthermore, this rush was based on the desire to capture an early-mover advantage as described in the previous paragraph. These firms erroneously assumed that this would create barriers to entry, which would eventually lead to substantial market positions. This practice artificially lowered prices, which led to obvious increases in demand, albeit spurious and temporary. Next, customer curiosity triggered unnaturally high demands for Internet sales. Porter predicted that once this bubble burst, many customers would return to more traditional sales channels. Lastly, many companies who supposedly amassed large "revenues" through the Internet did so through stocks rather than cash. This meant that these companies were highly exposed to the volatile stock market.

Building on the last point, Porter also states that the current stock valuation of these companies is unreliable because it no longer reflects the economic value that these companies generate. Rather, it reflects speculation and overblown "revenue" which is also based on the expectations of investors. This was especially true with the dot-com companies that were able to raise significant capital over mere speculative investments. They did not demonstrate the ability to sustain competitive advantage and generate consistent economic value. In essence, the Internet has blown the value of companies, dot-coms and traditional ones alike, out of proportion in the unfounded belief that the Internet will somehow bring a sea-change to the business environment.

So what should be done to correct the current practices? Porter's suggestion is simple yet powerful: return to the fundamentals. Porter makes an important distinction between the use of the Internet and Internet technology itself. This distinction is important because while the Internet as a technology itself is standardized (which means anyone can use it in the business operation), the use of the Internet is what truly creates economic value. How, then, can the Internet be utilized properly in the strategic context? Porter asserts that businesses must look at two fundamental factors in profitability: (a) industry structure and (b) sustainable competitive advantage. These two factors, which have been extensively analyzed in Porter's previous works, transcend all technological innovations and types of businesses. At this point, Porter introduces a framework to visually describe how the Internet affects the industry structure (see Fig. 1).

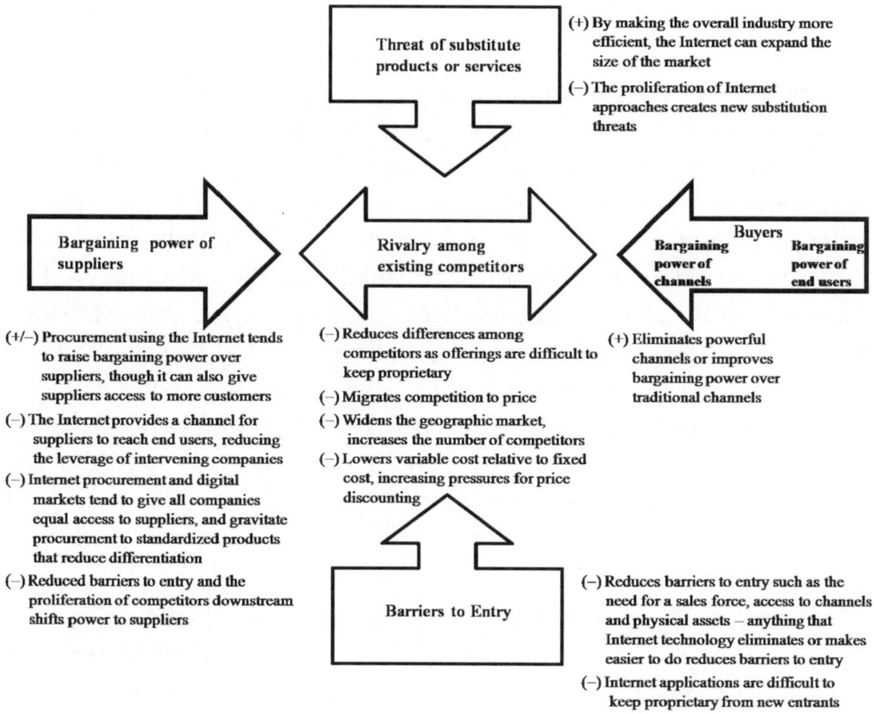

Fig. 1. The Internet's general impact on industry structure.[1]

As Fig. 1 demonstrates, the most pronounced influence of the Internet is that it enhances the bargaining power of the buyers. Since the Internet provides easier access to pricing and product information for the customers, companies have a more difficult time maintaining proprietary offerings. Customers can also take advantage of a wider range of firms, thus reducing the level of profit that can go to individual firms. Lastly, since the Internet has a standardizing effect and drives firms to compete based on the level of fixed cost (initially required to install the interface to operate on the Web) and reduce the average variable cost, firms engage in destructive price competition which reduces the overall attractiveness of the industry structure.

[1] Porter (2001).

Ironically, as the Internet grants easy access to information and reduces barriers to marketing, purchasing and distribution, it creates a more difficult environment for firms to capture profit.

However, this does not mean that firms do not have opportunities to enhance their potential through the Internet. As Porter has repeatedly emphasized, firms do not have to accept the pre-existing industry structure. Truly successful firms are those that are able to reshape the industry structure to their utmost advantage. The Internet can provide a very useful conduit in achieving this extraordinary feat. Porter implies that, depending on how firms fuse their traditional advantage with this exciting new technology, they can fundamentally alter the industry structure to create new economic value and unique services for their customers. In order to ground out the basic principles for firms to follow in achieving this, Porter returns to the two basic fundamentals of all successful businesses:

- *Operational Effectiveness* — This refers to performing the same things as your competitors, but in a more efficient manner. The Internet is a standardized platform that all firms can utilize to enhance their operations. Therefore, any innovation can be replicated quickly and will unlikely be a continued source of competitive advantage for firms.
- *Strategic Positioning* — How a firm decides to implement this concept is crucial, as strategic positioning is where the winners and losers differ. Rather than simply trying to differentiate through the Internet, firms must thoroughly integrate the Internet into their existing value chains in order to bolster their core competence and provide something unique to the customers.

Porter concludes that the Internet, contrary to popular belief, will largely have a neutral (if not destructive) effect on industry structure. The so-called "new economy" is nothing new. Rather, it is an old economy with access to a highly useful yet potentially destructive (in terms of industry structure) tool that can move competition in an unhealthy direction. Companies must utilize the new technology, but should not expect to distinguish themselves based solely on utilizing the Internet since everyone will be able to utilize this standardized feature. Instead, firms must look to more traditional sources of strengths, complemented and enhanced by the power of the Internet. Only then can firms create true economic value and specialized services for the customers, which will then lead to a sustainable, long-term competitive advantage.

Analysis

The Internet is an exciting new technology that can transform various aspects of business. However, it must be properly integrated into the firm strategy and value chain, or it may actually compromise the firm's strategic fit and further lead to destructive competition for the industry as a whole. Many firms and investors alike, swept away by the overhyped prospect of this new technology, forgot the fundamentals of competitive advantage, which are a unique positioning and a value proposition that enable firms to differentiate themselves from competitors and provide unique economic value to the customers. Although the Internet enhances operational effectiveness, it is a standardized feature in itself. Therefore, a firm that relies on the Internet to distinguish itself from the rest of the pack has made a critical error by forgetting what the fundamental sources of competitiveness are. Furthermore, Porter correctly points out how firms, in their hasty drive to achieve an early-mover advantage, have engaged themselves in destructive competition based on low price. Firms are then forced to run faster to maintain the same pace, and eventually all firms participating in the industry must suffer decreased profit margins and cut-throat competition.

One possible way to circumvent Porter's skepticism can be found from Prahalad and Ramaswamy's (2000) customer co-opting strategy (see Chap. 2 for details). Although Porter is largely correct in that increased consumer bargaining power decreases industry attractiveness, firms can actually turn this apparent disadvantage into an advantage. An increase in consumers' bargaining power could have negative effects on the industry structure, but Porter reminds us that firms which truly succeed are those that can alter the industry structure to their utmost advantage.

Consider Microsoft Windows 2000's beta-testing process, which Prahalad and Ramaswamy (2000) used to prove their point. Microsoft, before launching its Windows 2000 operating system, distributed a beta version of the new software to various consumer groups and encouraged them to test it out. After receiving feedback from its customers, Microsoft was able to create a more polished and complete version of Microsoft Windows 2000. In this process, Microsoft was able to save up to US$500 million in terms of R&D and software testing costs. Of course, Porter is generally correct in his overall analysis that the Internet is largely a negative rather than a positive influence on the industry structure. However, as the Microsoft case demonstrates, firms that creatively co-opt customers through the Internet can actually benefit instead of suffer, which shows that parts of Porter's skepticism can be circumvented through innovative and creative business practices.

3.2 Strategy and Philanthropic Organizations

Max Weber (1930, reprinted 2002) once stated that profit, when ethically generated and used for the greater good of society, can be the fundamental building block of a healthy capitalist society. Weber's extensive analysis on the relationship between the traditional Puritan emphasis on thrift, hard work, ethical profit and the normative fabric of a modern capitalist society can be regarded as the original conception of philanthropy through private foundations.

As Weber's grand reconciliation between profit and ethics prescribed, wealthy Americans went on to build various philanthropic foundations that tackle many social issues. From Andrew Carnegie to modern figures such as Bill Gates and Warren Buffett, the most successful individuals of the American (and perhaps global) capitalist system have altruistically given away billions of dollars for the greater societal cause. However, the normative nature of these foundations has somewhat prevented an objective and precise strategic analysis of the activities they perform.

Porter and Kramer (1999) boldly defy such taboo and identify several problems associated with the current state of practice in philanthropic foundations, and give several suggestions to fix the current problems and enhance their performance. Their central question asks whether society is efficiently maximizing the full benefit of philanthropic foundations. The simple answer is "not quite", and the authors begin to present their case as to why the current practices are problematic.

Foundations exist because they can channel funds to solve social problems more effectively than individuals or governments. Since foundations are subject to tax exemptions and other benefits, the society expects foundations to achieve more social impact than if the same amount of resources were channeled through governments or individuals. For example, if a donor gives away $100 to a foundation, the society as a whole loses about $40 in tax revenue. Therefore, the $40 must be better utilized to service society than it would have been if given to the government. However, this is under the assumption that all of the $100 is effectively used by the foundation. In reality, foundations only utilize 5.5% of their total assets for charitable purposes. This is far less than the $40 that would have gone to the government, which would have been channeled for societal services if the $100 were taxed instead of given away to philanthropic foundations.

Furthermore, by holding so much money (say, $330 billion) and not spending it for charitable purposes, the society is incurring a substantial cost in terms of deferred social benefits. Since donations receive tax exemptions and foundations are not taxed for the appreciation of their financial assets, the amount of tax revenue that would have been collected by the government accumulates substantially over time. Also, one must consider the fact that these foundations have substantial administrative costs such as staffing and screening of appropriate candidates. From this discussion, one can easily see that foundations are actually a very expensive way to allocate capital for social services.

Foundations, by withholding the money, have an obligation to provide social benefit which exceeds the withheld purchasing power.

How can foundations achieve this? The key to this answer is "strategy". Just as businesses set up strategies to achieve their goals, foundations must do the same. Porter and Kramer (1999) suggest four specific areas that foundations must focus on.

- *Selecting the Best Grantees* — This process must start out based on a unique position upon which the foundation can best utilize its expertise to generate the most social value. Instead of trying to provide funds for all disadvantaged students, foundations must focus on a certain segment of the population. Also, instead of focusing on a vague goal, foundations must set up a specific goal such as "we will reduce high-school dropout rates in a certain area". In essence, foundations must develop their unique capabilities to specialize in creating societal services. Furthermore, foundations must be able to critically examine their own performance, not just their recipients'. Only through constant self-assessment can foundations innovate in order to create more value for less. Foundations, just like firms, cannot be all things to all people. They must choose their battleground and must make decisions regarding the tradeoff they will face in terms of the scarce resources they have.
- *Signaling Other Funders* — Just like how a corporation markets itself to potential investors, a foundation must do exactly the same to its potential donors. By promoting the foundation as a specialized and effective organization in providing societal services, donors will have more confidence in the money that they give away, knowing that it will be spent most effectively.
- *Improving the Performance of Grant Recipients* — Instead of simply giving away money, foundations should also monitor and help recipients in enhancing their performance. If the money is simply given away, there is no guarantee that it will be spent for the intended purposes. Through engaging and monitoring the recipients on a long-term scale, a foundation can ensure that it achieves its fundamental purpose, which is to create more societal value from every dollar spent. This is linked to the above two

activities, as monitoring and engaging the recipient will further improve the foundation's self-assessment as well as its ability to signal other funders.

- *Advancing the State of Knowledge and Practice* — Since foundations are uniquely positioned to be active in achieving a certain societal goal along a long time horizon, they can fund research and support a systematic progression of projects. The knowledge and experiences accumulated through this process can then be transmitted to other organizations, such as the government and other philanthropic organizations, to further enhance the impact of the entire system.

In essence, just like successful firms, foundations must also be highly specialized, systematic and focused in their approach to create social services. In order to achieve this, the foundation's staff, methods and activities must be tailored to best fit the target segment and societal service that it wishes to provide. However, the reality is that the operations of most foundations are far from Porter and Kramer's (1999) prescriptions. According to available data, foundations are spread too thin in terms of money and staff. This is a major problem because foundations cannot focus or take a unique position without concentrating their resources into specific target areas.

Problems in the foundations' self-assessment methods are also discussed in detail by the authors. Foundations rarely assess themselves properly because of inappropriate performance criteria, which only focus on whether the money was spent as intended rather than whether the money has actually generated the desired societal impact. Also, recipients themselves do the evaluations, thus raising questions over objectivity. Lastly, most evaluations are done in a very limited scope since they rely primarily on interviews with individual grantees. This is highly problematic, and a more comprehensive and general self-assessment approach is critically required for foundations.

The authors conclude that current foundation practices not only diminish effectiveness, but inevitably reduce the satisfaction that donors, staff and trustees derive from their work. Unless foundations accept the fact that they must enhance their accountability, expertise and productivity, they cannot truly perform their intended functions.

Analysis

To some people, applying an analytical business framework to a philanthropic foundation may seem rather inappropriate. The idea of fusing the cold and calculating nature of business strategy to the warm and altruistic purpose of philanthropic foundations may not sit comfortably. However, as one can see from Porter and Kramer's (1999) brilliant article, they were able to clearly identify the true strengths and weaknesses of philanthropic foundations and make valuable suggestions to enhance their performance through a business framework. Just as a successful business must generate more value with every penny that it spends, a philanthropic foundation must generate more social value for every dollar that comes from donors. The general lesson that can be learned from this analysis is that productivity, positioning, innovation and specialization are the keys for both business and non-business entities alike.

3.3 Strategy and Society

Corporate social responsibility (CSR) has been receiving increasing attention from various segments of academia, managers and policy makers. International organizations such as the United Nations, for example, have taken proactive measures to promote and implement CSR as a measure to fight global poverty, especially in the context of its ambitious "Millennium Development Goals". This reflects the recognition that spurring a healthy and responsible entrepreneurial environment is one of the most powerful drivers of economic, social and political development. Therefore, it is no surprise that many publications and research studies have focused on this important issue. Also, many scholars have identified and analyzed various dimensions of CSR, such as the relationship between CSR and business ethics

(Balmer *et al.* 2007), CSR and finance (Cochran and Wood 1984) and CSR and politics (Jeurissen 2004).

More systematically, Porter and Kramer (2006) look at the relationship between CSR and business strategy. The authors then point out two major problems with the current state of CSR. The first problem is that many view the relationship between society and businesses as inherently conflicting. CSR is viewed as an obligation that firms must begrudgingly perform in order to appease people's concerns that corporations negatively affect society. The second problem is that, because of this erroneous perception, firms promote CSR in generic terms, as if it is a chore that must be done. It is largely done carelessly and without much effort. Therefore, it is not surprising that the current state of CSR practices is inefficient and insincere.

The authors suggest that it is time for firms to take a different approach to CSR: firms should regard CSR as a fertile ground for opportunity, innovation and competitive advantage. Fundamentally, the relationship between firms and society is not a zero-sum relationship, but a mutually beneficial one in which both the society and firms can enhance each other through CSR. How can we achieve this? The starting point in answering this question is for firms to start looking at CSR in the same strategic mindset in which they operate their day-to-day business. Currently, most CSR ranking systems focus solely upon superficial data such as the number of hours, amount of money and number of volunteers mobilized for CSR activities. These are rather meaningless, as the true measure of effective CSR should be the impact of CSR, not the input.

At this point, the authors analyze the four prevailing justifications for CSR:

- *Moral Obligation* — This is the most common and traditional dimension, which describes the normative obligation to be good citizens and perform positive citizenry. Commercial success must be achieved without breaking societal moral codes of conduct and without harming the environment.

- *Sustainability* — Companies are obliged to operate in ways that will not harm the society's long-term economic potential. For example, using hazardous materials to enhance short-term profitability should be avoided, since it can destroy the environment and lead to negative externalities.
- *License to Operate* — A firm consists of various stakeholders whose interests must be protected. Traditionally, this obligation was merely confined to the shareholders' profit maximization, but now the concept has been expanded to incorporate a wider range of groups. For example, if a company is to operate in a certain area, it must be aware of the concerns that the residents of that area have. This principle can be applied especially well to extractive industries and others that could potentially create hazardous materials or harm the people in the area.
- *Reputation* — Corporate image is crucial, especially with the rise of environmental and political awareness. Sophisticated consumers with environmental and political awareness will prefer companies with a good CSR track record. This is important for firms because it translates into corporate image, which affects sales and profitability.

The underlying premise of the above four categories is that firms must sacrifice a certain degree of their profitability in order to achieve socially beneficial outcomes. In other words, the prevailing notion of CSR regards firms and societies to be locked in a zero-sum battle between profit and CSR. Porter and Kramer (2006) assert that this view is not only outdated, but also socially inefficient. Firms are not separate from society, as firms have a tremendous capability to enrich society through providing various resources to increase social capital. Society, in turn, can help firms become more profitable and competitive through providing better human resources and business environments. The two entities can engage in a positive-sum game instead of a zero-sum one. Porter and Kramer suggest five ways in which this transformation can be realized.

Identifying the Points of Intersection

These intersections are where CSR should take place in order to be most effective. The authors make a very important distinction between inside-out linkages and outside-in linkages when viewing the points of intersection between firms and society. Inside-out linkage refers to the firms' capability to influence society. For example, firms that create hazardous waste material create a negative influence, while those that offer sound on-the-job training create a positive influence on society. Outside-in linkage is how society affects firms. Social conditions are very important in deciding whether a firm can be profitable and competitive. Available human resources, customer sophistication, infrastructure, and rules and regulations all have significant impacts on firms. Understanding these linkages is the first key to identifying the specific areas in which a firm can perform the most effective CSR (see Fig. 2).

Choosing Social Issues to Address

Porter repeatedly asserted that no firm can be everything to everyone. Therefore, firms must pick and choose their most advantageous battleground in order to succeed. The same principle can be applied for CSR. Firms must concern themselves with those social issues which they are most capable of solving and also those that will help

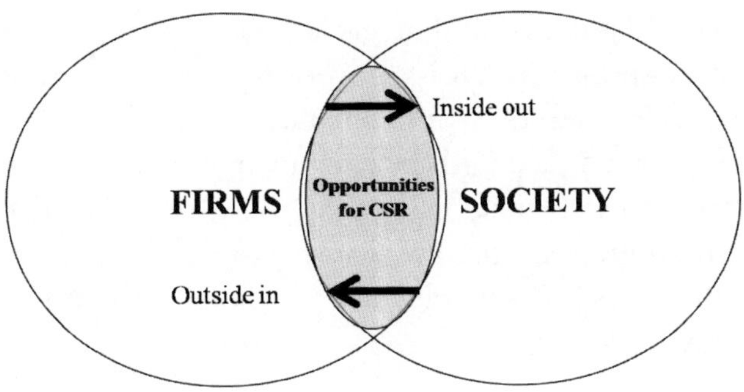

Fig. 2. Interdependence of firm and society through linkages.

enhance their competitiveness and profitability. Depending on the firm, the same social issue may be categorized differently. For example, carbon emission is a generic social issue, but for Honda, it has both a value chain impact and a social dimension. Furthermore, even within the same industry, different companies may have a different weight of priority on the same social issue. Porter and Kramer (2006) give the example of automobile safety in which Volvo has clearly made it its priority, while for Toyota, environmental friendliness is more of a priority than safety. The point here is that firms must perform CSR in areas where they are most affected and will be the most effective. All social issues are important, but certain firms are better equipped and motivated to tackle certain social issues. GE is better equipped to perform CSR in healthcare than Honda, while Honda is more willing to allocate its resources in CSR activities related to carbon emission.

Creating a Corporate Social Agenda

This refers to setting a corporate social agenda that enables a firm to move on from simply solving social problems to making CSR profitable for firms. In other words, CSR helps not only the society, but also the firm itself. In order to help refine this concept better, the authors suggest two types of CSR:

- *Responsive CSR* — Every corporate activity has some kind of impact (both positive and negative) on the society in which it operates. Responsive CSR is a corporate measure designed to mitigate adverse effects from business activities. For example, companies which deal with hazardous materials can allocate additional resources to make sure that these materials do not harm society. It should be noted that responsive CSR may stop adverse effects, but does not generate any additional benefit to the firm or the society.
- *Strategic CSR* — Contrary to responsive CSR, strategic CSR is a more proactive and evolved way of performing CSR. In other

words, CSR activities not only prevent adverse effects, but also generate positive externalities which benefit both firms and societies. For example, Microsoft works with the American Association of Community Colleges (AACC) to provide better equipment, human resources and other aid in order to enhance the quality of IT programs in these colleges. As a result, more students are able to obtain better jobs (societal benefits), while Microsoft is more easily able to recruit IT specialists suitable for its operations (firm benefits).

Integrating Inside-Out and Outside-In Practices

This describes how firms can further magnify the positive effects by performing CSR in such a way that it reduces the constraints put on the firm's value chain activities. For example, Marriott provides paid on-the-job training for unemployed job candidates who have been approved by the local community. Ninety percent of those in the training program take jobs with Marriott. This way, society benefits with more employed constituents, while Marriott can reduce the administrative cost in screening potential candidates. This kind of fully integrated model is the most sustainable, mutually beneficial and influential type of CSR that corporations can perform.

Another example is Nestle in India. Nestle needed a stable and fresh source of milk in Moga, India, in order to establish its business. However, local farmers in Moga were suffering from low calf-survival rates, poor logistics, lack of infrastructure and overall poverty. Nestle achieved a remarkable task by establishing refrigerated collection points for local dairy farmers, and then used those points as a fulcrum for strategic CSR. From these collection points, Nestle deployed trained veterinarians and other experts to local farmers in order to transfer the knowledge, technology and equipment necessary to enhance the calf-survival rate and set up a better farm infrastructure. The once poverty-stricken area of Moga transformed into a bustling dairy industry hub of India, while Nestle was able to benefit from the fresh dairy that local farmers produce.

Creating a Social Dimension to the Value Proposition

The last point is to perform CSR that benefits not only the value chain, but the entire firm strategy. For example, Whole Foods, which specializes in organic food products, makes sure that its commitment to environmentally friendly practices is reflected in every aspect of the firm's strategy. Not only does it encourage buyers to screen out food that is unhealthy, but it is also committed to using 100% wind energy for all of its facilities and stores. Furthermore, the company sponsors other environment-friendly agendas such as the Animal Compassion Foundation, which develops methods to raise livestock in a more humane manner. In essence, the entire value proposition of this firm — and hence the whole strategy — is built on safe, organic, natural and environmentally friendly food. The core message behind these discussions is that firms must integrate CSR into their firm value chain rather than viewing CSR as a separate activity. Figure 3 summarizes

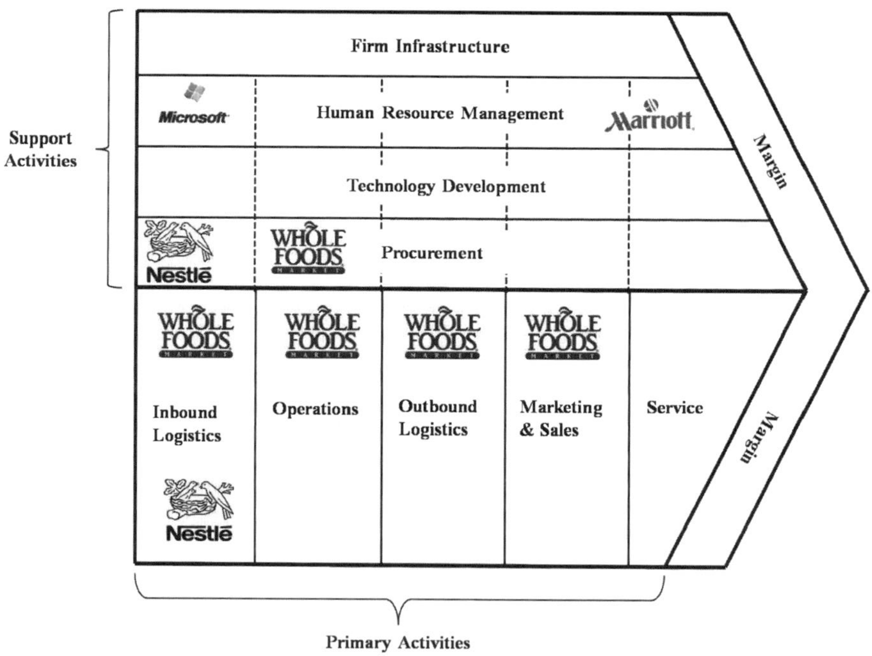

Fig. 3. Value chain analysis of CSR (Nestle, Marriott, Whole Foods and Microsoft).

how Microsoft, Marriott, Nestle and Whole Foods have incorporated CSR into their value chains.

In conclusion, Porter and Kramer (2006) urge firms and social constituents to stop looking at CSR as a burden, but more as an opportunity. At the same time, society must also stop regarding firms as immoral entities that will sacrifice social benefits for the sake of profits, but as an integral part of society which can generate immense economic and social value. Instead of regarding CSR as a "responsibility", the concept should evolve to "corporate social integration". There are plenty of dimensions and arenas in which both firms and society can harmoniously interact to create immense social value. The key step is for both parties to realize this and transform their mindsets to a more positive and proactive one.

Analysis

The strategic CSR paradigm presents a new framework for understanding and executing CSR. For many years, the general public has held a skeptical view regarding corporate motivations and promoted CSR as a buffer to keep business entities in check. However, firms are not only an integral part of society, but also entities that can generate immense social capital through their vast resources and capabilities.

One possible extension would be to expand Porter and Kramer's (2006) article into analyzing the multiplying effects that the positive externalities generated by corporations can have on society as a whole. The authors focus primarily on redefining the relationship and interaction between firms and society in terms of CSR, as depicted in Fig. 2. In other words, the focus is limited to the two-way transfer between the two sectors. However, as the authors emphasized towards the end of the article, the concept of CSR must change from responsibility to integration. In order to depict this idea more aptly, one must also be aware that the CSR performed according to this article will have a much more far-reaching consequence than that described by the authors. As Fig. 4 depicts, what Porter and Kramer propose can be extended to a more comprehensive mechanism for generating positive externalities, which all social constituents can enjoy. While the authors have aptly described the dynamics that should occur between the targeted segment of society and firms, they did not mention how this will emanate throughout the society.

Consider the Microsoft–AACC example mentioned previously to explain strategic CSR. As Microsoft allocates its human and financial resources to various community colleges around the United States, the recipients benefit from increased employability and job stability, while Microsoft benefits from an enhanced pool of human resources. However, this increased pool of human resources benefits not only Microsoft and the recipients, but other firms as well. Furthermore, since community colleges generally cater to more underprivileged students, this CSR activity also generates additional social capital by reducing the wealth divide and enhancing livelihood in poorer areas of America. Thus, what we witness is not just a two-way interaction between the firm and the target segment of society, but a creation of immense social capital that benefits others who are not directly involved in this CSR, as shown in Fig. 4.

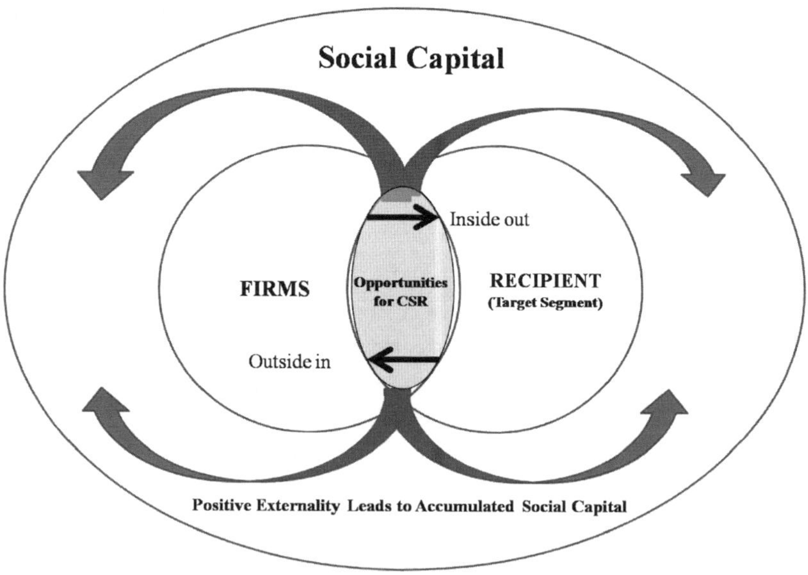

Fig. 4. Extended view of strategic CSR.

Case Study 1: Giordano of Hong Kong[2]

Giordano is one of Asia Pacific's leading apparel retailers. It has grown from a simple manufacturing company, based out of Hong Kong, to a global retailer in over 19 countries worldwide. Originally, most of the company's success came from the Asian region, but it is now beginning to venture into North America and the Middle East. More recently, Giordano made notable progress in the online strategy. Like many other retailers, Giordano has hedged its bets on expanding its business and consumer market through the online shopping industry. In 2006, in China alone, Giordano was able to hit online sales of RMB40 million (US$5.5 million) with only two IT employees assigned to the task of website maintenance and no further investments made.

Using the five-forces model, we can analyze just how attractive the apparel retail industry is and then compare that analysis with a post-Internet strategy implementation. Figure 5 shows the pre-Internet industry analysis.

As we can see from Fig. 5, the apparel retail industry is not very attractive: competition is stiff, barriers to entry are low and buyers hold a strong bargaining power. Giordano has suffered due to the high level of industry competition from others such as UNIQLO and Who.A.U. However, if a particular firm were to extend its brand recognition to the Internet, it could potentially increase its sphere of influence over competitors and grab a larger share of the market. Giordano has done this and has become one of the few garment retailers in Asia to offer online shopping through its website. If we apply the same five-forces model but include factors related to the Internet, we can see a difference in industry attractiveness.

As illustrated in Fig. 6, we can see that the Internet has enhanced the level of industry attractiveness. However, the Internet should not be solely considered in explaining the enhanced level of the firm's

[2] Information for this case study is abstracted from the Giordano website (www.giordano.com.hk), the Giordano online shopping website (hk.e-giordano.com) and *Hong Kong Trader* (2001).

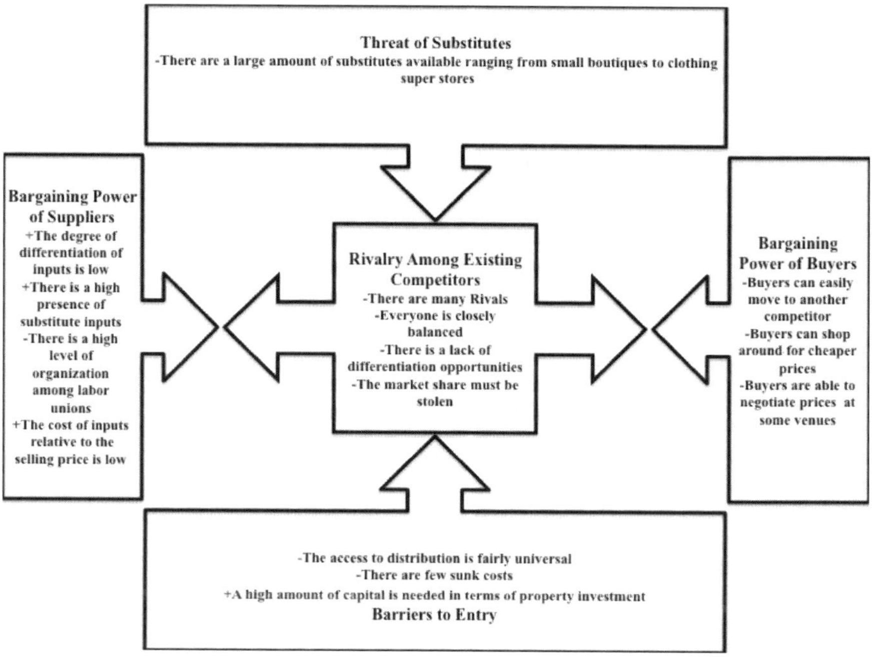

Fig. 5. Five-forces analysis of the apparel industry (before Internet).

competitive advantage, but should be used in conjunction with the firm's existing strategies and business plans. Giordano started with manufacturing, moved into retailing and is now reaching more customers than ever through taking advantage of the Internet technology.

Case Study 2: Temasek Trust of Singapore[3]

Temasek Holdings in Singapore established the Temasek Trust in 2007 with an initial endowment gift of S$500 million. The foundation was launched to focus on programs that contribute to the development of people in Asia, including Singapore. The foundation

[3] Information for this case study is abstracted from the Temasek Holdings website (www.temasekholdings.com.sg).

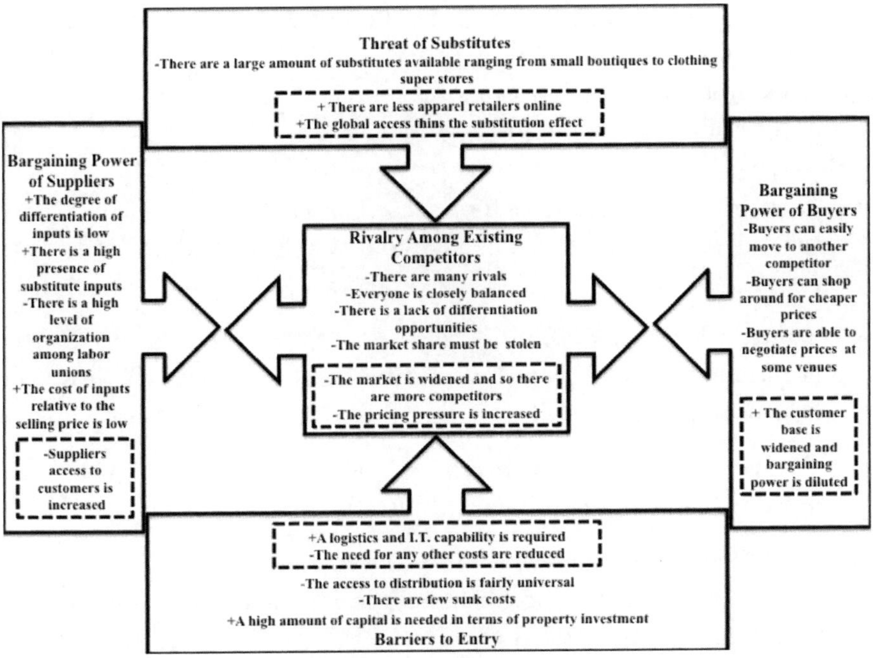

Fig. 6. Five-forces analysis of the apparel industry (after Internet).

is headquartered in Singapore, and its philosophy has been to both benefit from and contribute to the growth and development in Asia. Temasek Holdings sees its long-term future as anchored in a thriving and peaceful Asia, and thus it is in the company's best interests to cultivate the Asian community. So far, the institution has been playing a quiet role in sponsoring scholarships, supporting disaster relief, organizing youth exchange programs and funding research programs. It does accept gifts from third parties, but it does not actively solicit donations. The Trust also supports four nonprofit philanthropic organizations: (a) Temasek Foundation, (b) Singapore Technologies Endowment Program, (c) Singapore Millennium Foundation, and (d) Temasek Life Sciences Laboratory.

Does Temasek Trust have a strategy? Is it creating the maximum value with the resources it is holding back from society? The answer is no. The main problem is its purported goal of contributing to long-term growth in Asia. There can be hundreds, if not thousands, of milestones to be reached in order to fulfill this goal. Therefore, Temasek must reduce the scope of its aim and focus on a specific area along the following guidelines:

- *Strategy Depends on Choosing a Unique Positioning* — The Trust must decide which social challenge it wishes to address and focus on it.
- *Strategy Rests on Unique Activities* — Every other aspect of the foundation must then follow and be geared towards the position it has chosen for itself.
- *Positioning Requires Tradeoffs* — The Trust has to be willing to forego other opportunities and just say "no".
- *Goal Is Superior Performance in Chosen Area* — The Trust has to begin monitoring its performances in its chosen area and consistently improving upon them.

With a well-defined strategy in place, the Trust must now create value, which means that its activities must create social benefit. This can be achieved in four ways: (a) selecting the best grantees, (b) signaling other funders, (c) improving the performance of grant recipients, and (d) advancing the state of knowledge and practice.

Using the framework below, the Trust can provide a much greater social benefit overall (see Fig. 7).

Thus, the Trust, after selecting a focus such as higher education, would act to ensure that only the best applicants secure scholarships, thereby increasing the likelihood of a successful graduation. Furthermore, the Trust should ensure that it is able to improve the performance of recipients in order to improve the returns on the money it has spent. Signaling other funders would increase the amount of capital available to aid the project, and so a Trust must be willing to act interdependently with other funders. Lastly, the Trust should continuously advance its knowledge and practice by investing in research projects related to its area of expertise, and transmit its

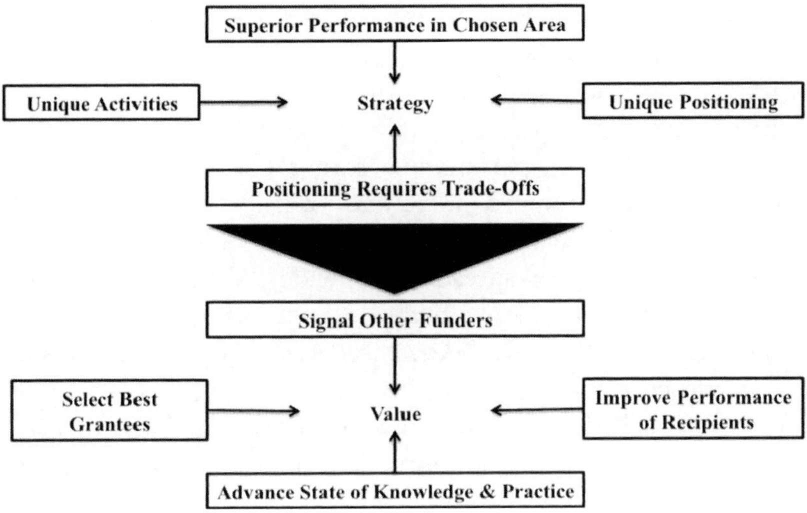

Fig. 7. Creating value.

experiences to other foundations to enhance the role of the entire philanthropic system.

Case Study 3: Yuhan-Kimberly Goes Green[4]

Yuhan-Kimberly is an example of a company that has truly leveraged itself on the basis of CSR. Its reputation precedes itself, and it is flooded with inquiries from other firms and various governments year after year regarding the secrets of its success. At Yuhan-Kimberly, the CEO title holds a different meaning. He is not known as the Chief Executive Officer, but rather as the Chief Environmental Officer.

Kook-hyun Moon, the former CEO of Yuhan-Kimberly, led the company from success to greater success with his self-created concept of "environmental management". He began his career at Yuhan-Kimberly in 1983 after spending a year in the United States developing

[4] Information for this case study is abstracted from the Yuhan-Kimberly website (www.yuhan-kimberly.co.kr), *The Chosun Ilbo* (2001) and *The Korea Herald* (2004).

new management concepts. Upon his return, he implemented a number of reforms within Yuhan-Kimberly based on two principles: (a) clean production/conservation of resources and (b) efficient and transparent management.

The company, a paper manufacturing company, imports only enough pulp to cover approximately 5% of its production, while 95% comes from recycled paper. Reforms were not only instigated within the company, but soon spread nationwide. Also, in 1983, Moon started the Forest For Life initiative, whose catchphrase was "Keep Korea Green" (*Uri Kangsan Purugae Purugae*). Over 20 years later, the Korean people are beginning to feel the impacts and benefits of this program, as their mountains have been reforested and their rivers cleaned after a period of rapid industrial expansion which ravaged the natural beauty of Korea.

Moon also realized that most companies only operated at about 34% of their equipment's capacity, as they did not run machines during the night or on holidays. By not operating at full capacity, many companies see their debt ratio grow while their profitability remains low. Great facilities do not equate to great efficiency; thus, he implemented a flexible work program, which allowed his factories to run for 24 hours per day. Workers work for four days of 12-hour shifts, but then rest for four days (three rest days and one education and training day). As a result, the company also sees one of the lowest staff turnover rates in the world and did not have to resort to lay-offs during the financial crisis of 1997 that severely hit Korea.

Many companies shy away from CSR, mainly due to the fear that it will result in another obligation which will eat away their profits. However, since 1970, Yuhan-Kimberly has maintained a high level of profitability. By focusing on environmental protection, employee protection and training that it has managed to streamline its business practices, the company can consistently save money, increase efficiency, enhance brand recognition and thus raise its competitive advantage to a level previously unseen. Indeed, it is now the benchmark for companies wishing to develop their CSR departments.

However, if the company were to apply the CSR strategy proposed by Porter and Kramer (2006), the effects would be further reaching and more beneficial within and outside the firm. Yuhan-Kimberly's CSR thus far has been more of the responsive-type CSR, which helps protect society as a whole and improves the company's image. But by moving to a more strategic CSR, it can create more benefits for both the firm and the society.

Yuhan-Kimberley is obviously toying with the concept of strategic CSR by the way it has altered its factory practices, but this impacts only one part of the value chain. Despite the limited application, the benefits of Yuhan-Kimberly's strategic CSR have been profound. It will be interesting to see whether Yuhan-Kimberly further integrates strategic CSR into its firm value chain, and what kind of impact this will have on its operation and business environment.

Discussion Questions

1. Do you agree with Porter's (2001) summation that the Internet can be more damaging than beneficial to industry attractiveness?
2. Can you think of a business type that could make a healthy, sustainable profit solely from the Internet strategy? Explain your case.
3. Can a pure business strategy really be applied so easily to other institutions such as philanthropic or charitable foundations? Explain.
4. What problems can be foreseen when applying the steps recommended by Porter and Kramer (1999) to a foundation-type organization? How can these be overcome?
5. Corporate social responsibility — useful strategy or merely an image booster? Discuss.
6. Can CSR really benefit everyone? Do you think it benefits one party more than another? If so, how and why?
7. Using Porter and Kramer's (2006) framework, how could we improve either Temasek Trust or Yuhan-Kimberley's lacking strategy? Discuss.

CHAPTER 4

Extension of Generic Strategy

Chapter Guideline

Now that we have a clear understanding of the far-reaching analytical power of Porter's frameworks, it is time to take a deeper dive into his methods. This chapter will extend Porter's discussion and will take a more in-depth and updated look into Porter's insights. How did Porter come up with his approach? What is Porter's definition of "strategy"? How are other prominent figures in business affected by Porter and how do they assess him? This chapter will provide answers to these questions in order to present the reader with a clearer and more comprehensive view of understanding Michael Porter's true contribution.

Summary of Previous Models

In the previous chapter, we witnessed the flexibility and far-reaching explanatory power of Porter's analytical framework. Furthermore, the previous chapter succinctly presented the most cutting-edge issues in business, such as corporate social responsibility (CSR), the Internet and philanthropy. The common theme that flows among all these works is that these issues must be dealt with in the context of strategy. For example, CSR needs to be dealt with in a strategic manner, while the Internet must be interwoven into a broader strategic context. Philanthropy must also be targeted and executed based on a strategy to maximize the value of every dollar spent. It is obvious that Porter's frameworks have had enormous staying power in a field in which short-lived fads are the norm. Therefore, this chapter will attempt to present the reader with materials that provide a more in-depth understanding of the impact and origins of Porter's various frameworks.

4.1 Operational Effectiveness versus Strategic Positioning

In understanding business strategy, one common error is to apply the military conception of strategy to the world of business. Of course, many of the ideas conveyed in military strategic thinking are highly applicable to business. However, it is also very important to bear in mind that the ultimate purpose of military strategy differs from that of business strategy. As the eminent Prussian military strategist, Carl Von Clausewitz (1832, reprinted 1982, p. 101), asserted, "War is an act of violence intended to compel our opponent to fulfill our will... physical force is therefore the means; the compulsory submission of the enemy to our will is the ultimate object." War, therefore, is inevitably a zero-sum struggle because the winner must inevitably subdue the loser. Business strategy, however, is far from a zero-sum game, unless firms erroneously engage in destructive competition. Porter (1996) lucidly explains how the appropriate application of business strategy can lead to a positive-sum game, which further maximizes the value created by individual firms.

Porter (1996) begins by lamenting the current business practice trend to neglect positioning (which is at the heart of strategy). Managers, in their attempt to cope with a dynamic and volatile environment, have engaged in destructive hypercompetition, which is purely based on productivity, quality and speed. These are, in Porter's terms, operational effectiveness aspects, which are clearly necessary but not sufficient in order to gain a real sustaining competitive advantage.

It is important to distinguish between operational effectiveness (OE) and strategic positioning (SP) because the two terms are often confused and misused. OE, in essence, is executing similar activities more efficiently than rivals, while SP means performing different activities from rivals' or performing similar activities in different ways.

OE is the basic necessary condition, while strategy is what gives the firm a true source of competitive advantage.

Examples of OE include organizational efficiency, advanced technology and better management practices. These are all areas in which Japanese firms were able to excel in the 1980s. Through this advantage in OE, Japanese firms were able to offer superior quality at lower cost. However, the problem with this kind of advantage is that other firms will soon catch up with these best practices and move closer to the productivity frontier, which leads to destructive hypercompetition. The gains from this competition benefit the consumers and suppliers at the expense of the firms' profit, as firms increasingly face diminishing returns on their enhanced OE. Therefore, the consistent source of long-term competitive advantage comes from occupying a unique strategic position and shifting the productivity frontier outward, as illustrated in Fig. 1.

How can firms achieve this? Porter (1996) suggests three ways in which firms can develop their true competitive advantages.

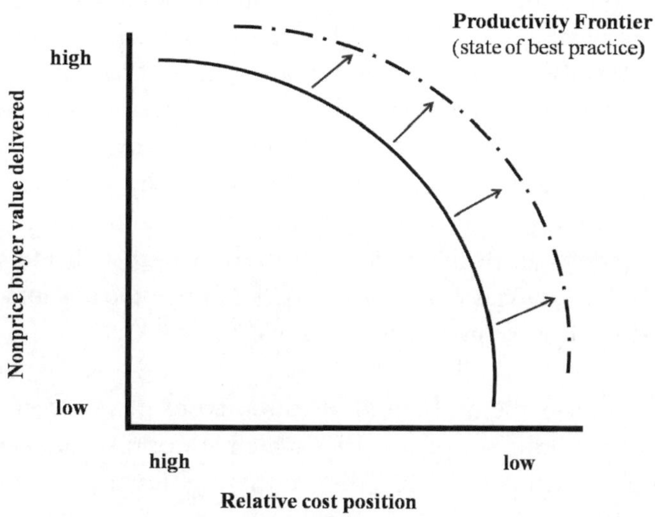

Fig. 1. Operational effectiveness versus strategic positioning.[1]

[1] Porter (1996).

- *Variety-based Positioning* — This positioning serves a wide variety of customers, but a very specific set of customer needs. For example, Jiffy Lube, an automotive lubricant company, does not offer any other service or product. The company's intense focus on lubricants gives customers a unique value proposition that rivals cannot match.
- *Needs-based Positioning* — This is based on targeting a particular customer segment and servicing its needs through a set of activities. It is crucial to understand that differences in needs will not translate into meaningful positions, unless the best set of activities to satisfy them also differs. IKEA, for example, seeks to satisfy all the needs of a specific segment of customers: young and price-sensitive customers. It provides various home furnishing options, but specifically caters mostly to newlyweds or younger couples.
- *Access-based Positioning* — Customer needs may be similar across segments, but the best configuration of activities to reach each segment is different. Elements of this configuration include geography, customer scale or any kind of differences in access channel. Access-based positioning derives its strength from segmenting customers who are accessible through different ways or channels. For example, Carmike Cinemas, a movie theater operator, has established theaters all across rural America. The company specifically targets towns with a population fewer than 200,000 and customizes all of its operations accordingly. Standardized, low-cost theaters suit the rural Americans' taste, thus creating a competitive advantage that is very difficult for competitors to replicate.

The common theme behind all three types of positioning is the presence of a unique set of activities which are optimized to serve the firm's target customers. This differentiating feature, according to Porter (1996), is what sets successful firms apart from mediocre ones. However, just picking a position is insufficient, as other firms will attempt to take over that position through various maneuvers. This can happen when rivals either reposition themselves to the valuable position or by straddling, which refers to a rival providing the same benefits in that position.

Does this mean that finding a unique position is futile? Not entirely! Porter (1996) asserts that occupying these unique and valuable positions for the long term requires tradeoffs. For example, a firm can choose to tailor all of its activities to serve the lower end of an industry, thereby occupying a unique position. This firm can then focus all of its resources to consolidate its position in a particular part of the industry.

Only when a firm makes tradeoffs to occupy these positions can it truly obtain strategic positioning. By making a tradeoff, the firm pushes potential imitators to also make tradeoffs, thus making it costly for them to compete. But how do these tradeoffs occur? The first source is inconsistency in image. For example, if a company that used to provide luxury products suddenly tries to reposition or straddle itself in the lower end of the market, it will suffer from image inconsistency. This is a significant risk for the potential imitator. The second source is the required changes in firm activity. Again, a former luxury product provider must reorganize certain parts of its organization and reallocate its resources to move into the lower-end segment. These additional costs create a barrier which protects the firm that already occupies a unique position in the lower-end market.

Therefore, a firm already occupying a unique position must strive to make the magnitude of this tradeoff as large as possible to fend off potential competitors. This can be achieved by what Porter (1996) describes as choosing the best "fit", which refers to combining various individual activities into a cohesive and unique system. When a firm creates robust fit, different activities create a synergistic effect that reinforces the entire system. This fit is difficult for competitors to replicate and overcome.

More specifically, Porter (1996) presents three types of fits which are most common among successful firms:

- *First-Order Fit* — It is important for a firm's overall strategy and its individual activities to be consistent. This brings cohesion to the position, as all activities are geared towards achieving a single goal.

- *Second-Order Fit* — After consistency is achieved, a firm can arrange its activities so that they reinforce each other to generate synergies. Then, the whole becomes larger than the sum of the parts as all the activities are not only being focused, but also creating a plus alpha to bolster the entire system.
- *Third-Order Fit* — The most sophisticated fit involves those who are not directly participating in the firm activities. In a third-order fit, outside players such as customers and suppliers magnify the synergy through their interactions with the firm.

The higher the order of fit, the higher the magnitude of the tradeoff that potential imitators have to suffer. This effectively enables firms to capture a unique positioning and long-term sustainable competitive advantage.

Then why do firms fail to achieve this? One of the main reasons is what Porter (1996) calls the "growth trap", which refers to a situation in which a firm's desire to promote increased growth comes at the expense of the firm's strategic position. For example, when a firm which was successful in one market segment determines that this particular segment is saturated, it is pressured to seek new fields to grow further. This in itself is not a bad maneuver, but the problem is that many firms sacrifice their original strategic fit to pursue new endeavors. Therefore, firms that wish to gain long-term competitive advantage must look to keep profitable growth by deepening their original strategic position rather than by trying to broaden it. This does not mean that firms should limit themselves to certain areas. Rather, firms must broaden their scope of operation only under the condition that the expansion does not compromise the fit.

In conclusion, successful firms must keep pushing the productivity frontier while also deepening their strategic position through upgrading the order of their fits. Without such commitment, firms will end up broadening at the expense of their unique positioning, while also damaging the entire industry structure by promoting hypercompetition based solely on superior OE.

Analysis

Porter's (1996) valuable insights appropriately identify the problems with current businesses and offer a clear-cut remedy. Furthermore, by pointing out that even in a dynamic, ever-changing business environment, there are still certain core principles that firms can hold onto and the ability to use them as their blueprint for success is very reassuring. Lastly, Porter's analysis on "fits" shows readers why truly successful companies with long-term competitive advantage are not those that are most efficient in terms of doing the same activities better than others, but rather those that focus on differentiating themselves from the rest of the pack by creating a unique "fit". This concept also shows why competitors who focus solely on operational effectiveness will have a very difficult time emulating and competing against firms that have made tradeoffs and distinguished themselves from the rest.

Nevertheless, there are several issues that need to be raised with this perspective. First is the elusive relationship between OE/SP and cost leadership/differentiation. According to Porter's logic, cost advantage is derived from more efficient performances of certain activities, while differentiation is generated from the choice of activities and method of performance. This logic is represented as the bold, straight arrows in Fig. 2.

However, the examples that Porter uses, such as Southwest Airlines and IKEA, have achieved their strong *strategic positioning* through a cost leadership strategy. Therefore, the question arises as to whether OE can actually be a source of both cost leadership and differentiation. Conversely, even SP can lead to both cost leadership and differentiation, as pursuing a unique fit can lead to lower cost. In other words, Porter's logic — which seems to equate operational effectiveness with cost leadership (and strategic positioning with differentiation) — does not hold in reality. As the dotted arrows in

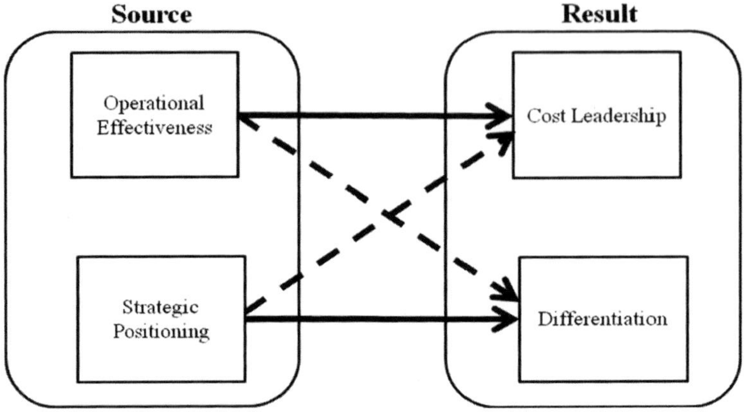

Fig. 2. Sources of advantage and results.

Fig. 2 represent, each source of competitive advantage can lead to cost leadership, differentiation or even both.

To make this point clearer, consider the example of three automobiles — BMW X3, Toyota Camry and Hyundai Sonata — in the context of Porter's productivity frontier (see Fig. 3). The Camry, just like IKEA and Southwest Airlines, is a cost leader which has reached that position through enhancing its OE. The BMW X3, on the other hand, is a luxury brand which has obtained its unique position through differentiation. Both are on the forefront of the productivity frontier, but have achieved their positions in vastly different ways. Now, Hyundai, which is lagging behind BMW and Toyota from either perspective, has a choice to either catch up with Toyota through enhancing its cost leadership or follow BMW into the luxury market through differentiation. Either way, Hyundai must improve its OE in order to do so.

The dotted arrow in Fig. 3 shows the potential trajectory that Hyundai might take in order to reach the productivity frontier. Is it making the mistake of being stuck-in-the-middle? Not really. It is simply pursuing its path and catching up with the leaders through enhancing its OE. Even Porter, who has been critical of the stuck-in-the-middle approach, implicitly acknowledged this point in his article (1996) by stating that improvement of both cost and

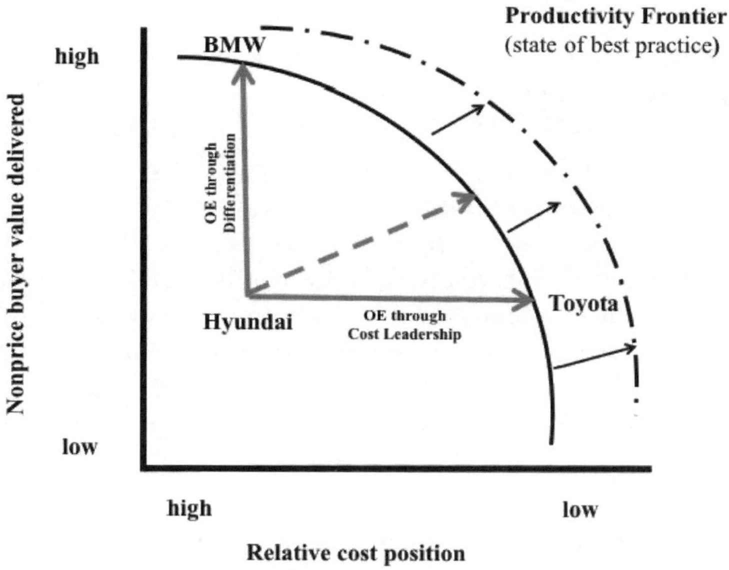

Fig. 3. Strategies of BMW, Toyota and Hyundai.

differentiation is possible when a company is behind the productivity frontier. Thus, Hyundai's strategy is valid, although it looks stuck-in-the-middle.

This example shows that OE through both cost leadership and differentiation can lead to a viable strategy. Unlike Porter's assertion that cutting costs and enhancing OE is not a long-term strategy option, Japanese companies are doing just that and are still being successful. Lexus, which is a luxury car, achieved its leadership within the luxury car market through cost leadership. Lexus is, in essence, a cost leader within the luxury car market.

Another problem with Porter's logic is the relationship between generic strategies (cost leadership and differentiation) and the three strategic positions (needs-based, variety-based and access-based). Needs-based positioning refers to serving a specific segment of customers; variety-based positioning is to serve a wide array of customers through a subset of an industry's products or services; and access-based positioning refers to differentiation by serving specific customers for specific needs. However, these three strategic positions clearly overlap with Porter's original two generic strategies of cost leadership and differentiation, and the distinction between these two sets of strategic options is unclear.[2]

This is not to discredit Porter's original work, but to point out that there are certain inconsistencies between this article (1996) and his previous approaches. Pointing out these inconsistencies in Porter's work may suggest some opportunities to expand and enhance Porter's framework. Therefore, it is always important to clarify these problems by first gaining a thorough understanding of Porter's framework and then improving it through an augmented or simplified analytical framework. It is clear from this analysis that one major recurring problem in Porter's discussion is the concept of stuck-in-the-middle. Although Porter criticized the stuck-in-the-middle approach, many firms have actually diversified and achieved success through this approach. Reconciling these apparent contradictions in Porter's model should provide us with a more comprehensive and accurate picture of appropriate firm strategy.

4.2 Why Do Good Managers Set Bad Strategies?

Michael Porter was invited for a special lecture at the Wharton Business School, USA, in 2006.[3] The key question raised was, why do most strategic errors come from within the firm? Porter pointed to three aspects in answering this question:

- *Destructive Competition* — As described before, firms can collectively engage in destructive competition by adopting the wrong approach. Managers often think of competition in terms of being the best in the industry. This notion in itself is harmless. However, the problem arises when managers attempt to be the best in all parts of the industry. Just like no one person can be the best in everything, no single company can become the best in all aspects of an industry. Rather, a company can be the best in a specific

[2] This issue will be further discussed in the next chapter.

[3] See *Knowledge@Wharton* (2006) for full interview.

segment of an industry or a specific target. However, the current practice has been extremely destructive, as firms have defined their goals in terms of advancing the interests and profit of shareholders. This leads to what Porter terms the "Bermuda Triangle of Strategy", in which firms sacrifice their uniqueness in order to achieve unprofitable growth just to increase shareholder value.

- *Confusing Strategy and Operational Effectiveness* — The appropriate corporate goal, therefore, should be to think of ways to deliver unique value to the customers through a set of differentiated fit of activities. Strategy, then, means devising ways to differentiate oneself from the rest of the competitors through doing things differently. As such, managers must constantly distinguish between whether the measures they are implanting fall under strategy or operational effectiveness. Without this distinction, companies will end up sacrificing their strategic objectives for the sake of operational effectiveness, which may generate short-term advantages but compromise their unique strategic position.
- *Capital Market Biases and Leadership* — This is a problem associated with a firm's valuation by financial analysts. Typically, they point to one firm in an industry that creates the largest value for shareholders and put pressure on other firms to emulate. This leads to homogenization of firm practices and hence leads to a no-win situation. Therefore, it is increasingly important for leaders and CEOs to communicate the firm's overall strategy, which is differentiated from those of its competitors, throughout the organizational chain. Because all individual activities must be aligned with the overarching strategy, it is not just the top managers that should have knowledge of a firm's strategy, but also those that are at the bottom.

Analysis

This section introduced Porter's more recent lecture on strategy (*Knowledge@Wharton* 2006), but there is nothing new with his perspective. The lecture was just based on his previous article (Porter 1996), i.e., strategic positioning versus operational effectiveness. Again, however, this does not mean that Porter is outdated. The system of analyses which Porter has established has truly revolutionized the discipline of strategic management. Ever since Porter first devised his frameworks in the early 1980s, his insights have remained highly valid despite all the fads and hypes business literature is susceptible to. Porter remained consistent in his view and has been more accurate than any other scholar. Despite several inconsistencies and criticisms on Porter, this lecture once again shows that his time-transcending validity proves why Porter is the undisputed leader in the field of strategic management.

4.3 Retrospective: An Interview with Michael Porter and Related Articles

This section discusses a series of articles containing an interview with Michael Porter along with several articles written by people in various fields of business and academia who have been profoundly affected by Porter's insights.

Michael Porter's Competitive Strategy

Argyres, McGahan, Barney, Brandenburger and Bachmann (2002) analyze and present the impacts that Porter's theory has had on the field of business strategy. They highlight two points about Porter. One is the profound influence of Porter's analytical framework in various academic disciplines and subject areas. For example, Porter's framework is extensively utilized not only for management strategy and policy, but also in education, health care, environmental protection and urban revitalization. Despite its broad application, one overarching theme is his belief in healthy and rigorous competition as the primary source of societal advancement. The second point is that Porter's idea has had unusual staying power in a field where fads are the norm and most theories are effectively refuted after a short while.

An Interview with Michael Porter

In his interview with Argyres and McGahan in Argyres *et al.* (2002), Porter begins by illustrating the process through which he came to devise his analytical frameworks. In the 1960s and 1970s, when Porter first entered into the world of business academia, the connection between industrial organization and strategy had not been clearly established. Both sides had strengths as well as weaknesses. On the industrial side, frameworks existed but there were too many exceptions to the rule; while on the business side, the traditional economic *ceteris paribus* (the practice of fixing all other independent variables and then looking at one variable's impact on the dependent variable) mode of thought was unrealistic. Therefore, all cases were taken individually and every case study required a separate SWOT (Strengths, Weaknesses, Opportunities and Threats) analysis, which did not really have any general applicability. This is why Porter decided to take the strongest points of both worlds and take a framework approach — this gave birth to the five-forces framework and the generic strategies, which were an attempt to encompass the most important independent variables into a comprehensive and readily applicable analytical framework.

This approach was first met with skeptics who doubted whether these frameworks could generalize all the complex and intricate inner workings of competition and strategy. Especially with the advent of new technologies and ever-volatile market conditions, many discredited Porter's attempt. However, contrary to the skepticism, Porter's analytical frameworks have had enormous staying power and can be applied to a vast array of social phenomena.

In the latter portion of the interview, Porter discusses some interesting possible extensions to his framework and theories that could be pursued in the future. One of the most prominent is the question of the evolution of industry structure. Although Porter's model appropriately dissects the existing industry structure, it does not show how the structure itself evolves. How do the five forces change and due to what variables? How do firm behaviors change over time depending on the industry structure? These are questions that are left open to explore.

Strategic Management, from Informed Conversation to Academic Discipline

Barney in Argyres *et al.* (2002) evaluates Porter's contribution as transforming the study of strategic management from "mere academic conversation" to a "rigorous academic discipline". It is interesting to note that the resource-based view of the firm, of which Barney is the leading proponent, has been one of the major alternatives to Porter's frameworks. Yet even the leading critics acknowledge that Porter has transformed the field of strategic management into a proper discipline. This is especially true because before Porter, there was no consensus even on the purpose of strategic management. However, Porter was able to aggregate all of the relevant points and visualize them into a cohesive framework and concept.

Of course, Porter's approach is not without problems, as it defines strategic management largely in terms of economic theory. Other psychological and sociological phenomena are also recognized as being important in the field. Nevertheless, Porter was the first one to comprehensively link strategic management with another field, thereby enhancing the validity of both fields in terms of applicability, conceptualization and theoretical rigor. Another contribution was choosing the right unit of analysis in strategic management, which is the industry structure. By focusing on the right level, Porter was able to uncover most of the main determinants of firm performance and choice of entry or exit.

Porter's Added Value: High Indeed!

Brandenburger in Argyres *et al.* (2002) points out that Porter's most important contribution is that his frameworks have been able to give a clear, visual representation of the most important variables which affect business performance and industry structure. Furthermore, they also give a more realistic picture than the diagrams and graphs in economic theory. Compare the supply-and-demand graph, which depicts a large number of small buyers and small sellers, to the five-forces model. The problem with supply and demand is that it makes unrealistic assumptions, whereas in real life there are many small buyers but a few big sellers. Business is not about small buyers and sellers, but about a few highly active and significant players — the five-forces model captures the reality of this situation.

Competitive Strategy: It's OK to be Different

Bachmann, who is managing partner of a prominent investment firm, Edward Jones, wrote the last article in Argyres *et al.* (2002). It is interesting to see how Bachmann (unintentionally) employed Porter's theory in creating his highly successful financial enterprise. Bachmann explains that in the early days of Edward Jones, the company suffered from lack of capital compared to its more established competitors. Therefore, Bachmann decided to tailor his firm's activities to service the needs of a very specific market segment, that being rural America. Since the firm had so little capital, it could not afford to service major investors or provide flashy and risky financial instruments. Instead, it took a more conservative approach and decided to add a personal touch to financial investment. Since the customers were mostly looking for stable, long-term financial instruments and wanted to have close and personal relationships with their investment manager, the firm's activities became customized to fit this segment. Without realizing it, Edward Jones was creating a robust fit, which Porter described as essential to achieving a long-term competitive advantage. The key contribution, which Bachmann highlights, was Porter's affirmation that it is not only okay to be different but also desirable. By making a tradeoff, i.e., not serving the major investors or offering elaborate financial instruments, Edward Jones widened the gap between itself and potential imitators and has been able to survive and prosper in the volatile world of investment firms.

Analysis

What distinguishes the greatest academics from other brilliant minds is their ability to build a system of thought. Many intellectuals throughout history have been able to advance a discipline through their insights, but only a select few have been able to actually synthesize their insights and build an entirely new system. In economics, for example, despite the numerous stellar minds that have advanced the discipline, no one has been able to surpass Adam Smith in terms of staying power. This is because Smith's seminal work, *The Wealth of Nations*, built a whole system of thought which transformed the entire *mode of thinking* in economics. He established the foundations of classical value theory and provided a revolutionary blueprint for understanding human progress in terms of economic growth. Furthermore, he founded a novel philosophy based on the doctrine of utility in an era when many people still thought that the optimum end of economic activities was accumulating a state stockpile of gold bullion (Ekelund and Hebert 1997, p. 124).

Just as Adam Smith built a new system of thought in his own time, Michael Porter also built an entirely new system of thought which transformed the *mode of thinking* in the discipline of strategic management. More specifically, when one looks at how Porter began by realizing the missing link between economic theory and industrial organization, one can clearly see how Porter's approach is a fusion of the two. If we summarize this process through an example, it is as follows:

One can formulate a basic econometric equation such as

$$\Upsilon = \beta_0 + \beta_1 X_1 + \beta_2 X_2 + \beta_3 X_3 + \beta_4 X_4 + \beta_5 X_5 + \cdots + \beta_i X_i.$$

What traditional economic theory would do is fix all X variables except for, say, X_3, which is barriers to entry. In this fashion, one can determine the impact that this single variable has on the dependent variable (Υ). This model is useful in determining the precise impact of individual variables on the dependent variable. However, the problem with this model is that it ignores the dynamic nature of real business contexts, in which all of the independent X variables simultaneously affect the dependent variable.

In contrast, the traditional SWOT analysis (Fig. 4) is highly tailored for individual cases and gives a realistic view as to how all variables affect a particular situation. By analyzing the strengths,

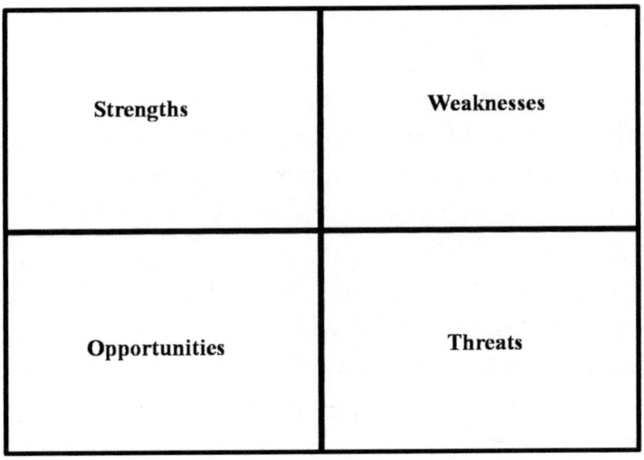

Fig. 4. SWOT analysis.

weaknesses, opportunities and threats, firms are able to analyze their plan of action to gain their objective. However, it is not clear which variables should be included in each cell of the SWOT framework.

Therefore, through numerous case studies and empirical analyses, Porter selected the most important *X* variables out of the hundreds that emerged from his research. By picking out the independent variables that mattered most in a large number of case studies, he then visualized them into a framework that is readily applicable and captures most of the important determinants of the dependent variable. Porter's frameworks, in essence, are a healthy balance between the economic approach and the SWOT analysis.

However, this is not to say that Porter's approach is without criticism. Barney and many other proponents of the resource-based view point out that by overfocusing on industry attractiveness, Porter neglects the fact that the attractiveness of an industry is not independent of the firm's resources. Firms have resources and capabilities that are not affected by outside determinants, and can even overcome the difficulty imposed on them by inherently unattractive industry structures. Furthermore, while Porter rightfully points out that cost and differentiation are the two main modes of strategic positioning, he does not properly identify the sources of these advantages. Adding to this criticism, some have noted that the threat of substitutability does not apply to highly sophisticated industries.

These may be constructive criticisms, yet many are based on an inappropriate understanding of Porter's work. In response to the criticism that Porter neglects the inelasticity of a firm's resources and capabilities, he clearly mentioned that firms not only participate in the industry, but also have the power to change the industry structure itself. As a matter of fact, Porter asserted that the most successful firms in any industry are those that have been able to change the industry structure to suit their advantages.

The resource-based view perceives the firm as a bundle of resources that, in order to be competitive, must be immobile and unique in nature. These resources are, in essence, the various administrative decisions and strategic choices that a firm makes throughout its value chain, as depicted in Fig. 5. Therefore, these aspects are comprehensively captured by Porter's value chain and his discussion

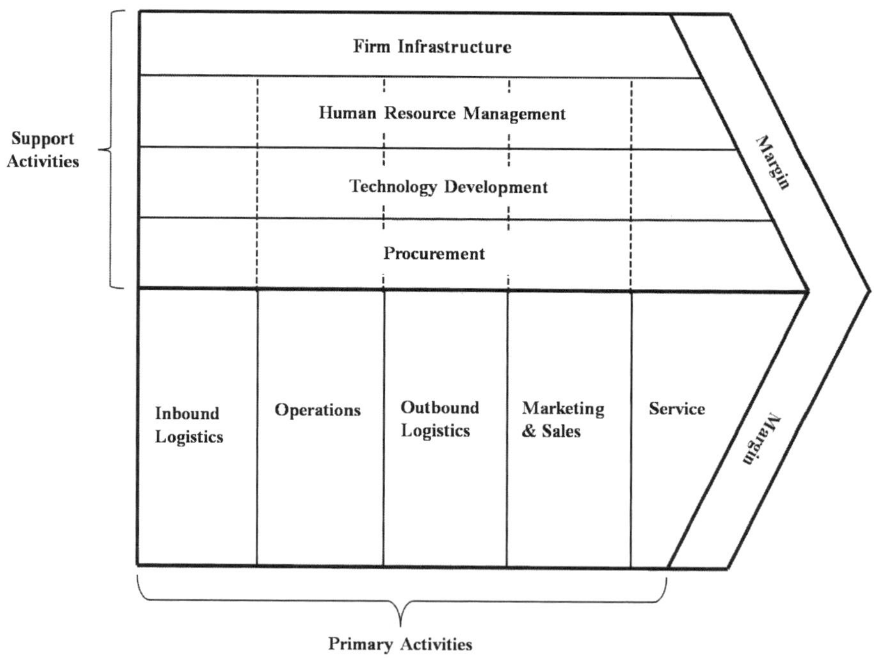

Fig. 5. Porter's value chain analysis.

on creating a unique fit of activities. The resource-based view is a very detailed and thoughtful extension of the dynamics of Porter's value chain analysis, and it shows how these individual elements interact to generate unique advantages for firms. However, this view is still largely within the frameworks that Porter has devised in the past. Furthermore, one prominent criticism of the resource-based view is that it largely ignores external factors and concentrates too much on endogenous variables which firms can control. Porter presents a comprehensive view of the external forces that affect industry structure and attractiveness through his five-forces model.

What we can see from these analyses is the far-reaching impact Porter has had over the years and how his view has consistently been proven valid despite the change of times. This is especially amazing when we consider the fact that strategic management is a field in which ideas tend to come and go in a very short span of time. Lastly, we can see that even Porter's critics largely acknowledge the sweeping and immense explanatory power that his various frameworks possess. However, this does not mean that we cannot improve Porter's model and devise an enhanced framework that can reconcile the various inconsistencies among Porter's frameworks. We will discuss this further in the next chapter.

Case Study 1: How Samsung Wins Over Sony[4]

The Samsung Group is South Korea's largest conglomerate by revenue (US$174.6 billion in 2007), leading several industries in the world. It is composed of numerous international businesses, all united under the Samsung brand, including:

- Samsung Electronics — one of the world's largest electronics company;

[4] Information for this case study is abstracted from the Samsung website (www.samsung.com), *BusinessWeek* (2003), Management and Accounting Web ("What is strategy?"), *Wired* (2002) and *The New York Times* (2004, 2007, 2008b).

- Samsung Heavy Industries — one of the world's largest shipbuilders; and
- Samsung Engineering & Construction — a major global construction company.

The Samsung brand is perhaps one of the best known South Korean brands in the world. In 2005, Samsung overtook Japanese rival Sony as the world's leading consumer electronics brand, and in 2008 was ranked 21st compared to Sony's 25th by *BusinessWeek's* Best Global Brands survey. This case study will focus on Samsung Electronics' strategy and, in particular, how Porter's concepts of positioning, tradeoffs and fit apply to Samsung's chosen strategy.

Positioning

As previously mentioned, Porter stated that there is a succinct difference between OE and SP, which if confused can cause problems in sustainability of competitiveness. Therefore, positioning can be subdivided into these two subsections: OE and SP.

Operational Effectiveness (OE)

According to Porter, OE is the act of performing similar activities to rivals but in a better way than rivals perform them. OE is not merely limited to efficiency though, but refers to the many practices that allow a company to better utilize its inputs.

This can be shown more clearly by using the value chain model. The value chain, depicted in Fig. 6, categorizes the generic value-adding activities of an organization. The primary activities include inbound logistics, operations (production), outbound logistics, marketing and sales, and service. The support activities include firm infrastructure, human resource management, technology development and procurement. Improving any one of the primary or support activities over competitors' allows Samsung to perform similar activities but in a superior way to rivals.

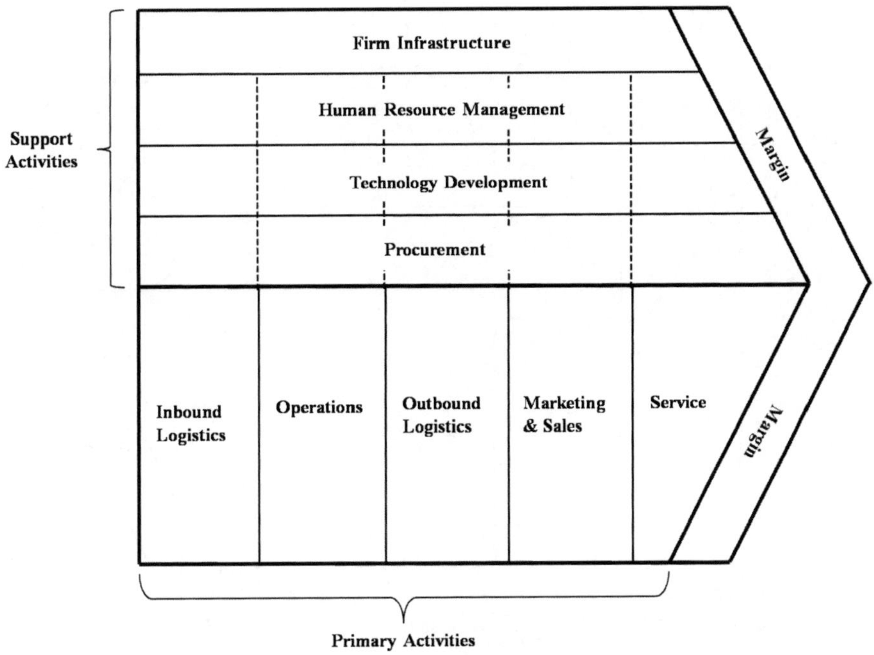

Fig. 6. The value chain.[5]

Samsung has indeed managed to improve multiple activities within the value chain, thus putting it a step ahead of its rivals, such as Sony, in the same market. Figure 7 highlights the areas where Samsung has made integral changes to its activities. Samsung has improved upon firm infrastructure, technology development and operations (and, by extension, human resource management) in order to gain a degree of advantage over its competitors.

Firm infrastructure, in particular, has transformed dramatically over the years. When Jong-Yong Yun took over as CEO in 1997, he drastically cut 24,000 workers and sold US$2 billion in non-core businesses. Furthermore, Samsung managers who have worked for other big competitors claim that at Samsung they go through far

[5] Porter (1985).

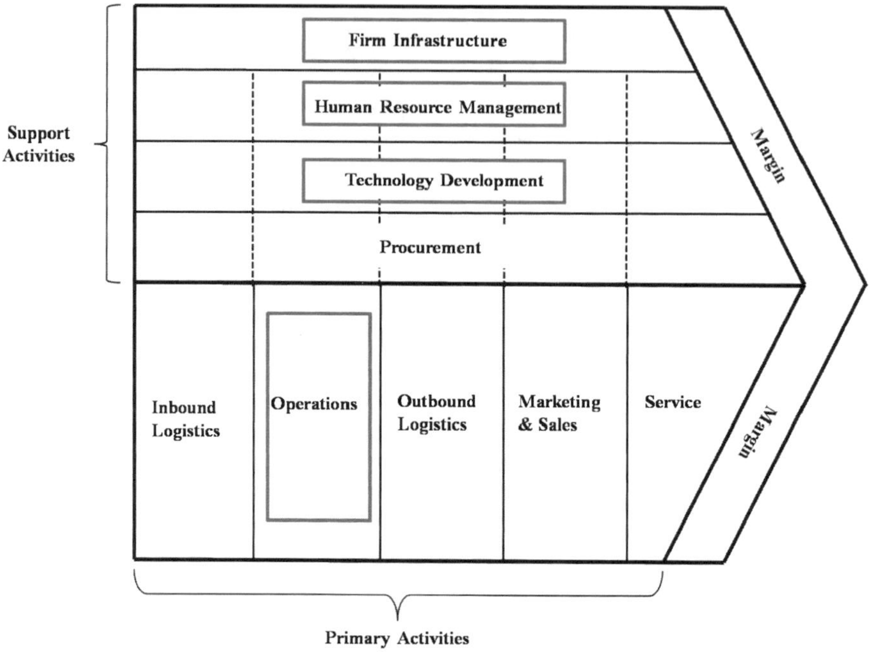

Fig. 7. Samsung value chain alterations.

fewer layers of bureaucracy to win approval for new products, budgets and marketing plans. Overall, this streamlining has improved Samsung's ability to seize opportunities. The Sony Chairman noted in a speech regarding Samsung's aggressive restructuring, "To survive as a global player, we too have to change."

With regards to technology development, Samsung is investing heavily in R&D and new factories across all product lines. In a span of just five years, Samsung has sunk in excess of US$19 billion into new chip facilities. Samsung has realized that to stay on top it must be willing to provide consumers with a constant stream of well-timed hits, and this means staying one step ahead of the pack in terms of technology development.

Operations is perhaps the most unusual segment for Samsung and where it differs almost completely from its competitors. While most competitors in the high-tech industry are developing proprietary software and content, Samsung has defiantly refused to enter the software business. It focuses on just developing the necessary hardware; and whereas most competitors outsource their hardware segments, Samsung refuses to outsource manufacturing and instead sinks billions of dollars into large-scale cutting-edge factories. CEO Yun was quoted as saying that "if we get out of manufacturing, we will lose." Thus, its diversification and vertical integration in manufacturing, while a negative aspect for competitors, act as a boon to Samsung.

As we have learned, while OE is necessary for a firm, it is not alone sufficient to maintain sustainability of competitiveness. Therefore, we now need to look at the second subsection of positioning, which is SP.

Strategic Positioning (SP)

SP refers to performing different activities from rivals, or performing similar activities but in different ways. Porter states that a company can outperform rivals only if it can establish a difference that it can preserve. While changes in OE can be easily copied and benchmarked, changes in SP are not as easily imitated. Furthermore, Porter argues that competitive strategy is about being different, and thus strategy is the creation of a unique and valuable position involving a different set of activities. SP, Porter claims, emerges from three sources: variety-, needs- and/or access-based positioning (see Fig. 8).

From this strategic point, Samsung has positioned itself in a variety-based position as well as a needs-based position. Samsung's variety-based positioning refers to its unwillingness to enter into the software market and its commitment to hardware. By manufacturing and selling only hardware, it is producing only a subset of the industry's products, and thus customers are forced to look elsewhere for their software needs. However, this works to Samsung's advantage, as it has been able to position itself as an absolute leader in the high-tech hardware industry, even above Sony in terms of revenue.

As for needs-based positioning, Samsung, through pricing, has targeted mid-level consumers. While the majority of its competitors

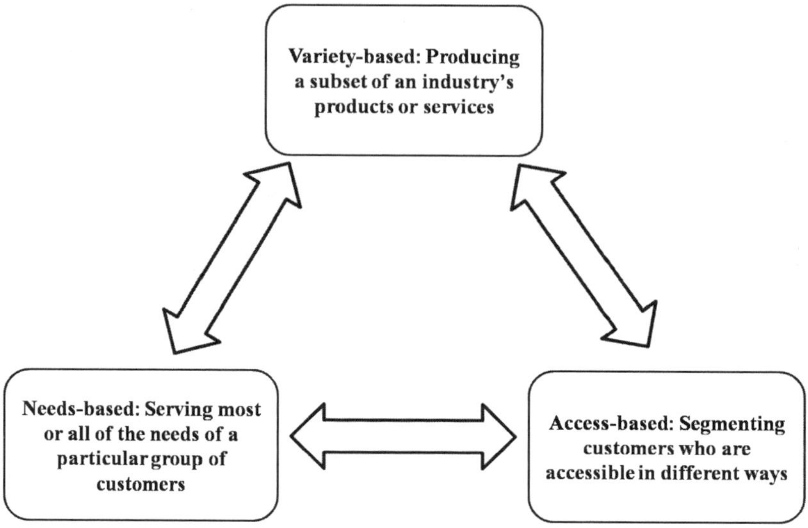

Fig. 8. Variety-, needs- and access-based positioning.

fight it out over the lower end of the hardware spectrum, Samsung is raising the stakes by providing superior design and quality for all kinds of mid-range products while remaining at a mid-range price.

Thus, through two different yet complementary positions, Samsung is managing to stay ahead of the pack. Combining its alterations to its OE alongside the company's SP makes it ultimately more difficult for rivals to benchmark its unique fit of activities. However, for Samsung to further safeguard its position, the company must focus more on tradeoffs.

Tradeoffs

According to Porter, a sustainable advantage cannot be guaranteed only by choosing a unique position, as competitors will imitate a position in two ways. A competitor can choose to reposition itself to match the superior performer, or can seek to match the benefits of a successful position while maintaining its original position (known as "straddling"). Thus, for a strategic position to be sustainable, there must be tradeoffs with other positions. Tradeoffs occur when activities are incompatible and arise for three reasons:

- *Inconsistency in Value Delivery* — This refers to how a company known for delivering one kind of value may confuse its primary customers and undermine its own reputation by attempting to deliver two inconsistent values simultaneously.
- *Tradeoffs from Activities* — These inevitably arise from firm activities if an activity is over- or under-designed.
- *Coordination and Control* — These are lacking if a firm tries to serve all things to all customers, thereby confusing various elements of firm operation.

Thus, strategy can also be defined as making tradeoffs in competing and choosing what not to do. Samsung has chosen what not to do quite clearly. Samsung, as previously mentioned, has remained distant from the software market, so customers have now come to expect excellence in hardware. If Samsung had moved into software, it may have ended up undermining its own reputation. In this case, the tradeoff was worth the risk. While software development could potentially be complementary to the hardware product line, Samsung would be forced to spend vast sums of money and time on developing the new product line in terms of product configuration, different equipment, different employee behavior, different skills and different management systems. The company would then dilute the funds and efforts funneled into new hardware development.

As Samsung is determined to focus on hardware, management is making its organizational priorities very clear. This will undoubtedly filter down to the employees, who are then provided with a very clear framework when making operational decisions. This contributes to the smooth everyday running of the firm and is likely to translate to customers as a well-organized, trustworthy and focused firm.

Fit

Lastly, to ensure a lockout of imitators, fit is required to create a configuration that maximizes the synergies among the various value chain activities. Fit among activities is generic and applies to many companies, but the fit which Porter refers to is more strategy-specific because it has the capability to enhance a position's uniqueness and amplifies tradeoffs. There are three types of fit: consistency between each activity and the overall strategy, reinforcing of activities, and optimization of efforts.

In essence, the whole matters more than any individual part when discussing ideas of fit. For Samsung, as it has a clear strategy with one overall goal, there exists a consistency among different activities. This can be identified when one looks at Samsung's main production locations. As Samsung is not attempting to be a low-cost provider in the market place, it is able to avoid low-wage countries where production quality might also be compromised. Therefore, Samsung tends to base its manufacturing and R&D facilities in more developed countries such as the US and Japan. Of course, it cannot afford to stay out of developing economies altogether, but it is important for Samsung to have customers see that the company has a strong presence in developed countries.

Furthermore, Samsung's improvements in overall company infrastructure are allowing the company to optimize its efforts. As a result, for example, rollout periods have become much shorter. It used to take at least 14 months for the company to progress from a new product concept to rollout, but now it takes merely 5 months. Faster rollouts also mean rapidly renewed product lines. Samsung renews its product lines every 9 months now compared with Motorola, which refreshes its product line every 12 to 18 months. Samsung is ensuring that none of the company's efforts is wasted. Thus, fit is vital to the company's strategy. Therefore, with its improvements in OE, Samsung performs similar activities better than its competitors; with its SP firmly targeted, the company increases its competitive advantages; and with a strong fit configured among its overall value chain activities, it is able to lock out competitors that are tempted to imitate the "Samsung way".

Although seemingly simple, management should target a consistent SP for the long term. Continuity is an important concept here, as it helps reinforce a company's identity. Frequent shifts in strategy may not only be costly, but also causes organizational dissonance. Samsung, however, seems to have dug itself in for the long haul and, as one of Korea's main players, is slowly taking over the world of high-tech hardware.

Why Not the "Sony Way"?

We have expounded fully on the "Samsung way", but it was not so long ago that Sony Electronics was the undisputed leader in consumer electronics. In recent years, Sony has lost ground to Samsung, and this begs the question: just what is Sony doing that is so different from Samsung? Exactly where have the two companies diverged? In many ways, Samsung and Sony are similar. They are both producing upper mid-range consumer electronics at reasonable mid-range prices; but unlike Samsung, Sony has become heavily involved in the movies, music and video game markets. A strong conflict between their main business segment, consumer electronics, and the digital media segment is hampering the company's operations. Sony is the only conglomerate to be in both consumer electronics and entertainment.

With regards to OE, Sony has made few significant changes over the years. In fact, the only significant change that the company has made is in the area of technology development (Fig. 9). Technology development has indeed been modified in that Sony has most significantly expanded its scope from hardware to software. In hardware, Sony continues to stay ahead of or equal to the head of the pack, and recently the company has moved into the digital media segment. Acting within a digital media segment has altered its value chain, but has not essentially altered its OE for the better.

The point of altering the value chain is to perform similar activities to rivals but in a better or more effective way. However, many of Sony's rivals are already performing a similar type of activity within their value chains. Companies such as iriver (a Korean firm)

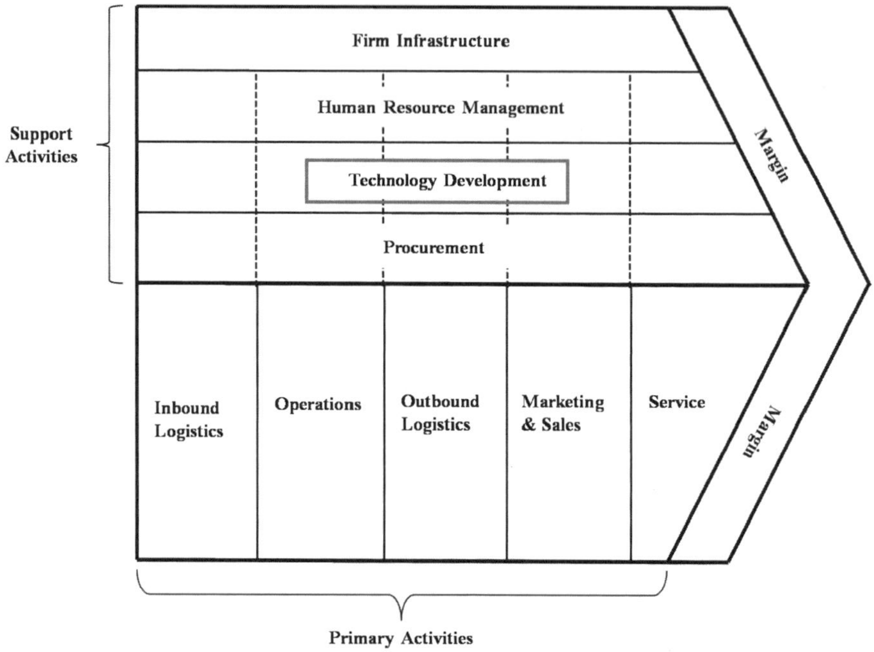

Fig. 9. Sony value chain alterations.

have already hedged their bets on both hardware and software products. After purchasing an iriver MP3 player, USB device or PMP, one can download a series of software to supplement and support the purchased iriver hardware.

However, after purchasing a similar hardware product from Sony, one might find the software slightly less accommodating. The problem is that, in a bid to increase profits, Sony has begun to spread itself too thinly over a number of markets, which Porter would refer to as having "no uniqueness". To make matters worse, there is a distinct lack of fit among these businesses. The digital media segment requires the hardware produced by the consumer electronics segment to function. However, the hardware division does not yet feel reliant on the digital media segment. Sony, in recent years, has been frozen by its fear of piracy and thus has not been able to find a resolution to this ongoing "civil war".

Sony's digital Walkman device is a good example, as Walkman users are hampered by the excessive procedures designed to block illegal file sharing. Furthermore, Walkmans are built without hard drives, as Sony's copy-protection mechanism does not allow music to be transferred from one hard drive to another. However, when we look at hardware products such as Apple's iPod touch, we witness almost flawless integration with other Mac software such as iTunes, iPhoto and App Store, which allow full integration of many aspects of the iPod such as photos, movies, games, music and so on.

Essentially, the conflict is that Sony's electronics division needs to let customers move files around effortlessly and create synergies, but the entertainment side wants to maintain barriers as it sees every customer as a potential thief rather than a "prosumer", as Apple or iriver does. Ironically, Sony's electronics division showed support for Napster, the file-sharing website, against the legal battles from Sony's entertainment division and other record companies. Sony Entertainment has also led the fight against companies that manufacture CD burners; and Sony Electronics joined in on a lawsuit against LAUNCH Media, an Internet radio service that is partially owned by Sony Entertainment.

Sony has attempted to expand outwards in OE, while failing to do so in SP. This has essentially created a conflict between the OE aspect of its business and the SP aspect, as well as a conflict within the SP aspects of its business. However, if Sony were to combine its strengths in hardware and in software entertainment, it could potentially create a synergy between the two and overtake Samsung's leadership in the consumer electronics market while simultaneously building a unique business model. There would be a complementary coexistence of both OE and SP. In order to do this, Sony has to go back to the drawing board and take a closer look at its OE and expand it beyond merely the technology development sphere. More importantly, the company has to re-evaluate its SP. Specifically, Sony needs to select which aspects of its business are going to correlate with which types of strategic positioning. In fact, it seems that Sony should take a leaf out of Samsung's book in this case in order to go head to head, and act even more extreme yet succinct in order to retake the lead.

Discussion Questions

1. Porter claims that not operational effectiveness but only strategic positioning can lead to a real sustainable competitive advantage. Do you agree? Why or why not?
2. Do you think that some aspects of operational effectiveness can lead to sustainable competitive advantage? If so, which aspects and why?
3. Porter highlights the need for top-level management to convey strategy to all levels of the firm. Why do you think this is so? How can this best be achieved in large firms?
4. The resource-based view of the firm is more pertinent than Porter's views and frameworks. Do you agree or disagree? Discuss.
5. It is argued that Porter is undoubtedly the guru of strategic management. Do you agree? Which aspect of his work do you most respect and agree with, and why?
6. What would Porter prescribe Sony to do next in order to enhance its competitiveness?

CHAPTER 5

New Models for Business Strategy

Chapter Guideline

Porter's model has provided a firm foundation for many fields in the discipline of strategic management. However, as evident from the various analyses done so far, Porter's model suffers from some inconsistencies. Like all concepts and theories, there are many avenues for improvement in order to present a more comprehensive view of strategy. This chapter will explain various attempts by scholars to reconcile and complement Porter's models in order to advance the state of knowledge in the field of strategic management.

Summary of Previous Models

In the previous chapter, we saw the profound impact Porter's theory has had on many aspects of management strategy. His seminal 1996 article, "What is strategy?", which redefined strategic management, demonstrates Porter's penetrating insight into the fundamental concepts of this field. These insights have had enormous staying power as evident from his recent interviews, which remain consistent and highly valid even after the phenomenal change in business environment over the past decades. Furthermore, we have read about business leaders, scholars and even critics who praise Porter's massive contribution to the field. However, even the most prescient scholars always leave some avenue for criticism and extension. Now it is time to look at the scholars who have tried to reconcile some inconsistencies in Porter's model and present new frameworks in order to advance the state-of-the-art knowledge in strategic management.

5.1 Blue versus Red Ocean: A Critique of Porter?

It is without a doubt that Michael Porter's definition of strategy has had a profound impact on business studies. However, just like any other academic landmark, many criticisms and new approaches followed Porter's seminal work. The most common criticism regarding Porter is that his strategic prescription of becoming either a low-cost provider or a differentiated niche player seems too limiting to fully convey the complexity of the real world. For example, Ridderstrale and Nordstrom (1999) tell readers to forget the old world order and make a difference in a new world order which they dub "funky business". This catchy phrase is further elaborated as finite and infinite dimensions. The former refers to the old world order and the latter refers to the new world order. According to them, the old notion of competitive strategy, which takes the beaten path over and over again, does not lead to success in the new world order. Indeed, the idea of creating uncontested, pristine and "funky" new dimensions sounds very alluring in a world swept up in a tidal wave of economic, technological, societal and political change.

The dichotomy of funky and non-funky, or infinite and finite, gained an even wider audience after Kim and Mauborgne (2005) introduced the catchy metaphoric dichotomy between Red Ocean strategy and Blue Ocean strategy, which describes the difference between a saturated unprofitable market space and a profitable untapped market space. Industrial organization economics thus far has emphasized the importance of competing within a pre-established structure. Therefore, competition, in essence, has been regarded as a zero-sum game in which a relative gain by one competitor leads to a loss for the other. Previous frameworks focused on how the industry space was divided among the various competitors within the industry. Kim and Mauborgne, on the other hand, assert that this is ignoring a much more profitable potential of creating industry spaces outside the pre-existing structure. This untapped space is dubbed the Blue Ocean, as opposed to Red Ocean.

The authors identified that 14% of firms which invested in Blue Ocean generated 38% of total revenues and 61% of total profits in their empirical study. The reasons behind these statistics are various, but the most important one is destructive competition. Production methods and technology have become increasingly standardized and easily replicable. Therefore, the best way to increase revenue is not by constantly struggling and edging ahead in the Red Ocean, but rather to find a new Blue Ocean in which firms can take advantage of untapped market space. The implication behind this theory is profound. For decades, strategy gurus have preached that the two viable strategic options are differentiation and low cost. However, according to the authors of the Blue Ocean strategy, firms have the opportunity to break the pre-established value/cost tradeoff and set a completely new rule for the game. The firm can create this Blue Ocean by focusing on the demand side rather than the production side, by reducing costs while driving up buyer value.

How does one achieve this marvelous feat? The authors offer several concrete steps that firms can take using the example of the US wine industry. The strategy canvas in Fig. 1 shows the seven elements

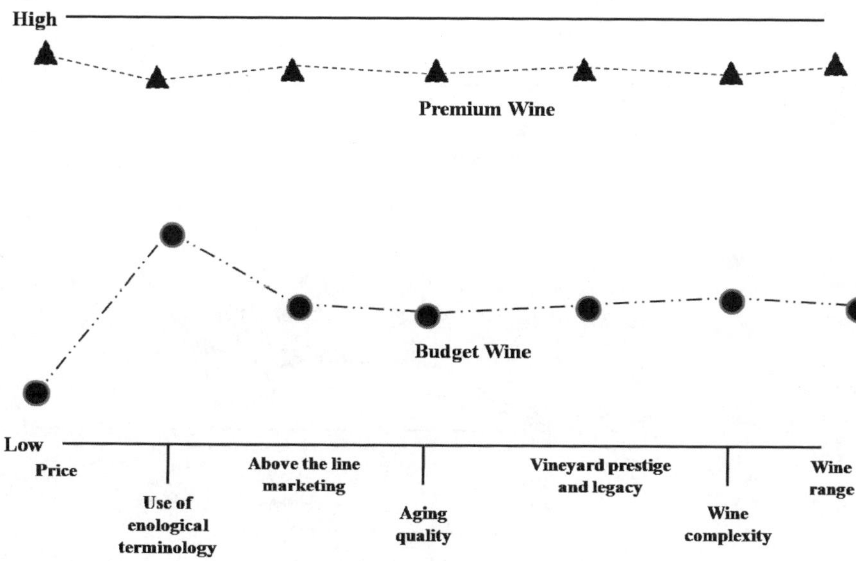

Fig. 1. Strategy canvas of US wine industry in the late 1990s.[1]

[1] Kim and Mauborgne (2005).

that determine the US wine industry: price, enological terminology, above-the-line marketing to enhance consumer awareness, aging quality of wine, prestige attributed to the vineyard, complex determination of wine taste and a wide range of wines depending on consumer preference. The remarkable feature here is that there is a convergence between premium and budget wines. Although they are highly different, they have identical strategic profiles based on the same seven elements on the canvas. In other words, despite claiming to be different, budget wines and premium wines all compete in the same criteria for a similar group of consumers.

The Blue Ocean strategy, on the other hand, requires a firm to compete based on *different criteria*. This is precisely what Yellow Tail, an Australian wine company, did in the US wine industry. Instead of trying to compete based on the same seven elements, Yellow Tail deleted all of the enological terminologies and lowered the prestige in labeling, and focused on creating a fun, easily approachable wine at a competitive price. Yellow Tail's strategy canvas is depicted through the square spotted lines in Fig. 2.

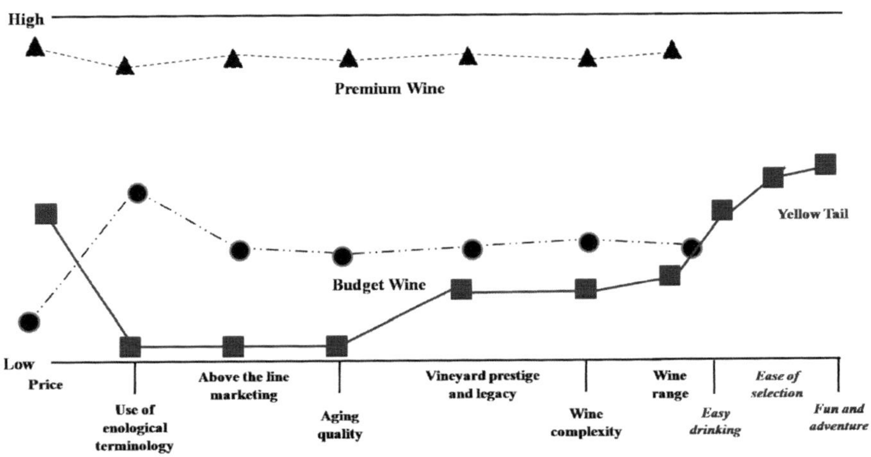

Fig. 2. Yellow Tail's strategic canvas.[2]

[2] *Ibid.*

The remarkable aspect to note about this new canvas is the creation of three additional criteria (far right of Fig. 2), which are represented at the right edge of the bottom axis. These three additional criteria represent the essence of Blue Ocean strategy, which is to alter the pre-existing structure and reap immense profits by doing so.

The authors also present a readily applicable framework that can be used to envision and implement their ideas (see Fig. 3). From this framework, we can see that creating a Blue Ocean requires eliminating and reducing pre-existing elements while creating and raising elements that did not exist or only had a weak presence in the industry. For instance, Yellow Tail eliminated enological terminology, aging quality and above-the-line marketing. Furthermore, the company also

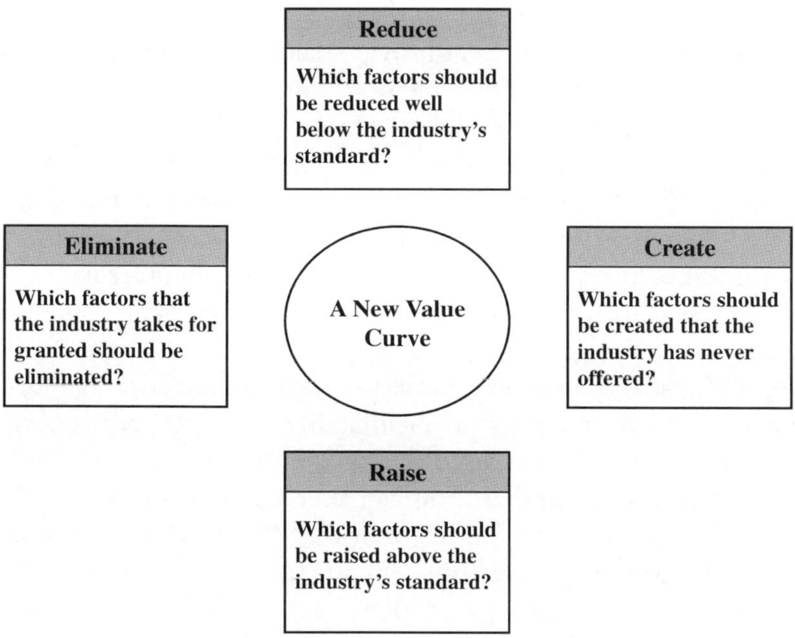

Fig. 3. The four-actions framework.[3]

[3] *Ibid.*

reduced wine complexity, wine range and vineyard prestige. The new wine brand raised the retail store involvement and created easy drinking, ease of selection and a sense of adventure into the wine industry. This induced a formerly neglected customer base (i.e., those who were reluctant to consume wine due to the complexity involved with wine drinking) to become Yellow Tail customers.

Kim and Mauborgne (2005) conclude that the Blue Ocean has always been present, yet has never been systematically analyzed. Therefore, they attempted to provide a comprehensive and analytical framework to create and analyze Blue Ocean and present a quantitative analysis of this exciting new concept.

Analysis

The Blue Ocean concept has been a sensational hit in many ways because of the message it entails. Firms do not have to remain prisoners of the pre-existing industry structure. Rather, firms can reformulate and even find new territory outside of the industry structure to reap high profits. This refreshing message was like an oasis in a desert to many managers who were struggling to find new ways to operate within the barren landscapes of established industry structures. However, as sensational as this concept may sound, we must be very careful before we accept the novelty of the Blue Ocean.

The first scholar to systematically analyze and present a framework for industry structure was Michael Porter. Porter, in his seminal 1980 book, *Competitive Strategy*, emphasized the importance of industry structure in determining firm profitability and competitiveness. In this book, Porter already discussed how industry structures are not static but dynamic, and that firms can alter the structure to their own advantage. Therefore, we can see that the Blue Ocean concept actually already existed, yet was not articulated to the extent that it has been by Kim and Mauborgne (2005). The Blue Ocean can also be regarded as one type of strategic positioning (SP) of Porter (1996).

Therefore, we can conclude that the Blue Ocean is not a completely revolutionary concept. Rather, it is a refinement and articulation of a pre-existing concept that Porter had devised in the

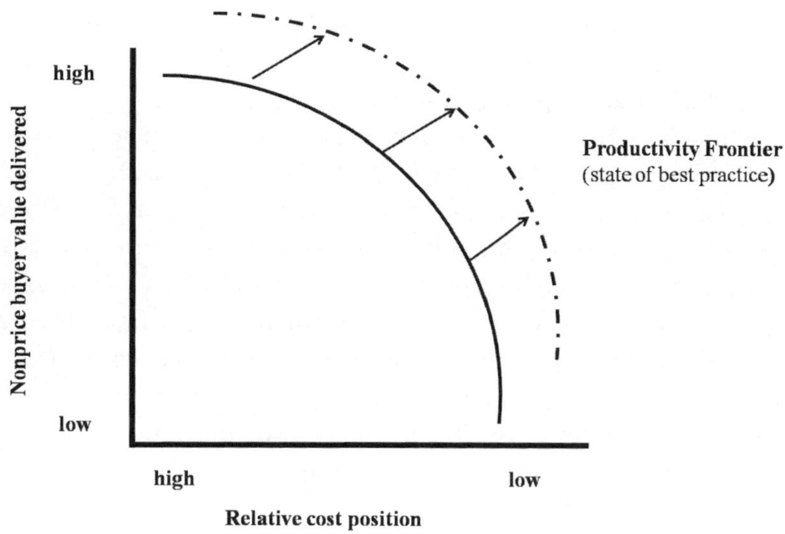

Fig. 4. Blue Ocean in terms of Porter's productivity frontier.

1980s. To be more precise, we can incorporate the Blue Ocean concept into the productivity frontier curve (Porter 1996). As shown in Fig. 4, the Blue Ocean can be seen as the act of pushing the productivity frontier outwards by altering the industry structure.

Kim and Mauborgne's (2005) contribution to this thought has been to formalize and refine the pre-existing concept in a readily digestible manner. While the Blue Ocean shows us a very precise and detailed analysis of how to alter the industry structure and create profitable business opportunities, the concept itself is not entirely novel.

5.2 Another Critique

As the analysis part of the above section demonstrates, a thorough understanding of Porter's work is necessary before making truly valid criticisms. The Blue Ocean concept is a refinement rather than a criticism of Porter's conception of strategy. Therefore, the next article by Moon (1993) starts off with a thorough review of Porter's generic strategies to provide the readers with a better understanding of Porter's view and its relevant critiques. Moon points out several issues with Porter's framework, and then presents a new and enhanced framework that attempts to reconcile these inconsistencies.

The starting point is Porter's ever-famous generic strategies (see Fig. 5). This simple yet powerful model succinctly summarizes Porter's mantra that successful firms must make a choice in order to acquire true competitive advantage. Firms cannot be all things to everyone and must make tradeoffs in order to formulate unique fits, which give the firm a long-term, sustained competitive advantage. Firms that are unable to make their choices and necessary tradeoffs are dubbed as "stuck-in-the-middle" and will eventually lose out to more competent competitors who have achieved their unique fits.

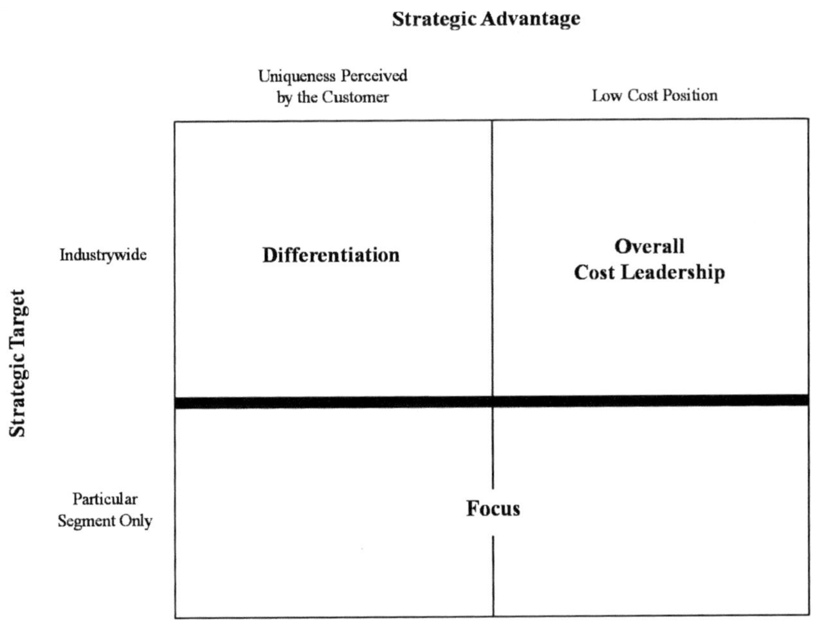

Fig. 5. Porter's generic strategies.[4]

[4] Porter (1980), p. 34.

However, one problem with this model is the concept of "stuck-in-the-middle", which views all strategies as mutually exclusive. To put it simply, can't firms shift their strategies depending on the stage of development they are in? Firms cannot simply start with a unique fit. There must be some kind of intermediate process that must be preceded in order to reach this advanced level of firm development. Therefore, the evolutionary nature of strategies, depicted in Fig. 6, can significantly enhance the generic strategies model.

Consider a typical new entrant to the international market. It usually cannot compete with its more established competitors based on technology, capital or experience. While there are exceptions (such as high-tech start-ups and consulting firms), most new firms gain their entry through advantages in basic factor conditions such as low labor cost. This is what Porter termed cost focus. As the new entrant accumulates additional experience, capital and resources, it will move on to either a differentiation focus or cost leadership, depending on whether it bases its advantage on differentiation or cost. After this stage, the firm will naturally gravitate to its final destination, which is

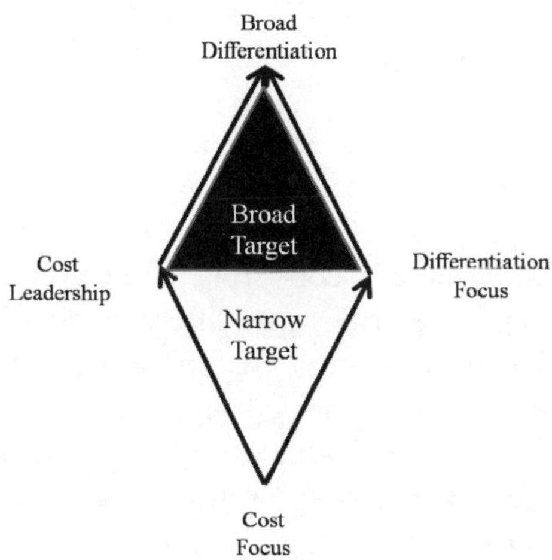

Fig. 6. Dynamic model of Porter's generic strategies.[5]

[5] Moon (1993).

broad differentiation (where a firm will compete based on its unique fit but serve a broad competitive scope).

The evolutionary path of certain Korean multinational corporations (MNCs) aptly illustrates this dynamic concept. Hyundai, for example, started out with a typical cost-focus strategy in the 1970s. It produced small cars based on cheap labor. As Hyundai accumulated experience, technology and brand value, it moved on to cost leadership in the late 1980s and throughout the 1990s, when it started to produce a wider range of automobiles but still at a significantly lower cost than its competitors. Note that even in this intermediate stage, cost leadership and differentiation co-existed in the Hyundai case. This, according to Porter, would be a classic "stuck-in-the-middle" situation in which firms would not be able to gain a sustainable competitive advantage. However, Hyundai incrementally increased its brand value, technology and scope of competition through this strategy, and it is currently slowly looking to move into the final stage of firm evolution — broad differentiation. Hyundai's recent focus on luxury models such as the Genesis and Grandeur is evidence of this. Did Hyundai fail? Hardly! Hyundai has been designated as one of the "compulsory success story" case studies for prestigious MBA schools such as Harvard and Stanford (Sa 2008).

The evolutionary path also shows how important it is to distinguish the dark-colored triangle depicting the "major league" (consisting of top global firms) from the light-colored triangle representing the "minor league" (consisting of new entrants) in Fig. 6. This is useful as it aptly describes two different spheres of competition that exist in global business and the strategies that firms will take depending on the "league" in which they compete.

Another major problem with Porter's framework is its unilateral focus on competition. While competition is the most important force dictating global business strategies, it does not represent the whole picture. Two alternative strategies, which are frequently adopted by emerging MNCs, must be taken into account in order to present a comprehensive framework. The first is the shelter strategy, in which firms seek protection from market (or competitive) forces in order to gain an initial foothold. Of course, this type of protective strategy is not sustainable in the long run, but many firms do indeed choose this strategy, at least in the initial stage. The second is the existence of a cooperative strategy or strategic alliance. Many firms choose to cooperate rather than compete, as frequently noted by many prominent scholars such as Ohmae (1989). Especially considering the complexity and broadening scope of global business, cooperation among firms is and will continue to increase in the future.[6]

Figure 7 incorporates all the points that have been made above. Global strategy can be divided into three broad categories: (a) protectionist, (b) competitive, and (c) cooperative strategies. Under these choices, firms can pursue a combination of various strategies according to the developmental stage and arena in which they wish to be.

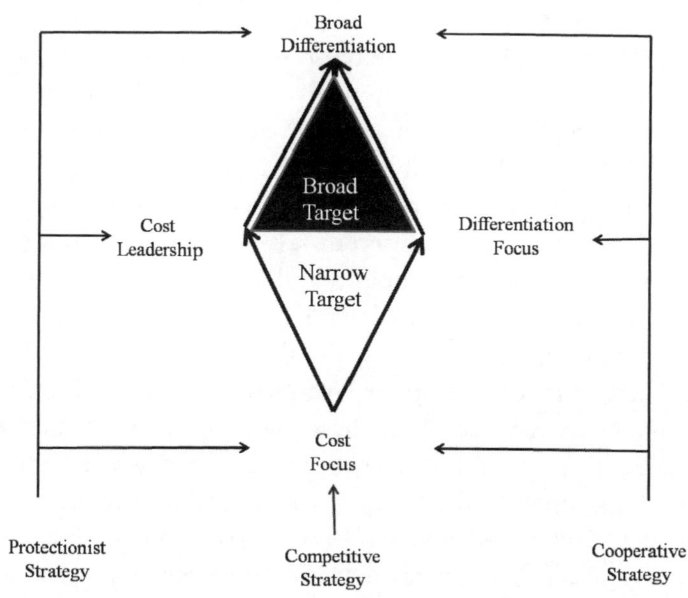

Fig. 7. Comprehensive global strategy.[7]

[6] This point will be further discussed in Chap. 7.
[7] Moon (1993).

In sum, the new model reconciles two problems Porter's model had. First, the static nature of Porter's model is transformed into a dynamic one. Most firms do not just stick with one strategy, as strategic choices evolve continuously depending on the stage of development. Second, competitive strategy, although important, is not the only type of strategy available. Many firms pursue various strategies including the protectionist and cooperative strategies.

The core message behind this discussion is that many of the strategies that Porter deemed mutually exclusive are not actually so. Stuck-in-the-middle is not a product of incorrect strategic choice, but rather a phase of evolutionary development. Lastly, although the path that individual global players have taken may differ, the ultimate destination for all of them is broad differentiation.

Analysis

The comprehensive global strategy presented above attempts to reconcile some of Porter's inconsistencies and adds other dimensions by incorporating the concepts of shelter, competitive and cooperative strategies. Although Porter always preaches that firms cannot be all things to everyone and that rigorous competition is the name of the game, the reality is quite different as many firms simultaneously engage in various types of strategies and cooperate with other firms.

What we can derive from Moon's (1993) model is that Porter's concept of tradeoffs and creating fits describes the path taken from cost focus to cost leadership or from cost focus to differentiation focus. After firms have reached these two points, regardless of how they reached the tip of the narrow target, they will all attempt to move on to the final destination, that is, broad differentiation.

Consider Toyota and BMW. Toyota started out with a cost focus and then eventually moved on to a cost leadership position through its good-quality yet reasonably priced cars. According to Porter, Toyota should stay in that position, make tradeoffs and create its own unique fit of activities for a sustainable competitive advantage. However, Toyota did not follow this path, but rather forged a new path by introducing the Lexus and other high-end models to cater to a much wider range of customers. Did Toyota lose its competitiveness and get stuck-in-the-middle? Not at all! Toyota is evolving to achieve the final stage of development, i.e., broad differentiation. The same could be said about BMW, which is a very well-known luxury carmaker. According to Moon's model, BMW was at the differentiation focus stage where it used to sell to a limited, high-end customer segment. However, rather than dwelling and solidifying its competitive advantage in that position, BMW has introduced the BMW 1 Series to target less high-end consumers.

Moon's discussion shows one overarching problem with Porter's discussion, which is Porter's over-focus on firms from advanced countries. Porter's discussions are based on his observations of firms that are active in developed markets, where market conditions are more stable and consequently more static. This is perhaps why, in some cases, scholars from developing or newly developed countries are in a better position to make observations that Porter might have missed. In Asia, global MNCs with worldwide brand recognition co-exist with many other firms relying heavily on traditional factor cost advantage. This is highly rare in the United States and other developed countries, where the level of economic development simply makes it difficult to observe both types of firms simultaneously. Therefore, scholars from developing countries are in a better position to observe and ameliorate the problems in Porter's static model. Figure 8 visually presents the difference between Porter's and Moon's points.

Since Porter mostly observes already-established firms operating primarily in developed nations, the majority of his observations are clustered around the productivity frontier. Firms already on the productivity frontier may show the end product of what a successful firm should be, but they do not show the evolutionary path that a firm can take in order to achieve the state of best practice. On the other hand, Moon bases his theory on a wider scope, as he observes both firms that are catching up as well as firms on the productivity frontier.

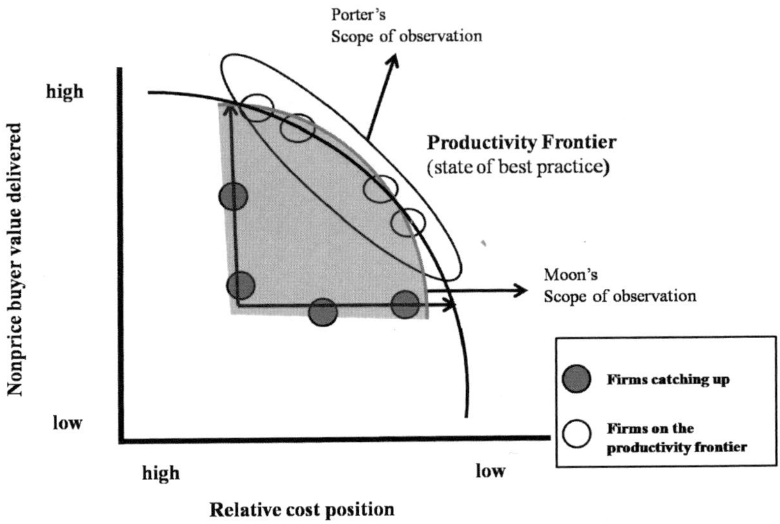

Fig. 8. Differences in scope of analysis between Porter and Moon.

5.3 Dynamics of How to Sell What to Whom

Moon and Hur (2008) continue the critical evaluation of Porter's framework. While the previous article (Moon 1993) resolved only one problem, namely the static nature of Porter's framework, this article attempts to enhance the model on a more comprehensive scale.

At this point, it is important to look at the evolution of Porter's generic strategies, as they have undergone significant changes since their inception in the 1980s (see Fig. 5). The three generic strategies neatly organize the most commonly used competitive strategies into a readily applicable framework. The key concepts introduced through this framework are the question of scope (industrywide or a particular segment) and the type of advantage (differentiation or overall cost leadership).

Porter further enhanced this version in 1985 by introducing an additional dimension in the focus arena (see Fig. 9).

Next, in 1996, Porter presented a further augmented version of his framework by adding the concepts of variety-based, needs-based

Competitive Scope	Competitive Advantage	Lower Cost	Differentiation
	Broad Target	**1. Cost Leadership**	**2. Differentiation**
	Narrow Target	**3A. Cost Focus**	**3B. Differentiation Focus**

Fig. 9. Four generic strategies.[8]

and access-based positioning.[9] Although Porter never actually created a framework that incorporates these new concepts, they can all be considered to be a subset of the focus strategy. They can be organized as in Fig. 10.

The above frameworks have been highly influential in transforming strategic management from a simply informed conversation to a rigorous academic discipline. However, they are not without flaws, and three general points can be made[10]:

- *Failure to Distinguish Scope of Product vs. Customer Group* —While Porter distinguished strategies according to competitive scope, the nature of the scope is rather elusive. Porter later introduced the concept of needs-based, variety-based and access-based strategies,

[8] Porter (1985), p. 12.

[9] See Chap. 4 for a more detailed analysis.

[10] For further discussion, see Moon and Hur (2008).

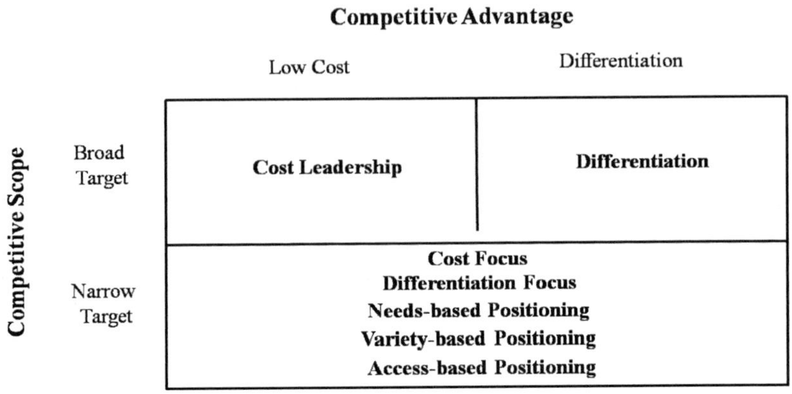

Fig. 10. Seven generic strategies.[11]

but they overlap to a significant degree and do not provide us with a clear-cut picture as to what exactly the firm's focus should be.

- *Stuck-in-the-Middle* — There are actually many firms who choose to pursue several strategies simultaneously and still succeed. Porter's framework fails to account for these firms.
- *Shifting Strategies* — Many firms constantly change their strategies according to business cycles and other variables. This goes against Porter's repeated assertion that strategies must be kept constant in order to create a sustainable competitive advantage.

In order to correct the three problems explained above, the framework must be altered as in Fig. 11.

Figure 11 refines Porter's existing frameworks to provide a more realistic picture, especially considering the realities of firms from developing countries. The core difference is the introduction of the product-based and customer-based strategies, which attempts to reconcile Porter's confusion when discussing the variety-, needs- and access-based strategies. The eight generic strategies are created to show a comprehensive and dynamic view. The unique feature of

[11] Moon and Hur (2008).

Product-Based Strategy	Customer-Based Strategy: Broad	Customer-Based Strategy: Narrow
Broad	**General** Differentiation	**Customer-based** Differentiation
Broad	**General** Cost Leadership	**Customer-based** Cost Leadership
Narrow	**Product-based** Differentiation	**Multi-scope** Differentiation
Narrow	**Product-based** Cost Leadership	**Multi-scope** Cost Leadership

Fig. 11. Eight comprehensive generic strategies.[12]

this model is the subcategorization of general, product-based, customer-based and multi-scope strategies. Each will be explained below.

- *General Strategy* — Firms in this category attempt to provide a wide range of product or service varieties for a wide array of customers. This can be done based on differentiation or cost leadership. For example, Mercedes (high-end manufacturer) and Hyundai Motors (lower-end manufacturer) both attempt to provide a wide range of automobiles for various customers, although the two firms have different strategic directions (i.e., differentiation for Mercedes and cost leadership for Hyundai).
- *Product-based Strategy* — This strategy attempts to meet particular needs of a wide array of customers. This can also be based on either differentiation or cost leadership. Land Rover and Jeep are both producers of off-road utility vehicles. However, Land Rover chose to take the differentiation route by providing sophisticated features at significantly higher prices. On the other hand, Jeep chose to offer value prices for the quality of the product that it offers.

[12] *Ibid.*

- *Customer-based Strategy* — Some firms attempt to provide a broad range of products or services to a narrow group of customers. Again, either a cost or differentiation approach can be taken, as demonstrated from the following examples. Caterpillar, a leading construction and mining equipment manufacturer, offers tough and durable machines with superior performance. Also, the level of customer service far exceeds that of its competitors in the same industry. Komatsu, another heavy machinery and mining equipment company, offers value products but at a lower cost. Komatsu, unlike Caterpillar, has taken the cost-leadership path to gaining competitive advantage within the customer-based strategy.
- *Multi-Scope Strategy* — This strategy is applied to meet the particular needs of a particular group of customers. Companies such as AM General Corporation utilize a multi-scope strategy, since it produces highly specialized military and special-purpose vehicles. The customer base is limited, the pricing is high and the strategy is heavily focused on providing specific value. It is rather difficult to take a cost-leadership approach in a multi-scope strategy because, for a company to pursue a cost leadership strategy, it has to have a certain degree of scale and scope economies to attain cost advantages. It is very hard to achieve this status in this kind of highly specialized industry.

The next question then arises: what is stuck-in-the-middle? Many companies have successfully pursued various strategies and survived. Stuck-in-the-middle is in fact not a result of the wrong strategic choice, but rather a broadening of strategy. The real question is not whether companies can or cannot broaden their strategy, but whether they can broaden it without losing their competitive advantages. Hence, successful companies will expand without diluting their previous advantages.

Consider Toyota and Honda's entry into the US market. Although the stellar success of numerous Japanese auto companies is considered public knowledge nowadays, they were looked down upon with doubt and lack of confidence in their early days of international entry during the 1980s. They were clearly not differentiators, as foreign luxury brands such as BMW and Jaguar dominated this segment. Even in the lower-end segment, Hyundai and Lada were competing fiercely based on their cost leadership. However, why is it that, 20 years later, four out of the seven best-selling sedans are those of Honda and Toyota which, according to Porter, have pursued a stuck-in-the-middle strategy?

The answer is quite simple. The majority of mid-size car buyers cannot afford expensive BMW 5 Series cars; at the same time, they are not willing to sacrifice their desire for quality and purchase a Sonata from Hyundai, which does not have a good reputation. In essence, these customers are both quality- and cost-conscious. By catering to these customers, Toyota and Honda were not being caught in the middle, but rather they were utilizing a customer-based strategy, which attempts to meet the broad needs of the middle-income buyers.

This new perspective can easily map out the evolutionary path of a firm. Consider two vastly different firms in the same industry, Hyundai and Mercedes. Hyundai started out in 1967 as a multi-scope cost leader with a single product catering to one customer group in Korea (multi-scope cost leadership). In 1976, it started to expand into the US and other countries based on cost-competitive automobiles (product-based cost leadership). In recent years, Hyundai has aggressively invested in overseas production bases and is becoming a general cost leader in a wide array of automobiles (general cost leadership). Hyundai was able to expand its product and customer base throughout the years without compromising its existing competitive advantage.

Mercedes-Benz, on the other hand, started out by catering exclusively to higher-end customers. The medium-sized C-Class and large-sized E-Class and S-Class cars were for more affluent customers (multi-scope differentiation). However, as time passed, it began introducing the smaller-sized A-Class cars that catered to a broader range of customers (product-based differentiation). It is important to note that the introduction of A-Class cars was not an attempt to be cost-competitive, but was to pursue differentiation within a different target segment. It targeted the customers who wanted a higher-end car within that class of vehicles. If the purpose were to compete on price, most would look for a Honda or a Toyota rather than a Mercedes. Mercedes is now increasingly offering a wider range of products in an array of classes to target such customers who look for luxury in different classes of automobiles (general differentiation).

The main concern for all firms is how to sell what to whom. The new model shows a more comprehensive framework to understand the answer to this question, as it shows the dynamic and complex nature of firm strategies much better than the previous models.

Analysis

The above discussion aptly summarizes Porter's existing frameworks and further enhances their explanatory power. As mentioned in the previous analysis, Porter's insights, as powerful as they are, still neglected the dynamic nature of global business and failed to account for many successful firms that shifted their strategies according to their needs. Furthermore, the ambiguity that constantly lingered over the relationship between Porter's new concepts of variety-, needs- and access-based categories and his previous analytical frameworks is cleared up as well.

However, Moon and Hur's (2008) study is limited to some industries and the only in-depth case study example presented is the automobile industry. Considering the fact that industry structure has a profound effect on firm strategies, it remains to be seen whether this framework can explain the inner workings of other industries that are vastly different from the automobile industry. Nevertheless, the contribution of this work is that the various frameworks succinctly ameliorate and further enhance Porter's previous frameworks. In addition, it gives a better context to analyze MNCs from developing countries, as most of the so-called "emerging giants" are still in the intermediary stages which cannot be captured by Porter's framework.

Case Study 1: An Indian Blue Ocean[13]

HCL is a leading global technology and IT firm with average annual revenues of approximately US$5 billion. HCL is composed of two firms, HCL Technologies and HCL Infosystems, both of which are based in India. HCL was founded in 1976 and is described as one of India's original IT garage start-ups. So just how did a garage start-up develop into a billion-dollar global IT company? One of the ways was through utilizing the Blue Ocean.

In 2005, Mr. Vineet Nayar took over as CEO of the HCL group. On the same day he took office, somebody left a gift on his desk, and that gift was the book *Blue Ocean Strategy* by Kim and Mauborgne (2005). Nayer claims that he decided to conceptualize the strategy and apply it directly to HCL. In essence, he wished to create uncontested market spaces within which his firm could grow and reap the benefits of an early-mover advantage. Nayer realized that the application outsourcing business was becoming increasingly commoditized and under pricing pressures. Thus, HCL had to chase larger deals that would bring a significant transformation to the firm. HCL made a concentrated effort to move up the value chain and go for multiservice deals with application and infrastructure components. Shortly after adopting its Blue Ocean strategy, the firm made a number of successful joint ventures and partnerships with the likes of Boeing, AMD, NEC and Celestica.

HCL's strategy now embodies a unique kind of disruptive innovation, which focuses on value centricity and a Blue Ocean approach to business. This has deepened customer relationships, created new markets and established strategic partnerships marked by collaboration, goal alignment and substantive engagement.

Firstly, however, HCL would have had to create a strategy canvas (see Fig. 12). The strategy canvas is a diagnostic and action

---

[13] Information for this case study is abstracted from the Blue Ocean Strategy official website (www.blueoceanstrategy.com) and *The Hindu Business Line* (2006a, 2006b).

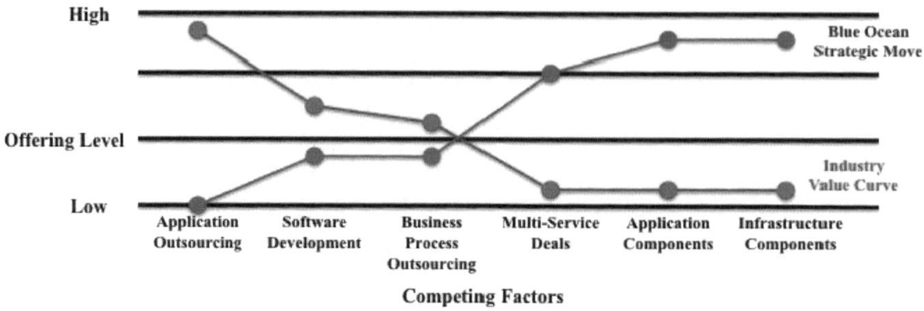

Fig. 12. HCL's strategic canvas.

framework for building an effective Blue Ocean strategy. The strategy canvas should include all of the current factors that the industry currently competes on and what customers receive from the existing competitive offerings on the market. Thus, its role is to first capture the current state of play in the known market space, and then secondly to propel the firm to action by reorienting its focus from competitors to alternatives and from customers to non-customers of the industry.

As depicted in Fig. 12, HCL became acutely aware that the application outsourcing, software development and business process outsourcing industries were intensely competitive, the margins were low and offerings were commoditized. Therefore, HCL organized its priorities according to the four-actions framework explained in the first part of this chapter (see Fig. 3). The framework, by first eliminating and reducing, allowed for insight into how to diminish investments in highly competitive areas. Secondly, by raising and creating, HCL was able to lift buyer value and create new demand. This ultimately provided HCL with a move from the existing industry value curve to a Blue Ocean curve. HCL's four-actions framework is shown in Fig. 13.

In Fig. 13, key points include the elimination of the pure application outsourcing business and a reduction of the software and business process outsourcing segments, where competition was high. Also, the raising of multi-service deals and the focus on

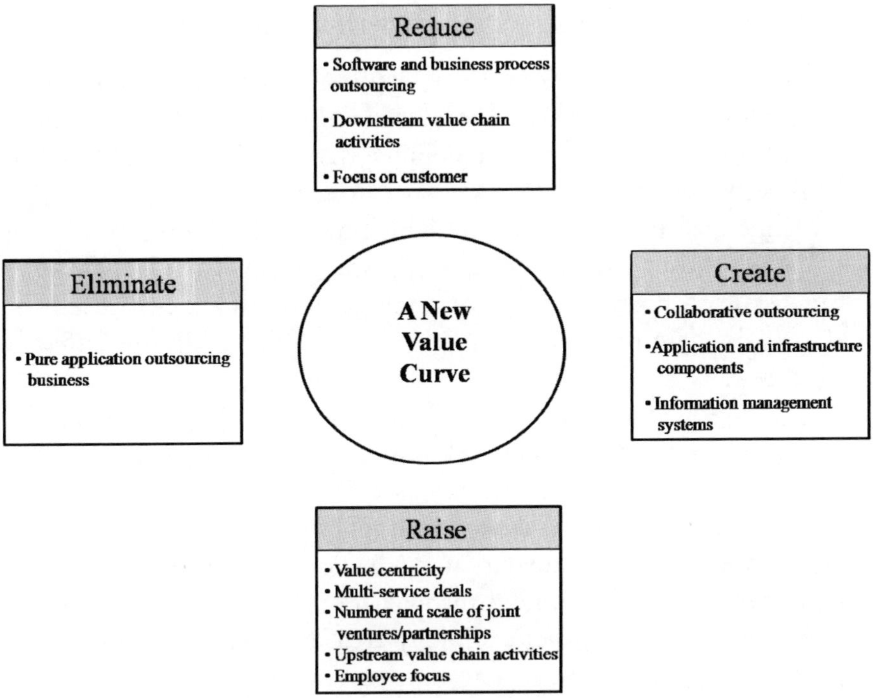

Fig. 13. HCL's four-actions framework.

upstream value chain activities were high priorities. By creating collaborative outsourcing, whereby client companies could select outsourcing criteria (application or infrastructure), and by focusing on information management systems, HCL was able to enter into previously unexplored business segments and thus swim in its own Blue Ocean.

Although HCL has been successful in its application of Blue Ocean, it should be made clear that this is a very difficult task to undertake. Furthermore, Blue Ocean should be considered an element of a whole strategy, not a strategy framework itself. The concept itself is heavily biased towards customers and does not take into consideration other forces that shape the industry structure.

Case Study 2: Toyota Stuck-in-the-Middle?[14]

The Toyota Motor Corporation is a global company that is headquartered in Japan and was declared the world's largest automaker in 2007 (BBC 2007). You may remember that we have already looked at a Toyota case study in Chap. 2, with regards to Nonaka's (2007) knowledge creation within a firm. This time, we are going to look at Toyota again, but from a different perspective. We have also previously discussed Porter's model of three generic strategies in Chap. 1, and we will again revisit this model but also from a slightly different perspective.

As mentioned before, although Porter's model is highly useful, there are two fundamental weaknesses within it. One is that the model views the generic strategies as being mutually exclusive, and the other is that the model does not show how to shift strategies from one to another. It is argued that while Porter warns against being "stuck-in-the-middle", some firms may actually benefit from competing in more than one generic strategy area. It is also argued that as a firm grows and develops, it may shift its strategy over time. We will thus highlight Toyota's simultaneous use of more than one generic strategy, and then look at how Toyota's generic strategy has changed over time along its evolutionary path.

Firstly, due to the 1973 oil crisis, US consumers began turning to smaller cars with better fuel efficiency. However, American car manufacturers considered small economy-class cars to be an entry-level product. Thus, the level of quality was kept low in order to maintain price competitiveness, even though US cars were not fuel-efficient. However, Toyota entered the US market with a different approach. Japanese consumers had a long-standing tradition of demanding small, fuel-efficient cars that were manufactured to high quality standards. As a result, Toyota began expanding beyond Japan and eventually into the US market. Using Porter's generic strategies

---

[14] Information for this case study is abstracted from the Toyota website (www.toyota.co.jp/en) and *The Economist* (2007c).

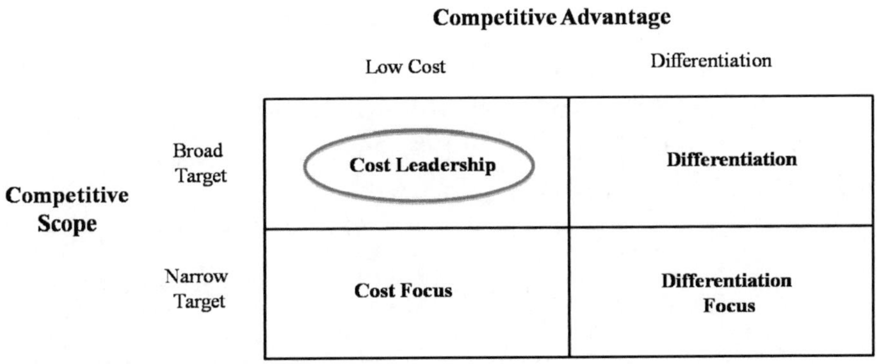

Fig. 14. Toyota's strategy.

model, we could place Toyota as initially having a cost leadership strategy, that is, a broad target market at lower cost. This strategy has been immensely successful for Toyota (see Fig. 14).

Until recently, Toyota has maintained this strategy and is still producing good-quality compact cars at reasonable prices. However, there has been further development in its strategy and that is the addition of the Lexus brand in 1989. Lexus is Toyota's luxury vehicle division and has become the highest-selling luxury brand of cars in the US. Toyota now runs both the Toyota and Lexus brands simultaneously, thus expanding its strategy in two different directions. The Lexus brand could be seen as a form of differentiation focus strategy, that is, a narrower target but a differentiated product. Thus, Toyota's generic strategy can be represented as in Fig. 15.

This proves that some firms, particularly larger firms, may be able to maintain more than one type of strategy at the same time without experiencing problems associated with being stuck-in-the-middle.

Regarding the second weakness discovered in Porter's model, i.e., the lack of dynamism, this model (see Fig. 15) first needs to be altered in order to make it more dynamic and thus easier to read. Toyota's strategic development will be shown using the new dynamic model. Cost focus is a common starting point for firms, as they usually have an advantage in terms of cheap labor or natural resources but lack vast

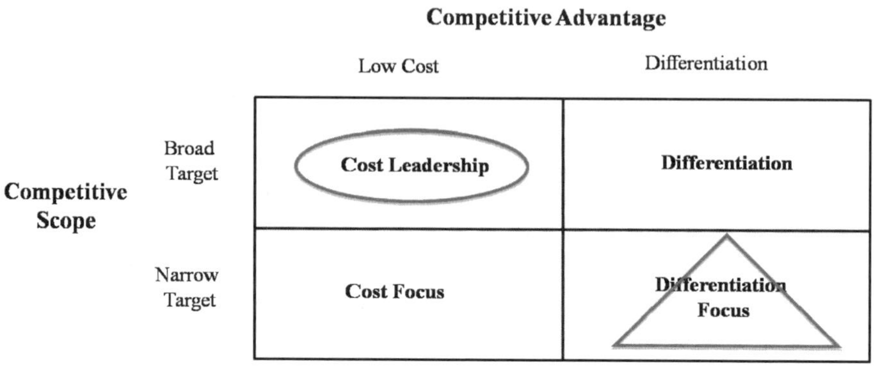

Fig. 15. Evolution of Toyota's strategy.

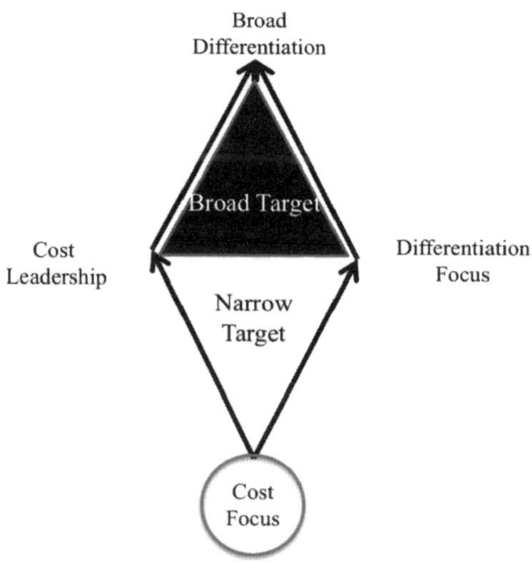

Fig. 16. Toyota's initial strategy.

amounts of technological know-how. Toyota, in a similar vein, launched its first prototype, the A1 passenger car, using the manufacturing process adopted by Ford Motor Company. This is represented in Fig. 16.

Toyota continued in much the same way for many years. That is to say, the company focused heavily on improving manufacturing

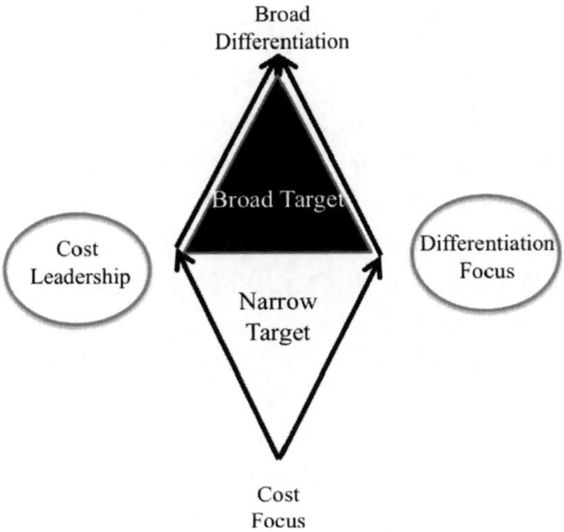

Fig. 17. Toyota's strategic evolution.

procedures to increase profits and relay the benefits to its customers mostly in the Japanese domestic market. However, following the 1970s oil crisis, Toyota changed its approach and started to export small, low-cost cars. The company maintained its cost focus, but widened its target. Through this strategic maneuver, Toyota moved from a cost focus to a cost leadership position. This evolution is represented in Fig. 17.

Lastly, as previously mentioned, Toyota initiated its luxury division with the Lexus brand. Toyota, therefore, has also moved into the differentiation focus segment and maintained it alongside its cost leadership strategy. This is a very common flow of events for a developing firm to follow, although it is usually only larger firms that are able to maintain more than one strategy at the same time. So what is next for Toyota? According to our model, the firm's final destination of strategy is broad differentiation. This is where the firm seeks to be unique in the industry and at the same time serves a broad competitive scope. It will be interesting to monitor Toyota's future developments with regards to this strategic position.

Case Study 3: A Make-Up Strategy[15]

Porter's generic strategies framework is of immense value to the strategist, both in its original and extended forms. We have already applied the three most basic generic strategies, the extended four generic strategies and the further extended seven generic strategies to previous case studies. However, we are going to take it a step further here and apply Moon and Hur's (2008) proposed generic strategies framework to this case study.

As mentioned before, Moon and Hur's model adds two competitive scope criteria, product-based and customer-based, which can be either broad or narrow. Within the competitive scope, there are four variables — general, customer-based, product-based and multi-scope — all of which can be classified as either differentiation or cost leaders. Thus, we have eight generic strategies (see Fig. 18).

		Customer-Based Strategy: Broad	Customer-Based Strategy: Narrow
Product-Based Strategy	Broad	**General** Differentiation	**Customer-based** Differentiation
		General Cost Leadership	**Customer-based** Cost Leadership
	Narrow	**Product-based** Differentiation	**Multi-scope** Differentiation
		Product-based Cost Leadership	**Multi-scope** Cost Leadership

Fig. 18. Moon and Hur's eight generic strategies.

[15] Information for this case study is abstracted from the Kanebo website (www.sensai-cosmetics.com), the Shiseido website (www.shiseido.com), the Jiangsu Longliqi Group website (longliqi.fuzing.com), the Etude website (www.etudehouse.com), the Amore Pacific website (www.amorepacific.com), the Isehan website (www.isehan.info) and the Kose website (www.kose.co.jp).

Product-Based Strategy	Customer-Based Strategy: Broad	Customer-Based Strategy: Narrow
Broad	**Kanebo**	**Shiseido**
Broad	**Jiangsu Longliqi**	**Etude**
Narrow	**Amore Pacific**	**Isehan**
Narrow	**Kose**	**???**

Fig. 19. Asian cosmetic firms in the eight generic strategies framework.

This case study will analyze the Asian cosmetics industry utilizing the new eight generic strategies. Seven prominent Asian cosmetics brands have been organized into the framework in Fig. 19.

Japan's Kanebo implemented a general differentiation strategy, as it not only offers a wide range of products to a wide range of customers, but also goes the extra mile with salon services that both utilize and advertise its products simultaneously. China's Jiangsu Longliqi is placed as a general cost leader, as it offers a wide variety of products to a wide customer base and does so at a very low price.

Japan's Shiseido has a customer-based differentiation strategy. Although it has a broad product range, due to its high cost and exclusivity, it has a narrow customer range. Etude is a Korean cosmetics firm that also offers a broad product range, but at a reasonable price. Its customer range is narrow, as it is geared towards teenage girls' cosmetic requirements.

Amore Pacific, another Korean cosmetics firm, has a much narrower range of products as it focuses only on skincare and make-up. It is pricey but not overly so, and thus is still accessible to a broad range of customers. Kose of Japan has a product-based cost leadership strategy. It has a narrow product range as it deals only in skincare, yet has a broad range of customers as it caters to both the young generation with its Awake line and more mature customers with its Sekkisei line.

Japan's Isehan has a differentiated multi-scope strategy as it offers only one product, which is a special nanotechnology-based skincare product. Due to its exclusivity, it also has an extremely narrow customer base. No cosmetics firm could match a cost leadership multi-scope strategy. Due to the problem of economies of scale, it is very difficult to have a narrow product range with a narrow customer base and do so at the cheapest price possible.

Applying this framework is a very useful method with which to base discussions around strategy. However, these firms' placement within the framework is by no means static. Further suggestion of movement from strategy to strategy is possible, depending on the firm's level of development. At the initial stage, a firm may base its strategy in the multi-scope area, and then at a later stage move to a product- or customer-based strategy. Ultimately, a general strategy is the most desirable one as the company becomes an all-around player rather than a niche player. Thus, the extension from three to eight generic strategies tackles the weaknesses found in Porter's previous work and, although daunting at first, is easy to understand and can be easily applied.

Discussion Questions

1. Do you agree or disagree that the Blue Ocean strategy is not an entirely new strategy proposition? Why?
2. Can you think of a product, similar to Yellow Tail wine, that has reformed the industry strategy canvas?
3. True or false: broad differentiation is the ultimate point for a developed firm. Why?
4. Does a firm have to choose only one strategy among protectionist, competitive and cooperative strategies? Can you think

of a firm which uses more than one of these strategies simultaneously?

5. Why does Michael Porter condemn the concept of "stuck-in-the-middle" so vehemently? Do you agree with him?
6. Besides the automobile and cosmetics industries, which other industries can we apply the eight generic strategies to? Can you find an example of multi-scope cost leadership in these industries?

CHAPTER 6

Measuring and Forecasting

Chapter Guideline

The previous chapter explained how different scholars utilized Porter's model and then further enhanced its explanatory power. Now, we need to look at another crucial aspect of business: measuring and forecasting the strategic success or failure of a business operation. Well-known methods include various indices such as financial statements, investor reports and so on. Since there is extensive literature available regarding these conventional indices, this chapter will introduce methods and frameworks of forecasting and measuring that are outside the conventional scope of analysis.

Summary of Previous Models

Various discussions on strategy are useful, since they provide a shortcut to understanding complex business realities. Through Porter, we were able to gain an understanding on the fundamentals of strategic management. Furthermore, scholars such as Nonaka and Prahalad presented insights into specific aspects of strategic management. Finally, the previous chapter illustrated a modified version which reconciled and further enhanced the explanatory power of Porter's models. However, businesses need to measure their success or failure in order to set realistic goals. Furthermore, effective forecasting is required to make plans for the future. In this chapter, we will turn our attention to these matters.

6.1 Measuring the Intangible

Many great thinkers in history have repeatedly emphasized the importance of assessing oneself objectively. Sun Tzu, the eminent Chinese military strategist, famously proclaimed, "If you know both yourself and your enemy, you can come out of hundreds of battles without danger (知彼知己 百戰不殆)" (Sun and Qin 1996, p. 122). This timeless wisdom is also highly valid in the world of business and, therefore, numerous methods for objectively tracking a firm's performance have been developed. Typical examples of business assessment tools include return on investment (ROI), return on assets (ROA) and cash flow, which most business majors are bound to encounter somewhere along their academic and professional careers. However, as important as these measures are, they are limited to measuring "hard" performance, which is strictly related to the tangible aspect of managing a firm. As we learned from Nonaka (2007) in Chap. 2, harnessing the intangible has become just as important as managing the tangible.

The Balanced Scorecard is a popular example of such a managerial tool designed to measure the intangible. Since its introduction in the early 1990s, this method has had a profound impact on strategic management and has led to various spinoffs and criticisms. Some have clarified the often nebulous link between Balanced Scorecard and strategic management (Ahn 2001; Brewer 2002; Butler *et al.* 1997), while others have questioned the validity of the Balanced Scorecard concept itself (Mooraj *et al.* 1999; Nørreklit 2000). Good or bad, what is evident is the massive stir created by the Balanced Scorecard concept. Therefore, comprehending the Balanced Scorecard is the first key step to gaining a balanced view of firm performance measures.

The Balanced Scorecard, as the name suggests, is a managerial tool that provides managers a method to strike a balance between the tangible and intangible aspects of measuring and keeping track of firm performance. While financial measures are well developed and can give very important insights into the condition of firm operations, they alone are not sufficient. The Balanced Scorecard is a management performance and assessment framework that tries to complement the existing financial statement to give a more comprehensive view on the efficacy of firm activity.

As Fig. 1 illustrates, the Balanced Scorecard is comprised of four major components, of which three are new perspectives: (a) customers, (b) internal business processes, and (c) learning and growth. These three additional perspectives are highly important for managers because financial measures alone cannot fill the void between strategy development and its implementation. Therefore, the Balanced Scorecard provides a performance management framework which connects the long-term strategic objectives with everyday, short-term actions.

Based on this framework, Kaplan and Norton (2007a) present four concrete new processes that managers can follow to implement the additional three perspectives into the firm's strategic management (see Fig. 2). Each of these components will be explained hereafter.

Translating the Vision

The starting point of the explanation is the top part of Fig. 2. Translating the vision is simply aligning individual employees' everyday actions with the company's mission statement or strategic vision. Consider, for example, the mission statement "to provide superior service to targeted customers". While this may seem like a very clear goal, the understanding of the terms "superior service" and "targeted customers" may differ widely among employees. The "translating the vision" portion of Fig. 2, in essence, is a parameter which clearly defines the firm's vision so that employees can ensure that their everyday activities are aligned with the firm's overall strategic goal or vision.

Communicating and Linking

The next step is communicating and linking, which is a critical process since the translated vision must be disseminated down the organizational hierarchy. The Balanced Scorecard provides a clear way to follow and understand the firm's vision, since it signals to all employees what

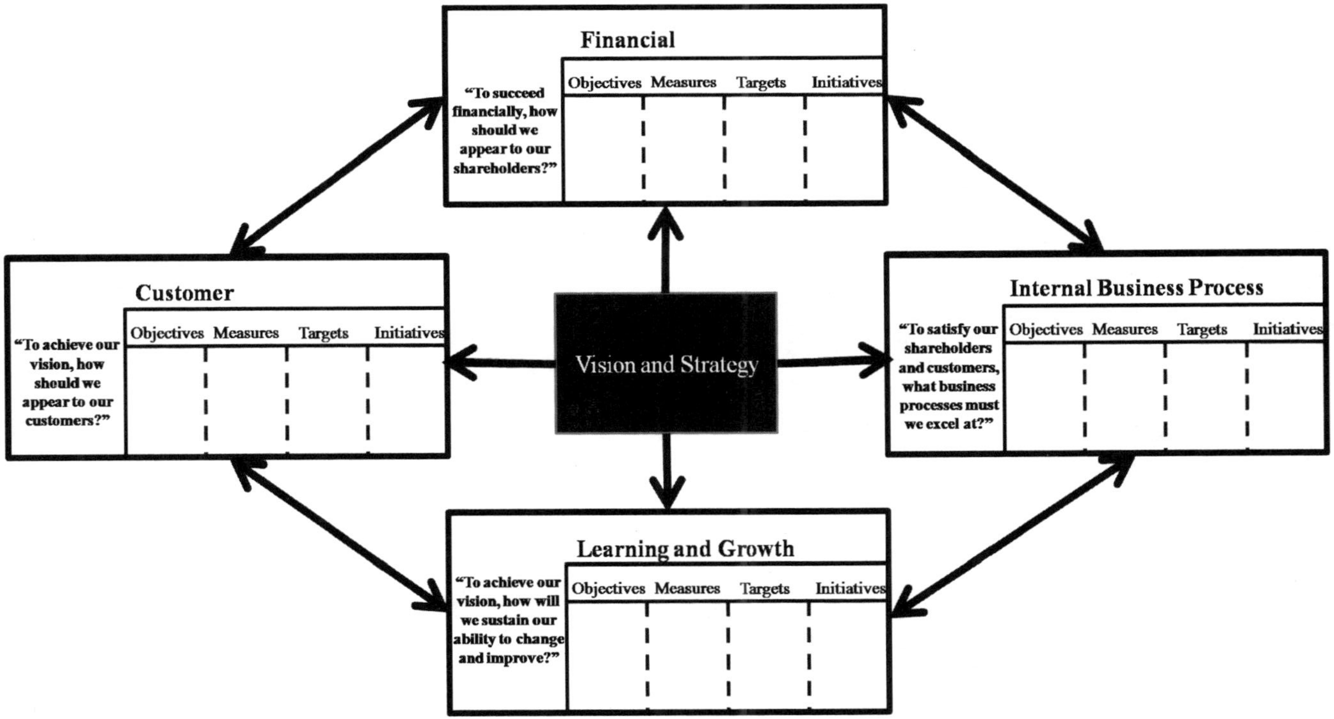

Fig. 1. Translating vision and strategy: four perspectives.[1]

[1] Kaplan and Norton (2007a).

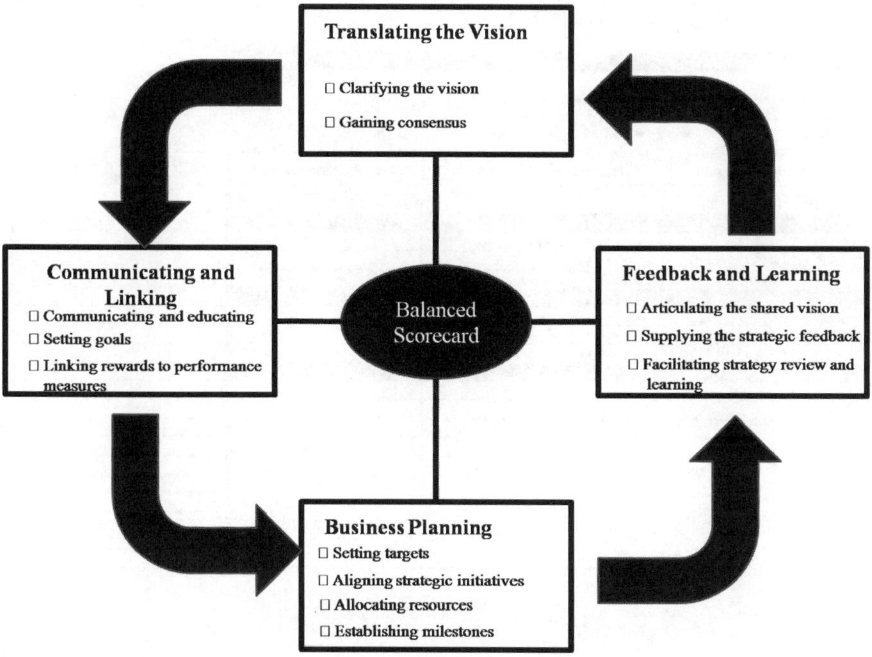

Fig. 2. Managing strategy: four processes.[2]

the firm is trying to achieve as a whole. Three specific steps can be taken to successfully achieve this feat (see Fig. 2):

- *Communicating and Educating* — Unlike the traditional top-down method of strategy execution, this step requires the upper-level managers to disseminate the strategic vision all the way down to the lowest echelons of the firm. Furthermore, reverse communication from bottom to top must take place for any other input to be incorporated into the firm's strategy. For this purpose, the Balanced Scorecard can provide everyone involved in the process with a method to quantify and effectively communicate the strategic vision to each other.

[2] *Ibid.*

The Personal Scorecard

Corporate Objectives

- ☐ Double our corporate value in seven years.
- ☐ Increase our earnings by an average of 20% per year.
- ☐ Achieve an internal rate of return 2% above the cost of capital.
- ☐ Increase both production and reserves by 20% in the next decade.

Corporate Targets					Scorecard Measures	Business Unit Targets					Team/Individual Objectives and Initiatives
1995	1996	1997	1998	1999		1995	1996	1997	1998	1999	1.
					Financial						
100	120	160	180	250	Earnings (in millions of dollars)						
100	450	200	210	225	Net cash flow						
100	85	80	75	70	Overhead and operating expenses						2.
					Operating						
100	75	73	70	64	Production costs per barrel						
100	97	93	90	82	Development costs per barrel						
100	105	108	108	110	Total annual production						3.
Team/Individual Measures						**Targets**					
1.											
2.											
3.											4.
4.											
5.											
Name:											5.
Location:											

Fig. 3. Personal scorecard.[3]

- *Setting Goals* — The next step is transforming this vision into concrete sequences (objectives and measures) that everyone can follow. The personal scorecard (see Fig. 3) is the embodiment of this idea. With this scorecard in every employee's pocket, all firm constituents can constantly measure and check whether their actions are in line with the firm's overall strategic vision.
- *Linking Rewards to Performance Measures* — Incentives are powerful tools that drive people towards great achievements. Naturally, it is crucial to establish a connection between Balanced Scorecard measures and compensation. Employees should be rewarded when they successfully implement the strategic vision in the Balanced Scorecard. Of course, Kaplan and Norton (2007a) note that this carries a certain level of risk since, if the company does not have the proper measures included, it could lead to inefficiency. The best

[3] *Ibid.*

approach is still rather unclear, but it will become more evident as more and more companies are adopting the Balanced Scorecard approach.

Business Planning

In order to coordinate the activities of individual departments and divisions, firms have to expend a significant amount of time and resources. Furthermore, because each part of the firm makes decisions on a different timetable, managers also have to deal with time lags that could occur among different departments. The Balanced Scorecard can help alleviate this problem to a significant degree because it can integrate the different units within the firm under one strategic vision without separate coordination. As Fig. 1 demonstrates, the Balanced Scorecard gives a comprehensive guideline to link all important parts of a firm into one strategic direction.

After the strategic direction is clarified, the companies must also select the most important variables and incorporate them into the Balanced Scorecard. This affords an important fulcrum upon which all the business units can mobilize and direct the firm's resources in the appropriate direction. The next process of business planning requires setting specific short-term targets for the Balanced Scorecard measures. Tangible goals are always very important because the scorecard users can constantly check whether their actions are in line with the overall strategic vision and make changes if necessary. The final stage is to define the long-term objectives, for which managers must set tangible milestones for individuals to follow.

Feedback and Learning

The final point of the entire loop (see Fig. 2) is the feedback and learning process. The above three processes are crucial in actuating the strategic vision of a company, but the process in its totality needs to be re-examined in order to correct mistakes and further enhance the entire loop. Corporate reviews have existed in the past, but they have usually been focused on one aspect of the entire business and rarely assessed the efficacy of the strategic vision as a whole. With the Balanced Scorecard, the firm can now conduct thorough research and make necessary changes in the end.

Analysis

Kaplan and Norton's (2007a) Balanced Scorecard has been immensely popular among firms and has been adopted by consulting firms worldwide. Prior to the Balanced Scorecard, most firms relied heavily on tangible (mostly financial) indicators to assess the position and condition of a firm. While these are important tools, they are no longer sufficient as firm operations have become much more complex and multidimensional. Firms making financial profit may still be heading towards disaster if the profit is being generated based on activities that are not in line with the firm's overall strategic vision. This is precisely why the authors' emphasis on measuring and integrating non-financial and intangible firm assets into the corporate strategy is a highly important aspect of strategy formulation in the business environment, which requires constant innovation.

There are several criticisms, however, with the Balanced Scorecard. First, and the most prevalent, is the subjective nature of the judgment criteria. When one looks at the specifics of the Balanced Scorecard, one can easily see that these are not based on tangible statistics. Rather, it is an amalgamation of subjective indicators which the strategic planners of a company assess as being valid towards the overall corporate-level strategy. While strategic vision itself inherently contains subjective elements, there is another inherent difficulty in trying to objectively quantify a firm's intangible assets. This is associated with the next problem: if the Balanced Scorecard is used recklessly, it could end up being a list of positive metrics without accounting for the various tradeoffs which arise when pursuing all of the "positive" goals. Despite these criticisms, Kaplan and Norton have presented us with a fresh new way to look at how to assess a firm's performance more comprehensively.

In order to put the Balanced Scorecard in a broader perspective, it is important to incorporate it into a more systematically designed framework. The diamond model (Porter 1990) for competitive advantage offers an analytical framework that systematically organizes the determinants of competitiveness into four categories: (a) factor conditions; (b) demand conditions; (c) firm structure, strategy and rivalry; and (d) related and supporting sectors. Although it was originally designed to analyze national competitiveness, the model is widely used for industry- and firm-level analyses.[4] Figure 4 represents the Balanced Scorecard in terms of Porter's diamond model.

The Balanced Scorecard can be viewed as a detailed framework for a subset of the diamond model. For example, the customer perspective is a method to measure the demand condition that a firm faces, while learning and growth can be seen as an advanced factor condition, as illustrated in Fig. 4. Thus, what we can see from this analysis is that Kaplan and Norton's contribution is to advance our understanding of a subvariable of each corner of the diamond.

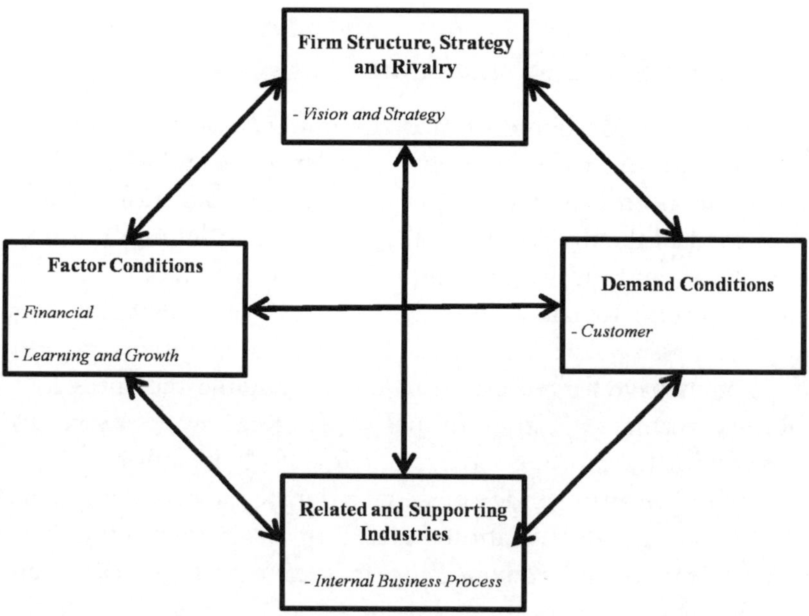

Fig. 4. Porter's diamond model and the Balanced Scorecard.

[4] For the evolution of the diamond model, see Rugman and D'Cruz (1993), Moon *et al.* (1998), Cho (1994), Cho and Moon (2000) and Cho *et al.* (2008).

It is always very important to organize the new knowledge that we gain into a single perspective so that we can have an all-encompassing and integrated view. Porter's diamond framework is one of those powerful analytical frameworks that enable us to do so, and it is very important that we do not forget the big picture even when we are talking about specific subvariables.

More recently, in *The Strategy-Focused Organization*, Kaplan and Norton (2007b) introduce a new tool — strategy maps — and a new approach that makes strategy a continuous process owned not just by top management, but by everyone. As a result, they describe how the nature of the Balanced Scorecard has changed from a valuation tool to a comprehensive value-based management tool. Several innovations and additional dimensions are included in the updated model and, for those who are interested, it is worth tracking the evolution of this influential framework.

6.2 Measuring Globalization

If the above section demonstrated the importance of measuring the intangible, now we turn our eyes to a wider scope and look at how to measure the hottest buzzword of our times: globalization. The word itself is used all the time, but the dearth of precise definitions or measurements of the term is quite surprising. This may be because of the highly complex, dynamic and transformative nature of the term as well as its massive scope of impact. However, some bold scholars and professionals have forged ahead to create tangible measures for this nebulous term, and the annual A.T. Kearney/*Foreign Policy* Globalization Index is a good example of this brave effort.

The Globalization Index presents a detailed analysis of globalization. Measuring globalization in and of itself is a difficult task, but A.T. Kearney and *Foreign Policy* magazine present a comprehensive index that analyzes the "globalness" of a nation by combining four major criteria: (a) economic, (b) personal, (c) technological, and (d) political.

The Globalization Index attempts to illustrate a balanced view of globalization, which is often myopically defined or measured

Table 1. Globalization Index 2006.[5]

			Dimension				Item												
							Economic Integration		Personal Contact			Technological Connectivity			Political Engagement				
2006 GI Rankings		Change from 2005	Economic	Personal	Technological	Political	Trade	FDI	Telephone	Travel	Remittances and Personal Transfers	Internet Users	Internet Hosts	Secure Servers	International Organizations	U.N. Peacekeeping	Treaties	Government Transfers	2005 GI Rankings
1	Singapore	0	1	3	12	29	1	1	1	4	49	10	12	13	33	10	42	47	1
2	Switzerland	1	9	1	7	23	17	7	2	6	2	17	15	5	33	9	42	10	3
3	United States	1	58	40	1	41	62	36	18	33	52	6	1	1	1	25	58	38	4
4	Ireland	-2	4	2	14	7	4	5	3	3	9	26	20	8	11	1	31	23	2
5	Denmark	2	8	8	5	6	20	6	6	16	16	12	3	7	11	13	6	8	7
6	Canada	0	23	7	2	10	30	12	4	20	57	7	14	2	2	14	6	32	6
7	Netherlands	-2	21	11	6	5	11	52	8	11	40	9	2	11	5	17	6	6	5
8	Australia	4	18	36	3	27	55	3	14	32	50	3	5	4	33	18	31	37	12
9	Austria	-1	15	4	13	2	15	18	10	2	29	19	7	14	11	3	6	7	8
10	Sweden	0	19	12	9	9	21	16	11	9	39	1	9	9	25	8	6	15	10
11	New Zealand	0	35	15	4	24	41	26	5	23	54	8	8	3	33	22	6	26	11
12	United Kingdom	1	25	14	8	4	48	10	12	15	42	4	17	6	5	7	6	20	13
13	Finland	-4	31	21	10	14	33	30	19	12	45	5	4	12	11	6	31	18	9
14	Norway	0	39	23	11	18	29	46	17	24	30	24	6	10	25	16	6	29	14
15	Israel	2	20	9	17	40	19	20	7	27	12	16	16	17	48	4	61	4	17
16	Czech Republic	-1	5	6	22	35	5	14	31	1	27	14	22	26	11	43	31	11	15
17	Slovenia	3	13	13	20	15	10	28	22	7	22	18	25	20	11	19	6	16	20
18	Germany	3	41	28	16	11	32	45	15	21	48	20	23	15	2	12	31	13	21
19	Malaysia	0	3	19	28	48	2	11	29	10	18	23	39	34	33	45	42	49	19
20	Hungary	3	7	17	27	20	7	13	41	5	34	29	19	27	11	32	1	24	23
21	Panama	3	2	46	32	39	8	2	35	39	32	42	44	21	48	55	1	31	24
22	Croatia	-6	14	5	29	32	13	19	21	8	7	27	33	25	33	49	1	22	16
23	France	-5	40	18	21	1	50	24	16	13	38	22	21	19	2	5	6	9	18
24	Portugal	-2	29	20	25	3	34	17	23	17	20	28	18	23	5	11	6	5	22
25	Spain	1	22	31	24	16	45	9	26	18	33	25	29	18	5	21	6	19	26
26	Slovakia	-1	6	45	26	19	3	29	28	34	37	21	28	33	11	28	1	54	25
27	Italy	0	50	25	23	8	51	40	13	22	47	15	24	24	5	15	6	12	27
28	Japan	1	62	58	15	13	61	57	42	44	59	13	11	16	33	2	6	46	29
29	South Korea	-1	32	39	19	33	26	41	25	38	24	2	13	29	33	27	31	58	28
30	Romania	5	11	30	36	28	22	8	37	30	10	32	43	43	11	46	1	36	35

because of the abstractness of the concept itself. By categorizing four major dimensions (see the Dimension column in Table 1) and then subdividing each variable into several important subvariables (see the Item column in Table 1), A.T. Kearney and *Foreign Policy* attempt to measure globalization in an objective manner (in this case, for 2006).

After presenting the Globalization Index, A.T. Kearney and *Foreign Policy* (2006) proceed to provide an in-depth analysis of some of the most interesting trends of 2006:

- *Waiting for the Heavyweights* — The recent rise of the BRIC (Brazil, Russia, India and China) countries is an exciting

[5] A.T. Kearney and *Foreign Policy* (2006).

phenomenon with various implications for managers, and there is an immense potential of the untapped market segments of these countries. If these countries turn their eyes to rural development, the global market will expand to an unprecedented level. These new consumers will bring a new dimension to globalization and economic integration.

- *Rich Man's World* — Many countries in the developing world have utilized the wave of globalization to their advantage and have achieved remarkable material wealth. They are now joining the elite tier of global capitalism. This phenomenon has significant economic as well as political implications, as these *nouveau riches* have the muscle to alter their countries in various ways.
- *The Toxic Few* — Globalization generates negative as well as positive effects, and one of the most pronounced negative consequences of globalization is environmental degradation. This report presents a graph which shows the high positive correlation between emissions and globalization.
- *Cash on the Side* — An informal economy is the level of business activities that should be taxed by the government, but are not. The less globalized a nation is, the larger its informal economy is, according to the report.
- *Latin America's Soft Left Turn* — Latin America has been a hotbed of leftist ideology for a long time. From Fidel Castro to the recent Hugo Chavez, many Latin American leaders tout the validity of their socialist agendas and appeal to the public in such a manner. However, an in-depth analysis of Latin America's recent globalization index shows a slightly different picture, as nations in this region have made significant strides in the ranking. Despite the leftist facade, Latin America is increasingly becoming an integral part of the global free market system.
- *Buying into Dubai* — The United Arab Emirate's recent aggressive move towards globalization has made international headlines.

> Dubai is ambitiously aiming to become a new global financial powerhouse in a similar vein as London and New York. As a result, policies have been highly business-friendly and many immigrants from various corners of the world are moving to Dubai for new opportunities. The influx of human and financial resources promises an exciting future for this ambitious city.

The subsequent annual reports have used the same methodology, as can be seen from the 2007 version depicted in Fig. 5. The top-ranking country is Singapore, followed by Hong Kong and the Netherlands. Surprisingly, the United States ranks seventh, even though all of the countries ahead of the US are noted for their small geographic size. Equally remarkable is the inclusion of Jordan and Estonia in the top 10.

Analysis

No word has generated as much discussion in recent years as the term "globalization". However, despite the ubiquity of this term, there has not been much success in providing a successful measure of this phenomenon until A.T. Kearney and *Foreign Policy* collaborated to formulate the Globalization Index. The usefulness of this Index is immense as it not only gives a concrete standard of measurement, but also provides a comprehensive overview of the meaning of globalization. While many people tout globalization, they usually talk about one or two aspects of this phenomenon. By identifying the major variables and subvariables, this Index provides us with a more scientific and quantitative approach to globalization.

However, the Globalization Index is not without problems, as several aspects can be called into question. First, the major classifications are economic, personal, technological and political (see Fig. 5). These classifications are rather ambiguous and it is doubtful whether these categories can be seen as equal in terms of the level of scope. For example, the economic category seems to be much more encompassing than the personal or technological category.

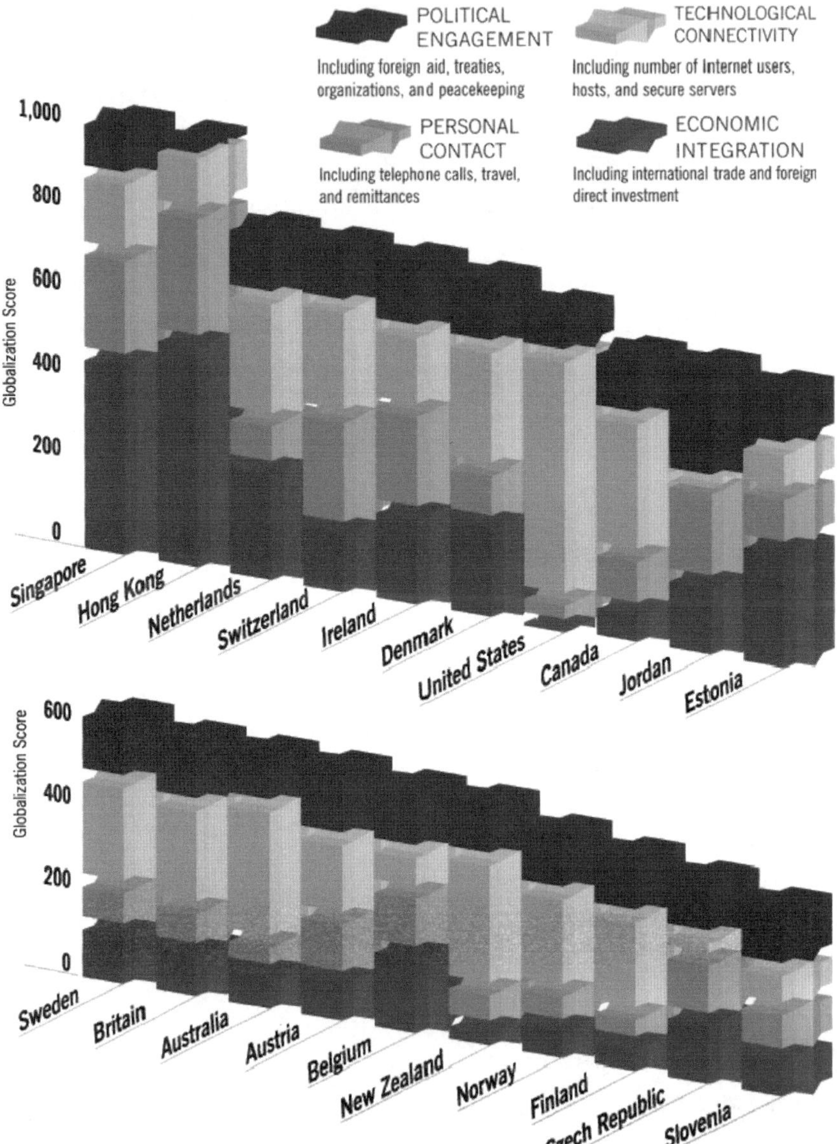

Fig. 5. Globalization Index 2007 — top 20.[6]

[6] A.T. Kearney and *Foreign Policy* (2007).

Intuitively, one can assume that the weight of one subvariable in the economic category may possibly outweigh the effect of that in the personal or technological dimension. A possible enhancement could be made by using economic, political and social as the major categories. Second is the possibility of missing variables. Although the four variables are relevant to explaining globalization, other important variables such as migration are missing. While further analysis is required, this Index leaves a lot of room for extension in terms of adding more variables to enhance the explanatory power.

The A.T. Kearney/*Foreign Policy* Globalization Index is but one of its kind. In order to gain a more balanced view of the level of globalization of each country, we should attempt to compare and contrast its results with other such indexes. In order to achieve balance, we will also look at the rankings provided by the World Investment Report (UNCTAD 2007), the Global Competitiveness Report (World Economic Forum 2007) and the National Competitiveness Research Report (Institute for Industrial Policy Studies 2007). By comparing their rankings and data compilation, we should be able to gauge whether the Globalization Index is a reliable and competent source.

World Investment Report (UNCTAD 2007)

The World Investment Report analyzes inward foreign direct investment (FDI) performance and potential, and ranks countries by their attractiveness in terms of investment environment. Using inward FDI data, a matrix can be created regarding potential and performance (see Fig. 6). The front-runners are countries with high FDI potential and performance; those with above potential have low FDI potential but strong FDI performance; those below potential are countries with high FDI potential but low FDI performance; and under-performers are those with both low FDI potential and performance.

However, it should be noted here that there seems to be an error in naming the middle band as "above potential" and "below potential". It would be more appropriate to categorize those with low FDI potential but high FDI performance as "above-expected

	High FDI performance	Low FDI performance
	Front-runners	Below potential
High FDI potential	Azerbaijan, Bahamas, Bahrain, Belgium, Botswana, Brunei Darussalam, Bulgaria, Chile, China, Croatia, Cyprus, Czech Republic, Dominican Republic, Estonia, Hong Kong (China), Hungary, Iceland, Israel, Jordan, Kazakhstan, Latvia, Lithuania, Luxembourg, Malaysia, Malta, Netherlands, Panama, Poland, Portugal, Qatar, Singapore, Slovakia, Thailand, Trinidad and Tobago, Ukraine, United Arab Emirates and United Kingdom.	Algeria, Argentina, Australia, Austria, Belarus, Brazil, Canada, Denmark, Finland, France, Germany, Greece, Ireland, Islamic Republic of Iran, Italy, Japan, Kuwait, Libyan Arab Jamahiriya, Mexico, New Zealand, Norway, Oman, Republic of Korea, Russian Federation, Saudi Arabia, Slovenia, Spain, Sweden, Switzerland, Taiwan Province of China, Tunisia, Turkey, United States and Venezuela.
	Above potential	Under-performers
Low FDI potential	Albania, Angola, Armenia, Colombia, Congo, Costa Rica, Ecuador, Egypt, Ethiopia, Gabon, Gambia, Georgia, Guyana, Honduras, Jamaica, Kyrgyzstan, Lebanon, Mali, Mongolia, Morocco, Mozambique, Namibia, Nicaragua, Republic of Moldova, Romania, Sierra Leone, Sudan, Suriname, Tajikistan, Uganda, United Republic of Tanzania, Uruguay, Viet Nam and Zambia.	Bangladesh, Benin, Bolivia, Burkina Faso, Cameroon, Democratic Republic of Congo, Côte d'Ivoire, El Salvador, Ghana, Guatemala, Guinea, Haiti, India, Indonesia, Kenya, TFY Rep. of Macedonia , Madagascar, Malawi, Myanmar, Nepal, Niger, Nigeria, Pakistan, Papua New Guinea, Paraguay, Peru, Philippines, Rwanda, Senegal, South Africa, Sri Lanka, Syrian Arab Republic, Togo, Uzbekistan, Yemen and Zimbabwe.

Fig. 6. Matrix of inward FDI 2007.[7]

performers", and those with high FDI potential but low FDI performance as "below-expected performers".

It is interesting to note that nine of the countries ranked as front-runners also appear in the top 20 of the Globalization Index 2007 (A.T. Kearney and *Foreign Policy* 2007), including Jordan and Estonia; but ten of the top 20 appear in the below-potential band of countries, including Australia and the US. This means that the latter countries are regarded as poorly performing by the World Investment Report of UNCTAD, yet highly performing by the Globalization Index of A.T. Kearney and *Foreign Policy.*

Looking at Table 2, which is a performance index ranking, we can see that for inward FDI rankings only five of the top 20 countries listed in the UNCTAD study are included in the top 20 of the Globalization Index. Therefore, there is a substantial gap in ranking between these two studies. With regards to outward FDI, 12 of the top 20 countries in the UNCTAD study are included in the top 20 of the Globalization Index.

Global Competitiveness Report (World Economic Forum 2007)

The Global Competitiveness Report covers 134 major and emerging economies, and is compiled using the self-developed "executive

[7] UNCTAD (2007).

Table 2. Top 20 rankings by outward and inward FDI performance.[8]

Inward FDI performance index ranking			Outward FDI performance index ranking		
Economy	2006	2007	Economy	2006	2007
Hong Kong, China	2	1	Luxembourg	3	1
Bulgaria	3	2	Iceland	1	2
Iceland	4	3	Hong Kong, China	2	3
Malta	5	4	Switzerland	4	4
Bahamas	8	5	Panama	5	5
Jordan	7	6	Belgium	7	6
Singapore	6	7	Netherlands	6	7
Estonia	9	8	Kuwait	12	8
Georgia	15	9	Bahrain	11	9
Lebanon	13	10	Singapore	8	10
Guyana	20	11	Ireland	9	11
Bahrain	12	12	Sweden	13	12
Belgium	10	13	Spain	14	13
Gambia	11	14	France	18	14
Panama	16	15	Estonia	17	15
Mongolia	19	16	United Kingdom	21	16
Tajikistan	18	17	Israel	15	17
Cyprus	24	14	Norway	16	18
Moldova, Republic of	27	19	Austria	23	13
Egypt	31	20	Denmark	33	20

opinion survey". The survey, using a wide variety of variables, asks questions with a scale answering system on the current condition of a particular country's economic and business environment.

Table 3 shows the Global Competitiveness Report rankings for 2007. Fourteen countries out of the top 20 in the Globalization Index 2007 (A.T. Kearney and *Foreign Policy* 2007) are included, but the order in which they appear is significantly different. While the US is ranked seventh in the Globalization Index, it is ranked as first place by the Global Competitiveness Report. It should also be noted that

[8] *Ibid.*

Table 3. Global Competitiveness Report ranking 2007.[9]

Country/Economy	GCI 2007–2008 Rank	GCI 2007–2008 Score	GCI 2007–2008 rank (among 2006 countries)	GCI 2006–2007 rank
United States	1	5.67	1	1
Switzerland	2	5.62	2	4
Denmark	3	5.55	3	3
Sweden	4	5.54	4	9
Germany	5	5.51	5	7
Finland	6	5.49	6	6
Singapore	7	5.45	7	8
Japan	8	5.43	8	5
United Kingdom	9	5.41	9	2
Netherlands	10	5.40	10	11
Korea	11	5.40	11	23
Hong Kong SAR	12	5.37	12	10
Canada	13	5.34	13	12
Taiwan, China	14	5.25	15	13
Austria	15	5.23	15	18
Norway	16	5.20	16	17
Israel	17	5.20	17	14
France	18	5.18	18	15
Australia	19	5.17	19	16
Belgium	20	5.10	20	24

the smaller countries are dispersed throughout the ranking, and that Estonia and Jordan are not ranked in the Global Competitiveness Report top 20.

National Competitiveness Research Report (Institute for Industrial Policy Studies 2007)

The report by the Institute for Industrial Policy Studies (hereby referred to as "IPS") includes a total of 66 countries. As can be seen from Fig. 7, the IPS report ranking also places the US highly and is

[9] World Economic Forum (2007).

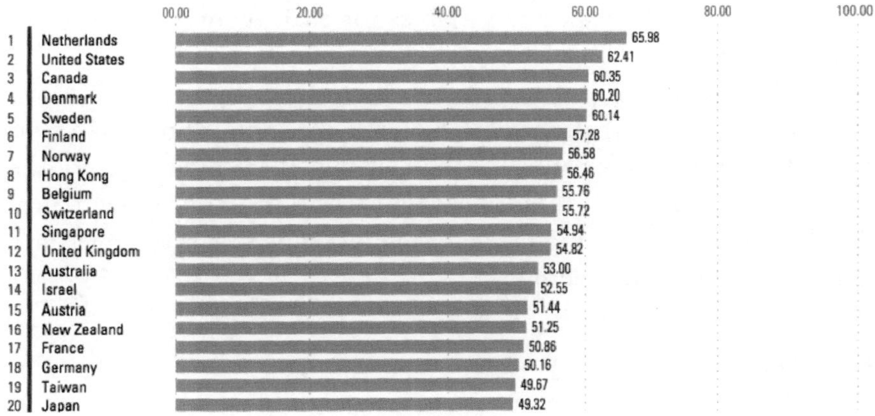

Fig. 7. IPS global ranking.[10]

the only report to rank France, Germany and Japan in the top 20. It should be noted that the smaller countries such as Hong Kong, Singapore and Switzerland are included in the rankings, but are rated no higher than eighth place. Estonia and Jordan are not included in the top 20 countries of this report.

While this analysis only skims the surface of the differences that exist among the many reports available, it does highlight the need to be aware of the risk in taking these reports at face value. In order to understand the reports' ranking, we first need to understand how the data are collected, how the data are analyzed and, most importantly, for what purpose the data are collected. For example, the IPS report specifically divides countries according to "country groups" in order to present a more accurate picture. In other words, comparing Hong Kong with the United States is rather meaningless because of the immense difference in size and structure of these two economies. Rather, Hong Kong should be compared with other economies such as Dubai and Singapore, while the United States should be compared with Japan and other larger economies. Other institutes have their own, different approaches.

[10] Institute for Industrial Policy Studies (2007).

Furthermore, the specific variables for each report differ greatly. Extensive analysis will not be made here, since it will take at least a whole chapter or two just to give a meaningful analysis on this topic. However, the point that needs to be made for serious business scholars is that they must be wary of the fact that these indices are prone to mistakes and biases. Quoting them without a thorough understanding of the underlying mechanisms and constituent variables may lead to substantial problems.

6.3 Measuring the Future

Futurology, the study of postulating probable futures, is an interesting field as it combines the aura of ancient soothsayers with the practical, objective analytical methods of modern science. Many prominent scholars (without actually calling themselves futurists) have provided us with a way of understanding the future. However, not many have actually attempted to provide a concrete guideline for measuring the future.

This concept is promoted by Paul Saffo (2007), a famous technology forecaster, who discusses concrete methods to effectively forecast the future. Unlike the popular myth of a person in robes, chanting mystical incantations, futurists and forecasters use highly scientific and objective methods to analyze future trends. Forecasting looks at how hidden currents in the present signal possible changes in direction for companies, societies or the world at large. The difference between a prediction and a forecast is that the latter is based on firm logic and thorough analysis of the available current data. Having defined what forecasting is, Saffo proceeds to present clear steps to making an effective forecast.

Define a Cone of Uncertainty

The cone of uncertainty is the process of visualizing the possibilities of various events that could stem out from a moment or event. Various elements must be included in this cone, such as the relationships among variables and the probability of realizing each event. However, the most important process is to define the "breadth" (of the cone), which is a measure of the overall uncertainty. One may visualize this process as drawing a net to capture all the elements of uncertainty in order to make an effective forecast. This is a very difficult yet important task, as it provides the basic platform for future forecasting. The key to accomplishing this feat is to assign the proper weight to each probable event. Designating the probability of each possible outcome defines the breadth of the cone and thus the scope of analysis.

However, this task is inherently difficult due to the natural tendency for people to avoid uncertainty. People prefer a "yes or no" approach to future events rather than acknowledging the fact that every event, no matter how certain or uncertain, has a certain degree of possibility to materialize. Consider the Y2K scare which engulfed the entire world right before the year 2000. One group completely dismissed the event as improbable, while others went out to stockpile supplies in order to prepare for Armageddon. Although, in this case, the former group was correct, it only became probable after the tireless work of many programmers who created systems to avoid the Y2K catastrophe. As such, the probability was certainly there, although human effort and other circumstances mitigated digital Armageddon.

Look for the S-Curve

Contrary to intuition, most changes do not come incrementally. Rather, according to Saffo (2007), change comes in an S-curve pattern: it starts off relatively quietly and then a drastic change occurs through some catalyst. Consider Moore's Law, which predicted that circuit density on silicon wafers will double every 18 months. This forecast, made in 1965, has turned out to be largely true. The explosion point (or where the curve of the "S" starts to form) was the so-called digital revolution, which completely changed the industrial landscape in many fields including IT and electronics (see Fig. 8).

As one can see from Fig. 8, the key to effective forecasting is to identify the S-curve before it explodes and also forecast where the inflection points are going to be. The current digital revolution is still

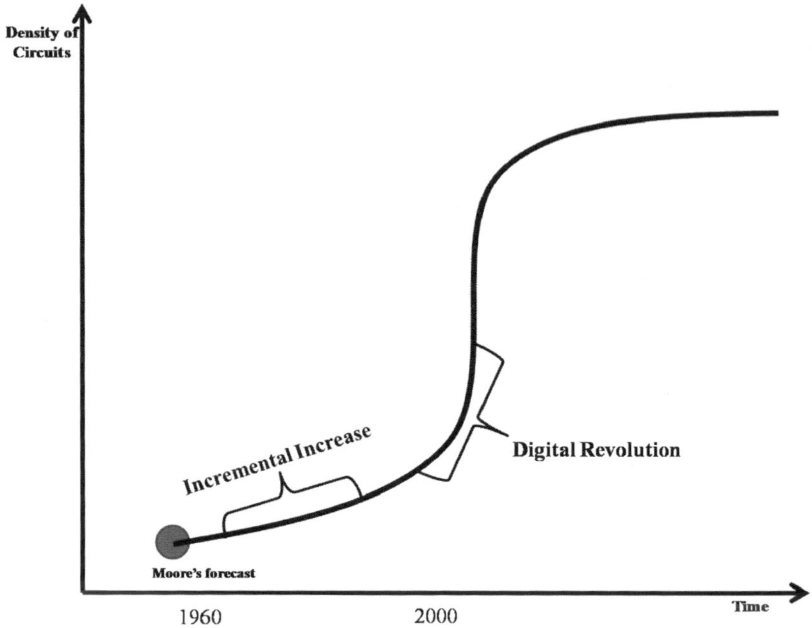

Fig. 8. Visual representation of Moore's forecast.[11]

at an inflection point, and whoever wants to get ahead of the trend must figure out when and how the trend will stabilize and plateau.

This curve also shows why so many forecasters often make mistakes when analyzing future trends. Many have the right idea, yet miscalculate the speed at which the new trend will arrive. The Internet, for example, has been around since the 1980s, and many predicted it to spread a lot faster than it has. However, it still took a decade to reach the public and spread rapidly.

Another point to note is that we should not eliminate the possibility of a trend reversal. External shocks such as government regulations might eliminate the trend altogether. For example, advances in embryonic stem cell research in the US have taken a significant dent after President Bush banned federal funding of the

[11] Drawn based on Saffo (2007).

technology during his administration. The current Obama administration is predicted to reverse this policy, but it is without a doubt that this shock may, at least temporarily, have slowed the progress in embryonic stem cell research.

Embrace the Things That Do Not Fit

As clarified in Fig. 8, an effective forecaster must predict the inflection point before it actually hits. But how does one get to achieve this marvelous feat? One suggestion by Saffo (2007) is to pay attention to things that do not quite fit the current picture. Since humans have a natural tendency to avoid uncertainties, the general public tends to reject these unfitting signals as an anomaly or an outlier and not pay attention to them. Consider the Roomba, the smart vacuuming robot designed by iRobot. Although quite a few have been sold in the market, people still do not believe that the age of robots has arrived. The Roomba seems like a small anomaly or, at best, an enhanced version of the traditional vacuum cleaner. However, when one considers the recent strides made in robotics through various competitions such as the Defense Advanced Research Project Agency's (DARPA) Grand Challenge, the Roomba is a clear indication that the robotic future is not a very distant one.

Hold Strong Opinions Weakly

It is always easier to shoot an empty wall first and then draw the target around the shots. This is precisely the kind of trap many forecasters fall into. One would forecast that a certain event would unfold and use one piece of strong evidence as proof that his or her claims will materialize in the near future. However, this can often lead to erroneous conclusions because the real world is far more complicated and intertwined to be explained by one or two major variables. Rather, Saffo (2007) suggests that it is much more important to look at various interlocking information. Many people have difficulty in following this prescription because once one formulates a strong hypothesis and finds a couple of strong pieces of evidence, all other signals are blocked out as negligible. In order to avoid this pitfall, a forecaster must constantly be critical of his or her own forecast by collecting weak evidence that could potentially derail his or her hypothesis. This way, a forecast will truly be complete and effective, as all variables will have been considered.

Look Back Twice as Far as You Look Forward

Another common mistake that people make is to look for lessons from the not-too-distant history. History may be a good indicator for what is to come in the future, but an effective forecaster must ensure they are looking back far enough, instead of focusing on recent history. So when you look back, always look back at least twice as far as you look forward, and look further back if you are still not sure of forecasting the future.

Know When Not to Make a Forecast

Many people get swept away with drastic changes and overestimate the impact that the new trend will have. The advent of the Internet brought everyone into the "dot-com bubble" and erroneous predictions about the "new economy", in which the rules of economic success would fundamentally change. However, after the dust settled, it became apparent that most of the traditional economic logic was left intact and that the Internet, although an efficient and useful tool, was simply a conduit and not a game changer. Therefore, in order to make effective forecasts, it is important not to overstate the impact of the drastic changes that happen, and to make an informed and critical forecast about what will happen once the dust settles and reality sinks in.

Analysis

As Thomas Kuhn (1962) once wrote, a scientific revolution is based on the accumulation of numerous anomalies which defy the pre-established scientific theory and widely accepted paradigm. These anomalies, according to Kuhn, are generally ignored or considered as outliers by most people. However, these anomalies have various levels of significance to the real innovators of the time and are the basis for forecasting the impending paradigm shift. In other words, revolutionary paradigm shifts inherently cannot come in a linear format. Rather, when several phenomena, which cannot be explained by the previous paradigm, accumulate and stretch out, a paradigm shifts into a new dimension. The underlying logic behind Saffo's article (2007) is largely similar to that of Kuhn's book. Of course, Saffo has refined and significantly enhanced the explanatory power of the logic through various cases and further explanations. However, the core message does not deviate significantly from that of Thomas Kuhn.

Nevertheless, Saffo's article is illuminating in that it offers the readers a very comprehensive look at how to understand the nature of revolutionary change. It is interesting to note that Saffo's analysis of the "dot-com bubble" is similar to that of Porter's 2001 article, "Strategy and the Internet". Porter, at the time, concluded that the Internet was overhyped and that when the hype subsided and the dust settled, the economic forces of the past would play a more significant role. While everyone was touting the "new economy", Porter's analysis turned out to be largely correct as the "dot-com bubble" burst and people finally realized that the new economy was not that different from the old economy.

Case Study 1: The Bank of Tokyo-Mitsubishi UFJ[12]

The Bank of Tokyo-Mitsubishi UFJ (hereby referred to as "BTMU") is one of the world's largest private financial institutions in asset size and market capitalization. It was created through a merger between The Bank of Tokyo-Mitsubishi (BTM) and the UFJ Bank in January 2006. BTMU's operations include retail banking, corporate and investment banking, and treasury operations.

---

[12] Information for this case study is abstracted from Kaplan and Norton (2006), the Palladium Group website (www.thepalladiumgroup.com) and The Bank of Tokyo-Mitsubishi UFJ website (www.bk.mufg.jp/english).

BTM's successful recovery from non-performing loan losses that plagued Japanese banking in the 1990s became a model to follow for many Japanese banks. In fact, the year prior to the merger with UFJ, BTM repaid the Japanese government more than half of the US$7 billion the bank owed for its bailout during the banking crisis. In June 2005, it was the first of the four Japanese megabanks to complete payment of its public debt. Today, BTMU focuses on building up its retail operations within Japan and expanding corporate banking into emerging economies such as China and Russia. How has it managed to attain this kind of success in such a short period of time, and how does it intend to continue doing so? In 2001, BTM adopted the Balanced Scorecard method (hereby referred to as "BSC") — a practice that has continued since BTM merged into BTMU in 2006.

Its long-term strategic goal is to become the world's premier financial group. However, this is largely dependent on the following: (a) gaining recognition as a globally active top Japanese brand, (b) sustaining growth in shareholder value, (c) enhancing operation quality and risk management, and (d) developing innovative products and services for its ever-expanding customer base. The bank once focused solely on the financial aspects of its business. However, it has since recognized the importance of these factors in order to become a top-tier financial services organization.

Initially, the bank could not see that it had a problem and was at first reluctant to implement the BSC method. The bank worked on a bottom-up basis and, when asked about its strategy, said, "Go to the workers and ask them, they will know." However, when the various business units compiled their strategy maps, it became obvious that there existed little or no clear unifying concept of strategy among the corporate ranks. Thus, the strategy maps were compiled, compared and analyzed, and ultimately a new strategy map was created whereby strategies were subdivided into those that were common to the whole group, shared by more than one unit or unique to a particular unit (see Table 4).

In this way, the organization was able to formulate both an overall strategy while maintaining each business unit's autonomy. The

Table 4. Strategy subdivisions.[13]

Type	Definition	Example
Common	Bankwide objectives, mandated throughout the organization on every scorecard	Enhance cost efficiency (financial-perspective objective)
Shared	Interdivisional objectives shared between two or more units that were expected to cooperate to achieve the result	Streamline credit approval process (internal-operational-efficiency-perspective objective)
Unique	Intradivisional objectives describing an activity expected to be fulfilled independently by that group	Maintain knowledge of your customer files (internal-risk-management-theme objective for treasury)

organization also realized that it had to move from a bottom-up to a top-down structure within each business group in order to disseminate aims, goals and strategies more easily, but retain a horizontal alignment between the business units themselves. Thus, despite its initial reluctance, the BTMU was able to achieve significant synergies among its business units by utilizing the BSC.

Case Study 2: Business Strategy on the Government[14]

The Ministry of Public Administration and Security (hereby referred to as "MOPAS") of South Korea was established in 1998 when the country's Ministry of Government Administration and the Ministry of Home Affairs were combined. MOPAS is responsible for government innovation, government organization management, e-government and decentralization. However, when the two ministries were combined, they discovered that they were lacking an

[13] Kaplan and Norton (2006).

[14] Information for this case study is abstracted from the MOPAS website (www.mopas.go.kr), the Balanced Scorecard Institute website (www.balancedscorecard.org) and the Palladium Group website (www.thepalladiumgroup.com).

organizational focus. It was an uncoordinated, disruptive and unorganized period of time. So, in order to bring the two ministries together and focus their efforts, the BSC was introduced.

At first, the organization lacked a strategic center, and thus, after completing its strategy maps, the organization realized that its top priority was to provide the best public service to its customers: the Korean people, central government agencies and the local governments. Thus, it shifted its focus to a more balanced indicator comprising customers, internal business processes, and a learning and growth viewpoint (see Fig. 9). This shift allowed the organization to more easily achieve its priority of satisfying its customers. Essentially, MOPAS determined that it needed to adopt various innovation-oriented methods used in the private sector in order to become more competitive.

Besides its already considerable financial accomplishments achieved through the merger of ministries, the newly formed MOPAS implemented a variety of changes and improvements in the areas of internal business processes, learning and growth, and customers. The following are examples of some of the multitudes of changes that were made in the organization:

- *Internal Business Processes* — A horizontal distribution of administrative functions of power between local authorities and a top-down structure were implemented.
- *Learning and Growth* — Continuous training for all government employees was implemented. In addition, regular workshops were held to which private- and public-sector guest speakers were invited.
- *Customers* — Information services and transparency regarding policy developments were improved, while the opportunity for customer feedback regarding new policies was also improved.

As a direct result, Minister Myung-Jae Park stated, "We are witnessing remarkable progress in meeting the strategic objectives of the ministry." Thus far, the outcome has resulted in MOPAS being

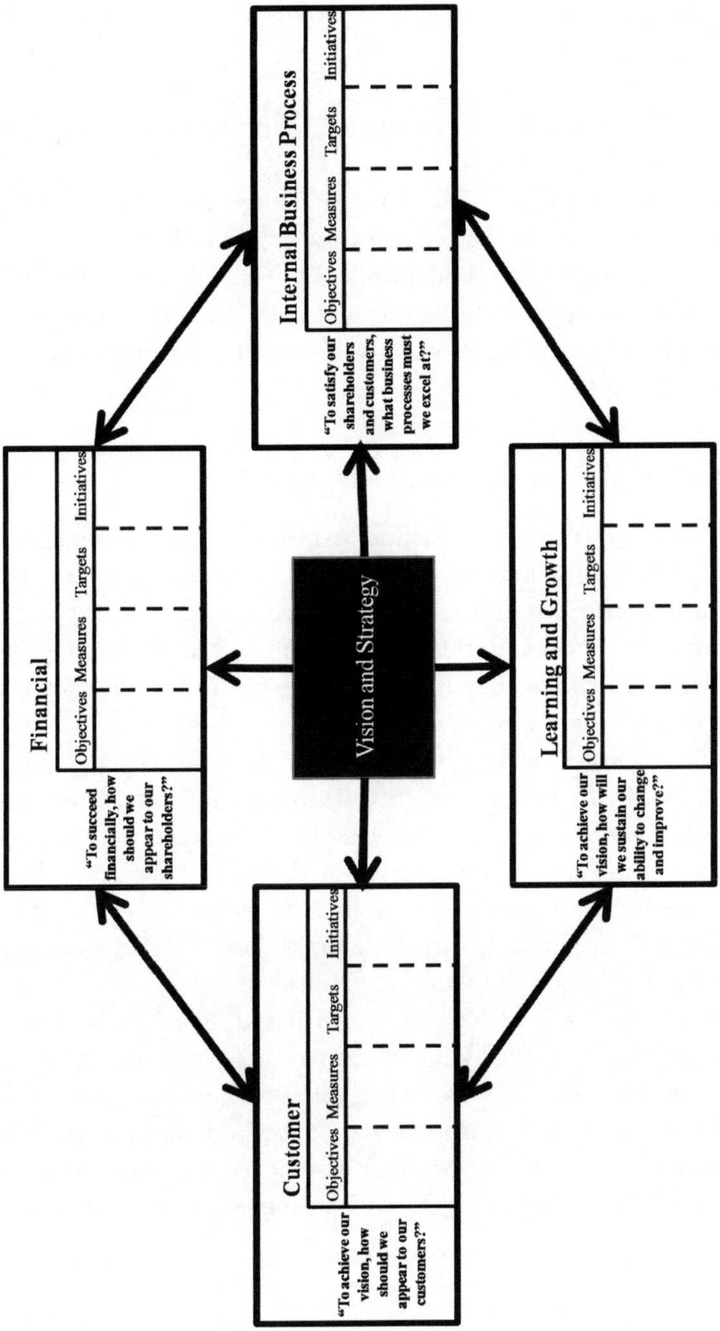

Fig. 9. The Balanced Scorecard.

inducted into the Palladium Group's 2007 Hall of Fame with respect to its effective use of the BSC. This achievement has afforded the Ministry the right to a consultation session with Dr. Robert Kaplan himself in order to solidify its future goals and its further implementation of the BSC.

Thus, with case study 1, The Bank of Tokyo-Mitsubishi UFJ, and case study 2, MOPAS, we have seen how effectively the BSC can be applied in both the private and public sectors. However, the earlier analysis in this chapter should be recalled and, with that thought, further development could be more effective using the diamond model rather than the BSC.

Case Study 3: New Zealand Robotics[15]

As mentioned previously, forecasting is not a case of looking into a crystal ball, reading the lines on one's hand or turning over tarot cards. There is a distinct difference between predicting and forecasting. Forecasting is based on sound logic and thorough analysis of available data. In order to make an effective forecast, one must define a cone of uncertainty; look for the S-curve; embrace the things that do not fit; hold strong opinions weakly; look back twice as far as you look forward; and, of course, know when not to make a forecast. Using these six basic rules, almost any firm can attempt to forecast its future.

Robotics firms are the enterprises of the future and have already made the seemingly impossible possible. So what is next for these robotics firms if we have already developed robots with manufacturing, cleaning, dancing and talking capabilities?

Wizard Robotics is a New Zealand-based R&D company and robot manufacturer, specializing in unmanned aerial vehicle (UAV) and autonomous underwater vehicle (AUV) technology (see Fig. 10). Both New Zealand and Australia are renowned in this specialized area of robotics. Wizard Robotics was one of the first companies to introduce civil robotics to New Zealand. It covers all areas of

[15] Information for this case study is abstracted from the Wizard Robotics website (www.wizardrobotics.com).

Fig. 10. Unmanned aerial vehicle (left) and autonomous underwater vehicle (right).[16]

autonomous aviation and marine vehicles, and provides autonomous solutions to agriculture, forestry, mining, gas and oil companies. While its work is undoubtedly vital as the development of robots can help human life, we must ask, what is next?

In order to best gauge what is next for this pioneering New Zealand firm, we must first define a cone of uncertainty. The cone of uncertainty (see Fig. 11) shows, on the left, the areas of current development such as Sony's development of a fully mobile dancing robot, Sanyo's development of a home guard robot, Toyota's development of service robots such as guides, and Wizard Robotic's development of UAVs and AUVs. These are all beginning to reach a convergence point, which is represented by the center of the diagram, such as full mobility, speech ability and little requirement for human control. Now the cone of uncertainty opens up into the future on the right-hand side. This represents the possible areas for further development with some suggestions that Wizard Robotics may or may not wish to consider.

Secondly, Wizard Robotics should look for the S-curve in order to understand the trends which are going to take place within the robotics industry. At the moment, the industry is seen as quite novel and quirky, but not exactly a very concrete and promising engine for future growth. However, with further technological advances, it is

[16] Images extracted from the South Atlantic Fishery Management Council website (www.safmc.net) and the Links999 — Technology and Information Directory website (www.links999.net).

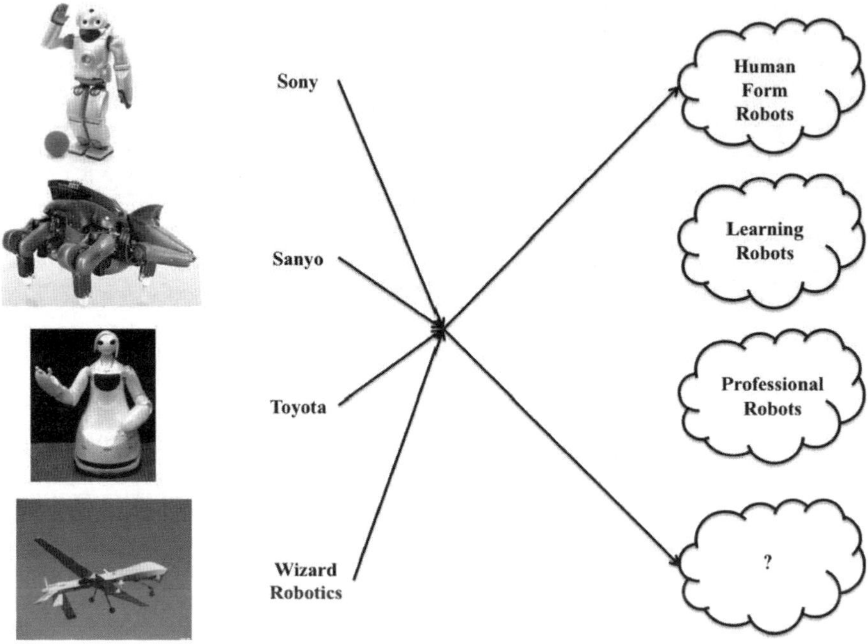

Fig. 11. The cone of uncertainty.

likely that robots will become an ever-increasingly large part of our lives and thus more necessary. When society reaches this stage (the lower curve of the "S"), there will be a massive and sudden increase in demand. Wizard Robotics would do well to stay a step ahead of this trend.

In order to stay a step ahead of this trend, we must embrace the things that do not fit. Currently, many people do not believe that the personalization of robots and the wide use of artificial intelligence (AI) robots will be an imminent reality. However, if we embrace this uncertainty, we will be more prepared when it occurs.

Saffo (2007) also advices us to hold strong opinions weakly. Wizard Robotics should not be overly confident that AI robots will be a surefire possibility. In fact, the firm should keep in mind the possibility that it could be wrong. Therefore, it should collect evidence that counters its future hypothesis to be prepared for the worst, but continue to hope for the best.

In addition, effective forecasting requires looking back twice as far as looking forward. Thus, Wizard Robotics should look back not only to the developments made in the robotics industry 5 years ago, but also to the general trends which developed over the past 10, 20 and 30 years. A detailed analysis starting from the birth of robotics technology in the 1950s would be a good starting point. From there, contrasting the rise of the Japanese robotics industry with the fall of the US robotics industry in the 1970s and 1980s would further enhance the understanding of the crucial elements for success.[17] As Saffo (2007) noted, history does not repeat itself but it does rhyme. Contrasting the success and failure of the two cases would be very useful in devising the company's future plans.

Lastly, it is true of human nature that we are fearful and yet fascinated by change, and as such the cone of uncertainty is not static. It can widen to the point where unprecedented uncertainty makes it wiser to not make a forecast. As the robotics industry overall is uncertain and open to endless possibilities, there will exist periods of time where Wizard Robotics would be better off not making a forecast and rather waiting until things settle down once more.

Discussion Questions

1. Would you add a variable to the Balanced Scorecard? If so, which variable and why?
2. The analysis suggests that the diamond model is a more comprehensive model than the Balanced Scorecard. Do you agree? Which do you prefer? Discuss.
3. How would you improve A.T. Kearney and *Foreign Policy*'s Globalization Index?

[17] See Porter (1990), pp. 224–238 for a historical analysis on the robotics industry.

4. Among the indexes presented for measuring globalization, FDI and national competitiveness, which do you think is the most representative? Discuss.
5. Do you believe forecasting is a viable source for firms to base their strategy on?
6. Saffo (2007) provides six rules for effective forecasting. Do you believe any of them are redundant or can you add a seventh rule?

CHAPTER 7

Global Perspectives on Strategy

Chapter Guideline

Now that we have looked extensively at the world of business strategy, it is time to add a more global perspective to our academic endeavor. This chapter will discuss some articles that have had a crucial impact on the field of global business strategy. These articles will lay the foundation for gaining a comprehensive overview of the meaning of global business strategy from various perspectives.

Summary of Previous Models

We started with Porter's analytical framework to establish a basic understanding of business strategy, and then proceeded to look at some alternative views by authors such as Nonaka, Prahalad and Fredrickson. Afterwards, we looked at works by authors such as Moon, Kim and Mauborgne, who attempted to further extend Porter's framework. Lastly, we looked at various ways to measure and forecast business opportunities. Based on a thorough understanding of business strategy, we now turn to the connotations of global business strategy and will look at several milestones that give us an overarching view of this dynamic field.

7.1 Global Competitive Strategy

During the 1970s, many Western companies faced a formidable challenge from Japanese companies armed with low-cost labor and efficient production methods. Many scholars analyzed this phenomenon and pointed out various determinants behind the Japanese success. Rehder (1979), for example, analyzed unique Japanese management practices which assume remarkable efficiency due to the country's cultural heritage. The prescription derived from this conjecture was that Western companies must adopt certain aspects of Japanese organizational know-how to counter the threat. Others, such as Drucker (1981), point to more comprehensive cultural reasons which he dubs Japanese habits, or rules, of competitive success, including (a) taking competitiveness seriously; (b) considering national interest ahead of personal interest; (c) making external relationships important; and (d) not seeking final victory over opponents with whom one still has to live with. As valid as these comments are, they have focused on characteristics derived from Japan's uniqueness. While this may provide a certain degree of explanation, it does not present a clear prescription.

Hamel and Prahalad (1985) take a more descriptive approach and analyze why Western companies failed to meet the Japanese challenge from a strategic management perspective. The main problem with the previous countermeasure by Western companies, according to the authors, is that it was squarely focused on expanding economies of scale. While economies of scale are important, there are many other variables that decide the winners and losers of global competition. Therefore, the Western companies' frantic outsourcing of their production activity to low-cost countries (at that time) such as Taiwan and Korea was not an effective countermeasure from a global strategic perspective. These authors proceed to illustrate the missing variables through a series of examples.

Thrust and Parry

The term "thrust and parry" refers to the new type of competition that unfolded between multinationals in the 1980s. For example, Michelin, a French tire maker, attacked the American market by utilizing the profit generated in Europe to drive out Goodyear. Goodyear, after suffering market loss in America, struck back in

Europe in order to drive Michelin out of America. In essence, the two giant tire makers attacked each other by cross-subsidizing their operations across the Atlantic. The lesson to note here is that the key to winning this competition was not in expanding economies of scale. Rather, the flow of cash into each other's home market was where the true game lay. The Japanese understood this nature of global strategy and utilized it to their best advantage in their assault on Western multinationals.

At this point, Hamel and Prahalad (1985) emphasize that it is important to distinguish between global competition and global business. Global competition, as seen from the Michelin vs. Goodyear case, requires cross-subsidization in order to gain global brand and distribution positions. Global business, on the other hand, remains in the more traditional realm, based on economies of scale and efficient (low-cost) production.

Identifying the Target

The battle between companies through cross-subsidization is aptly described in the section above. However, on a larger scale, the global war is focused on world brand dominance. Relying simply on scale economies and reducing production costs will not bring victory in this intense war for global brand positions. In order to provide a shortcut in understanding the complex global competitive landscape, Hamel and Prahalad (1985) present the framework depicted in Fig. 1.

The three major categories in this framework are building a global presence, defending a domestic position and overcoming national fragmentation. In the context of the 1980s, the Japanese competitors were in the process of building a global presence; while American companies such as RCA, GE and Zenith were desperately defending their domestic dominance; and, finally, the Europeans were overcoming national fragmentation. By following the corresponding segment in Fig. 1, one can see what kind of tactic each competitor (from left to right: Japanese, American and European) followed, in chronological order. Further explanation about these three categories will follow in the coming sections.

	Build Global Presence (Japanese)	Defend Domestic Dominance (American)	Overcome National Fragmentation (European)
1965	Access Volume		
		Response lag	Response lag
1970	Redefine cost-volume relationship		
		Match costs	
1975	Cross-subsidize to win the world		Reduce costs at national subsidiary
		Amortize world scale investment	
1980	Contiguous segment expansion		Rationalize manufacturing
		Gain retaliatory capability	
1985			Shift focus of strategic responsibility

Fig. 1. A global competitive framework.[1]

Loose Bricks in America

"Loose bricks" refer to ignored market segments that Japanese competitors exploited in order to make their initial landing in American markets. For example, in the 1960s, the Japanese gained a foothold in the small-screen portable television segment (see the first column of Fig. 1). Japanese local demand conditions overwhelmingly favored smaller-sized televisions due to typically small-sized Japanese homes, and Japanese companies were able to utilize this competitiveness from their home market to succeed in America. The American manufacturers were caught off-guard and soon paid for their mistakes, as the Japanese incrementally built their brand name through exploiting this "loose brick" and eventually dominated the entire market with more diverse product types.

[1] Hamel and Prahalad (1985).

Zenith and RCA were caught off-guard and desperately tried to defend their home markets through outsourcing and cutting production costs (see the second column of Fig. 1). However, the more desperately they tried to do this, the more ground they lost as the Japanese were cross-subsidizing their operations in the US market through the abundant revenue they were generating in the Japanese domestic market. The failure of these American multinationals to understand the true nature of global competition led to these half-hearted and ineffective countermeasures, which ultimately gave way to Japanese competitors' progress in the American television market.

Loose Bricks in Europe

The story was a little different in Europe, but the end result was the same. Japanese companies, just as they did in the American market, landed in the European market through the largely ignored, small and portable television segment. However, because of government protection, the Japanese were not allowed to export any other product types. The Japanese overcame this problem by establishing production bases in Europe, which allowed Japanese companies to sell products other than small-sized portable TVs in the European market. The Japanese companies also found partners and distributors within the European markets that helped them establish a strong brand presence in Europe. The end result was that Japanese companies were able to exploit a "loose brick" in both the American and European markets, and eventually expand their product lines along with their brand names.

Regaining Cost Competitiveness (European Companies)

In the European case, the problem is far more severe because of the fragmented nature of European television manufacturers. Philips, for example, after successfully building enough scale economies and aggressively reducing production costs, still faces the problem of a fragmented management structure. As shown in the third column of Fig. 1, the European manufacturers must overcome national fragmentation in order to compete effectively in the global competition. Hamel and Prahalad (1985) suggest three concrete steps that these firms can take in order to counter the Japanese competitive threat. Firstly, analyze the precise danger of national fragmentation. Secondly, create a system in which managers can track global competition and devise effective countermeasures. Lastly, educate executives on the need for cohesion and organizational reform.

New Concepts

From the above discussion, it is clear that three new concepts emerge. First is the concept of worldwide cost competitiveness, which refers to the minimum world market share needed in order to gain large enough scale economies to compete. Next — as explained through the discussion of cross-subsidization — is retaliation, which refers to the minimum market share the company needs in a particular country to be able to influence the behavior of key global competitors. The last is home-country vulnerability, which refers to the risk harbored by concentrating on the domestic market without branching out internationally.

New Strategic Thought

In conclusion, firms cannot survive global competition unless they look at global competition from a much wider scope. Without an effective incorporation of the three new concepts explained above, firms will lose further ground and ultimately perish.

Analysis

Hamel and Prahalad (1985) provide us with piercing insight into the reasons why many Western companies were taken over by Japanese competition in the 1970s and 1980s. Japanese manufacturers were able to rise from the ranks of low-cost manufacturers to world-class multinationals because of their aggressive and comprehensive approach in knocking the Western market's walls down. Japanese companies are now at the cutting edge of global competition in most manufacturing segments.

It is interesting to note that, after a couple of decades, the Japanese are now in the position of being chased by Korean, Chinese and other manufacturers from developing nations. The competitive landscape has changed significantly since the time Hamel and Prahalad's (1985) article was written, and these new competitors are competing in a fashion that is even more dynamic and complex than that described in their article. As this book progresses into the later chapters, we will see how global competition has changed from Hamel and Prahalad's description in their groundbreaking 1985 article. However, as is true for any intellectual development, it is important to know the roots before observing the leaves. This article provides us with a very firm foundation for understanding the nature of modern global competition, which we will further build upon.

Another more recent work by Hamel and Prahalad (1994) entitled *Competing for the Future* deals with the concept of future competition and how to prepare a firm to stay ahead. While the analysis is much more complex and in-depth, the core message is the same: managers must seek constant innovation, broaden their scope, and accept and integrate unfamiliar methods into their management practices. The answer to winning global competition is to always hold a much wider vision and scope than your competitors.

7.2 Global Cooperative Strategy

There is a famous Korean proverb: "Even lifting a piece of paper becomes easier with two people working together." The underlying moral here is that cooperation rather than competition may be more desirable in many situations. In the world of business, this age-old lesson is expressed in terms such as "strategic alliances", which facilitate the coordination of firms' relationships with partners. Such interdependencies affect firms' ability to compete and/or create economic wealth (Eng 2007).

While strategic alliances across borders are quite common nowadays, they were not as common during the 1960s and 1970s. However, starting from the 1980s, increased economic deregulation led to the increased flow of global capital and thus promoted more diversified entry modes. As Dunning (1995) noted, a series of new developments during the 1980s and 1990s has transformed the activities of economic agents. The world has moved towards embracing a new trajectory of market capitalism that is characterized by alliances, or relational and collective actions. What is implied here, as represented in the term "alliance capitalism" (contrasted with the "hierarchical capitalism" of the past), is that firms are moving towards a more eclectic mode of wealth creation which combines both competition and cooperation.

One of the first scholars to present a comprehensive view on this phenomenon of increased strategic alliances is Kenichi Ohmae (1989). While Hamel and Prahalad (1985) provide us with a framework for understanding modern global competition, Ohmae presents a comprehensive view on the importance of strategic alliances or global cooperation. The starting point of Ohmae's discussion is explaining the three main reasons why strategic alliances have become increasingly important in global business strategy.

Californization of Need

Globalization has led to an interesting phenomenon which Ohmae calls "Californization of need". This term refers to how consumer preferences and needs have increasingly converged due to the increased information dissemination and global lifestyle. In essence, everyone, more or less, wishes to live and shop in California. For example, Koreans, Japanese, Turks and French alike all have a McDonald's Big Mac for lunch and a Starbucks Chai Latte afterwards, whilst wearing Levi's blue jeans and carrying a Nokia cell phone in a Gucci bag.

But why does this phenomenon mandate strategic alliance? The answer is that firms must cater to a wider audience than they did in the past, which means that the scale of production must be substantially increased compared to the past. Therefore, firms must incur a high level of fixed cost in order to possess the capability to cater to a wider audience. The problem is that many firms do not have the capacity to do so, nor is it desirable to do so even if a firm possesses immense capital. Rather than trying to cater to this significantly wider customer base by incurring the fixed cost alone, it makes much more sense to forge alliances to distribute the necessary cost.

Dispersion of Technology

Dispersion of technology refers to the technological aspects that have fundamentally shifted global competition from a variable-cost game to a fixed-cost game. Technological complexity embedded in products has evolved drastically over the years. This means that a single product now requires so many other cutting-edge technologies that one firm cannot possibly have the expertise to become world-class in all categories. Combine this with the fact that all these firms wish to sell to as many customers as possible, and then we can see why every cutting-edge technology simply disperses so much faster than it used to.

Consider the evolution of cameras. In the past, cameras were analog devices that required very simple parts and components such as camera lens, gears, shutters, a plastic body and a good screen. A single firm could undertake the production of all the necessary components without compromising its competitive advantage. However, following the digital revolution, the camera has evolved drastically. It is now near impossible for one firm to be proficient in all aspects of production without incurring tremendous fixed costs. For example, a digital camera today needs cutting-edge software technology and solutions such as CCD (charge-coupled device) sensors, flash disk memory and CMOS (complementary metal oxide semiconductor) memories. Furthermore, even if these software technologies could somehow be produced in-house, it would make little sense to keep it in-house when these separate technologies could be sold to various other firms for increased revenue. The only solution in this case is to seek allies that are specialized in each of the necessary components and establish a long-term partnership with them.

The Importance of Fixed Costs

The need to cater to global consumers with similar needs and the wide dispersion of technology mean that firms must now play the fixed-cost game in order to succeed. Take building a brand name, for example. In the past, firms could go about it alone since the brand name had to be recognized by a much smaller group of consumers. Now, with global competition, unless the brand name is recognized by a wider audience, a firm does not even get a chance to sell its product. Achieving global exposure and recognition is a herculean task which requires immense fixed costs. Rather than incurring all the fixed costs, it is much wiser to seek alliances to amortize the risk associated with making such a significant investment.

Let's say that an American firm has developed a new pharmaceutical product that could be marketed all over the world. In the past, firms did not have a global consumer base to cater to, so it simply used its own sales force for domestic distribution. However, if the firm wants to distribute the new product in Japan, should it incur a massive fixed cost and establish its own sales force in Japan or should it seek an alliance? The answer Ohmae (1989) gives is the latter.

Dangers of Equity and the Logic of Entente

The question that we must ask at this point is, why do so many firms prefer to go it alone rather than establish alliances? The answer is equity control. When a firm invests in a joint venture or acquires another firm, the chief concern is return on investment (ROI) and the dividends that are generated with it. Based on this concern, firms want total control or at least dominance in the form of equity share in order to maximize ROI and the dividends. This is why most firms want a 51% equity share in an alliance, as this provides the majority of the control.

However, Ohmae (1989) criticizes such a control-obsessed approach for two reasons. The first is that this hierarchical mentality will inevitably lead to conflict between the partners. The parent company with a 51% equity share will frequently question the competence of the other side when ROIs do not increase rapidly and substantially. ROIs simply cannot increase very quickly, whereas most equity shareholders are very willing to pull the plug unless the investment pays chart-topping ROIs. The second problem is that even when this arrangement generates a good ROI, the parent firm will start to think of what would happen if it had 100% control instead of 51%. Looking at the cash flow and revenue generated, the parent firm forgets the massive fixed costs that it did not have to install due to the alliance and only focuses on the potential benefit of 100% ownership.

Ohmae (1989) insists that this kind of destructive relationship rarely, if ever, leads to success. Instead, two things must change. Firstly, firms must view alliances as a marriage rather than as a parent-to-subsidiary relationship. Secondly, firms must realize that the primary focus should not be on ROI, but on return on sales (ROS). Unlike an ROI orientation which demands the subsidiary to *work for* the parent, an ROS orientation means that both partners will focus on the sales of the operation for a mutual benefit and *work together*. Thus, the new logic of *entente* or strategic alliance requires a fundamental shift in perception from a parent-child relationship to a parent-parent relationship based on mutual respect and cooperation.

Analysis

Ohmae (1989) brings in a fresh new perspective to global business strategy by shifting the focus from competition to alliance. If Hamel and Prahalad (1985) presented us with a new perspective in understanding the nature of global competition, Ohmae adds another dimension by focusing on global alliances. The key message from Ohmae is that in the new global business landscape, firms cannot survive without a sound strategic alliance, which allows them to amortize the massive fixed costs needed to compete effectively. It is interesting to note that while Prahalad, Hamel and Ohmae all observed the same symptoms, they prescribe polar opposite solutions.

As useful as the above two articles are, they both need to be incorporated into a larger framework. While all of these authors are brilliant business intellectuals, it is important not to be overwhelmed

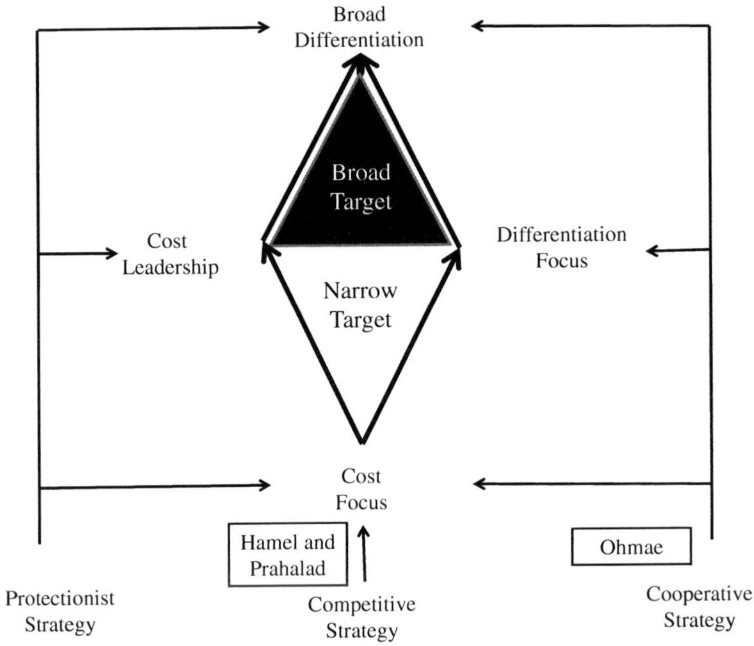

Fig. 2. Hamel and Prahalad (1985) and Ohmae (1989) in the comprehensive global strategy.

by their brilliance and keep a larger framework in mind when reading their articles. Figure 2 shows how these two articles stand in the context of a comprehensive global strategy (refer to Chap. 5 for further details about the model).

This illustration shows that, although both articles have presented the readers with luminous insights, they are still only describing part of the broader picture. Hamel and Prahalad (1985) have succeeded in shedding light on the true nature of global competition, but have missed the fact that alliances can significantly ease the process of competing in the new global arena. However, this does not mean that Ohmae's (1989) antithesis is entirely valid either. Ohmae's discussion of fixed costs and the need for alliance is highly relevant, but alliances are still only part of the global competitive game and one cannot replace the other entirely.

The nature of an appropriate alliance therefore needs to be better defined when discussing strategic alliances. Let's say that a firm has a certain core advantage within its value chain. Rather than indiscriminately looking for a strong and competent alliance partner, it is better to base the choice of partner on the weakness of the firm. In short, a thorough analysis of a firm's weakness in the value chain must precede its choice of partner.

Furthermore, the problem with Ohmae's (1989) logic is even more pronounced when seen from the larger context of the global economy. Strategic alliances are useful for firms to amortize the immense fixed costs and hence operate more smoothly in the global business context. This benefits the consumers, as it brings more consumption options at a lower cost and disperses technology more rapidly. However, when this trend is taken too far, we can imagine a scenario in which mega-alliances and acquisitions can create immense barriers to entry for newcomers. This has the potential to kill the competitive spirit so vital for a healthy business environment. Moreover, firms may not want to share their core competencies with each other (Porter 1990). In short, although Ohmae's article has added a very important new dimension to global business strategy, we should not regard it as a replacement to competition. Rather, it is simply another weapon which can be kept in the firm's arsenal of a wide array of strategic weapons that can be deployed.

7.3 Comprehensive Synthesis?

Cooperation or competition? What is the answer to global strategy? The obvious answer is both, but this impeccably logical response does not do much in terms of providing a practical prescription. Luckily, we have the genius of Sumantra Ghoshal (1987) to explore a synthesizing framework of the two extremes.

Ghoshal (1987) explains the need to provide managers with an organizing framework that synthesizes the various perspectives. As the concept of global strategy gained increasing prominence during the 1980s, related literature flourished, yet no one synthesized everything into a single framework (see Table 1).

Table 1. Global strategy: an organizing framework.[2]

	Sources of competitive advantage		
Strategic objectives	National differences	Scale economies	Scope economies
Achieving efficiency in current operations	Benefiting from differences in factor costs — wages and cost of capital	Expanding and exploiting potential scale economies in each activity	Sharing of investments and costs across products, markets and businesses
Managing risks	Managing different kinds of risks arising from market or policy-induced changes in comparative advantages of different countries	Balancing scale with strategic and operational flexibility	Portfolio diversification of risks and creation of options and side-bets
Innovation, learning and adaptation	Learning from societal differences in organizational and managerial processes and systems	Benefiting from experience — cost reduction and innovation	Shared learning across organizational components in different products, markets or businesses

The easiest way to follow this synthesis is to first look at the far left column in Table 1. This column outlines the strategic objectives that all firms must achieve in order to have a successful global strategy. Simply put, a global firm looks to achieve efficiency, manage risk and learn to innovate through its global strategy. However, an important point to remember is that each of these goals has tradeoffs and conflicting ends in the actual implementation process.

[2] Ghoshal (1987).

Next is to look at the sources of how to achieve these different objectives. National differences, scale economies and scope economies are the sources through which firms can find the means to achieve these important strategic objectives. Combining these two broad categories in a three-by-three matrix, Ghoshal (1987) presents a comprehensive framework that synthesizes all pre-existing works. Below is a detailed analysis of each objective.

Strategic Objectives

- *Achieving Efficiency* — Through global strategy, this is to visualize the cost advantages of global integration vis-à-vis the benefits of responding to national differences. In other words, different industries and companies gain or lose competitive advantages depending on the level of integration (i.e., standardization of the firm's value chain regardless of the market) or differentiation (i.e., tailoring of the firm's value chain depending on the market). For example, the consumer electronics industry would benefit from high integration and low differentiation; while the packaged foods industry, which depends highly on local consumer tastes, would benefit more from differentiation rather than integration. This classification can even map the difference in companies within the same industry. For example, in the automobile industry, Toyota is closer to integration, while Ford or Fiat is closer to differentiation. The level of analysis can go down to individual tasks executed by the firm (see Fig. 3).

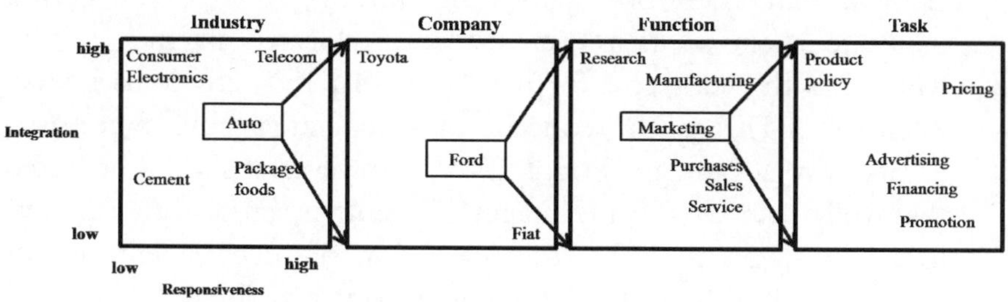

Fig. 3. The integration-responsiveness framework.[3]

[3] *Ibid.*

- *Managing Risks* — There are four types of risks that firms face in conducting their operations. First are macroeconomic risks, which are basically exogenous variables beyond the firm's control. Second are policy risks, which are government policies that affect the conduct of firms. Third are competitive risks, which are strategic responses by competitors that may undermine the firm's position. Last are resource risks, which occur under a situation in which the firm may not have the necessary resources to implement its global strategy. The key to a successful global strategy is to analyze all of these risks when making strategic choices.
- *Innovation, Learning and Adaptation* — These are the three methods with which a firm may enhance its capabilities through operating in multiple environments. Through exposure to diversity, the firm can internalize what it has learned and enhance its competitive advantage. This is quite different from the previous theories (e.g., Dunning 1995) which believe that a firm goes abroad in order to exploit the market imperfections based on its pre-established advantages in a new market, but is similar to an imbalance theory (Moon and Roehl 2001; Moon 2007) which explains that firms often go abroad to search for advantages.

Sources of Competitive Advantage

- *National Differences* — Different nations have different factor endowments, which lead to inter-country differences in factor costs. A firm can therefore gain cost advantages by configuring its value chain so that each activity is located in the country which has the least cost for the factor that the activity uses most intensively. This is the concept of comparative advantage-based competitive advantage (Kogut 1985). However, it should be noted that while comparative advantages of countries can provide competitive advantages to firms, the realization of such benefits is not automatic, but depends on complex organizational factors and processes. In essence, the difference between the traditional trade theory and Ghoshal's (1987) view is in the number of variables. The traditional view focuses on factors such as labor and capital; while

Ghoshal includes more variables such as quality, quantity and configuration of the firm's material, human and institutional resources.

- *Scale Economies* — Just like the first source, scale economies are also well studied and rich literature is available on this subject. This goes back to the basic economic principle that increased economies of scale lead to reduced production costs and ultimately increased competitiveness. However, again, this is still a limited and static viewpoint of scale economies. A dynamic view of scale economies can be adopted by adding the concept of a "learning effect". Firms with larger scales can accumulate more experience, thus leading to even more cost cuts. However, we must also note that scale economies may harbor negative effects. A larger scale also means an increase in the potential for a response lag. This may prove especially detrimental in a global business environment which is becoming increasingly complex and unpredictable. Therefore, it is very important to balance scale and flexibility.
- *Scope Economies* — The last and least well-understood source is scope economies. While economies of scale refer to the decrease of average total cost by expanding the production of a single product, economies of scope refer to a similar benefit reaped from expanding the production of multiple products. For example, there are scope economies if the cost of the joint production of two or more products is less than the cost of producing them separately. Scope economies focus on the synergistic effects created when a firm diversifies its products and markets. A more detailed explanation can be seen in Table 2.

The logic of scope economies arises from a diversified firm's capability to share costs across the value chain activities. This leads to a unique combination of activities that makes it difficult for competitors to imitate. Such sharing can take place across segments, products or markets (Porter 1985). For example, in the soft drinks industry, bottling and distribution are local in scope, while the designing of efficient bottling plants is integrated. Coca-Cola has thus externalized those functions which are purely local in scope. Similarly, IBM has

Table 2. Scope economies in product and market diversification.[4]

	Sources of scope economies	
	Product diversification	Market diversification
Shared assets	Factory automation with flexibility to produce multiple products (Ford)	Global brand name (Coca-Cola)
Shared external relations	Using common distribution channel for multiple products (Matsushita)	Servicing multinational customers worldwide (Citibank)
Shared learning	Sharing R&D in computer and communications businesses (NEC)	Pooling knowledge developed in different markets (Procter & Gamble)

externalized the PC business by setting up an almost stand-alone organization. As another example, Procter & Gamble may incur costs by developing a separate product for a specific market. However, this effort leads to knowledge creation, which creates a synergistic effect for other products as well.

Prescriptions in Perspective

As emphasized before, the usefulness of this model lies in its synthesis. This helps managers formulate a comprehensive global strategy that takes into consideration all of the important variables. Another very important contribution of this model is that it highlights the existence of tradeoffs between different strategies. When individual strategy prescriptions are analyzed separately, they all seem valid and useful. However, in reality, by choosing one strategy, one must forgo the opportunity to pursue another path. Consider, for example, the decision to choose from different sources of competitive advantages. If a firm wishes to exploit factor costs in some different locations, it must sacrifice some opportunities to enhance scale efficiency and thus forgo some synergistic effects. In sum, this framework shows that

[4] *Ibid.*

managers must make the appropriate strategic choices and be aware of the different tradeoffs, according to the objective and the surrounding context that they face.

Analysis

Ghoshal (1987) brilliantly summarizes and synthesizes the existing discussions into one coherent framework. As we have seen in Hamel and Prahalad (1985) and Ohmae (1989), a unilateral focus on one aspect of global strategy leaves several blind spots that are not accounted for. If a firm decides to follow Hamel and Prahalad's prescription of aggressively pursuing cross-subsidization and attacking the competitor's home market, it may miss the opportunity to forge strategic alliances, which can significantly reduce the firm's operating cost. However, if a firm decides to unilaterally follow Ohmae's prescription, then the firm may face the problem of lacking a competitive edge by compromising its own advantage in an obsession to forge strategic alliances. Instead, Ghoshal aptly points out the existence of various strategic options and, more importantly, the tradeoffs that inevitably accompany each choice that a manager makes.

Case Study 1: Arçelik Is No Turkey[5]

Arçelik is a household appliances manufacturer based in Turkey. The company is controlled by Koç Holding, one of Turkey's largest and most prestigious groups, and is the market leader in Turkey's appliance sector with its Arçelik and Beko brands. It is also the third-largest household appliances company in Europe. The company engages in the production and marketing of durable goods, components, consumer electronics and after-sale services. Its products include white goods, electronic products, small home appliances and kitchen accessories.

Arçelik now operates in more than 100 countries, including China and the United States, through its 13 international subsidiaries

[5] Information for this case study is abstracted from the Arçelik official website (www.arcelik.com.tr/english).

and over 4,500 branches in Turkey. It also operates 10 production plants in Turkey, Romania and Russia, producing a wide range of products including refrigerators, washing machines, dishwashers, cooking appliances and components. It offers products under its own nine brands, including Arçelik, Beko, Altus, Blomberg, Arctic, Leisure, Arstil, Elektra Bregenz and Flavel. However, the company's own branding was not always the case.

Before 2000, Arçelik was mainly a domestic original equipment manufacturer (OEM) firm with limited international presence. Turkey was hardly known as a country with a competitive edge in the white goods sector, so it is difficult to imagine how such a firm has gone from strength to strength when the odds were seemingly stacked against it. This case study will highlight all of the points mentioned by Hamel and Prahalad (1985), Ohmae (1989) and Ghoshal (1987), thus providing us with an excellent example of a firm that has gained global recognition through truly global strategic endeavors.

Hamel and Prahalad (1985) on Arçelik

Koç Holding is by far the largest and most important transnational corporation of Turkish origin, and is viewed as a dominant force in the Turkish economy and a rising giant in various sectors. What is more remarkable is the pace and aggressiveness at which Koç Holding has globalized its business in recent years, in particular its subsidiary, Arçelik. From the perspective of Hamel and Prahalad (1985), we will first look at how Arçelik has (a) built a global presence, (b) defended its domestic position, and (c) attacked the "loose bricks" in Europe.

Arçelik was founded in 1955 and originally focused on producing metal furniture, which was in high demand in Turkey at that time. However, as Turkey began to experience an industrial boom, the firm saw "bricks" come loose in the consumer appliance market and it quickly moved its operations into home appliances. By 1960, Arçelik had become a major Turkish manufacturer of washing machines and refrigerators. Had it not seized the opportunity of the "loose bricks" in the consumer appliance market at that time, Arçelik would probably still be producing just metal furniture in Turkey.

Arçelik licensed most of its technology from GE and Bosch-Siemens, and was permitted to utilize the technology only for the domestic market. However, as of the early 2000s, the majority of these licensing agreements expired and Arçelik began to devise ambitious plans to burst into the global market. Arçelik has taken a highly diversified path to building a global presence, through acquisitions of foreign firms subsidized by its domestic profits and by establishing international distribution channels, consistent with the global competition model of Hamel and Prahalad (1985) (see Table 3).

Arçelik made the majority of its acquisitions — including several prestigious Western multinationals such as Grundig and Blomberg — in order to acquire advanced technology, build distribution channels overseas and, more importantly, improve the disadvantageous brand image associated with being from a developing country. As a direct

Table 3. Arçelik's acquisitions, strategic alliances and joint ventures.[6]

Firm	Year	Country	Entry mode*	Purpose
LG	2000	Korea	JV	Technology
Beko	2001	Austria	A	Branding/Distribution
Blomberg	2002	Germany	A	Technology/Branding/ Distribution
Bregenz	2002	Germany	A	Branding/Distribution
Leisure	2002	UK	A	Distribution
Flavel	2002	UK & Ireland	A	Distribution
Arctic	2002	Romania	A	Branding/Distribution
Alba	2004	UK	JV	Technology/Production
Grundig	2004	Germany	A	Technology/Distribution
Alba	2007	UK	A	Branding/Distribution
Changzhou Casa-Shinco	2007	China	A	Distribution/Production
Fisher & Paykel	2007	NZ	SA	Distribution

* Entry modes: acquisition (A), strategic alliance (SA), joint venture (JV).

[6] Information sourced from www.arcelik.com.tr/english/.

result of its acquisitions, it has gone from strength to strength in Europe and is now beginning to enter the Asian market.

Many firms that expand this quickly and aggressively may be in danger of national fragmentation, so it is essential that the national subsidiaries continue to interact with the organization. Arçelik is obviously aware of this danger, and has implemented rigorous employee training and education programs across the board in order to make all employees aware of the connectivity that exists between the brands. The brands are not to be treated as separate entities, but as complementary arms to a central entity.

Ohmae (1989) on Arçelik

Ohmae (1989) emphasized the concept of the "Californization of need", which describes the general convergence of global consumer tastes. This integration has led to a wider base of global consumers, which increases the importance of scales of production. Therefore, Ohmae recommends strategic alliances as one course of action to relieve the burden of achieving increased scales of production. He also points out that, as products have become more technologically advanced, it has become increasingly difficult (if not impossible) for one firm to provide all of the essential components that are required to manufacture a product. There may also be hefty fixed costs associated with branding. While branding is essential for the success of any firm, firms often wish to avoid the associated costs. Arçelik has successfully managed to avoid all of the above pitfalls mentioned by Ohmae.

By pursuing a highly aggressive path of strategic alliances and acquisitions, Arçelik has been able to spread its costs and simultaneously increase its scale of production. This aggressive internationalization acted as an enabling switch for this previously domestic OEM company to advance into an original brand manufacturer (OBM) with solid technology and brand reputation.

Furthermore, strategic alliances have enabled Arçelik to distribute the high costs of technology development and acquisition. Had Arçelik attempted to internalize all technology development and manufacturing activities, the costs and time required would have made it an insurmountable task. Instead, the firm decided to establish partnerships with the Korean multinational LG for developing air conditioners and with the British firm Alba for distribution and finance operations. Arçelik's moves have been quite successful, as the company has been able to grow into the third-largest supplier of white goods in the European market without having to incur significant fixed costs.

Lastly, Arçelik has been successful in avoiding fixed costs associated with branding. As a Turkish firm, it has advantages in some Eastern European markets such as Romania, Uzbekistan and Azerbaijan, and does not have to work as hard at branding as it does in other markets. In markets such as Germany, the UK and the US, a Turkish firm may be looked down upon simply because of its country of origin (COO). As a Turkish firm, Arçelik faced significant COO disadvantages which could raise issues regarding the level of the quality of the good. Rather than attempting to build up its Turkish brand, Arçelik was able to circumvent this negative COO problem by purchasing recognizable, trustworthy, highly valued brands from more developed countries. Grundig is an excellent example of this strategy, as it has a 95% recognition rate in Germany, yet few even know that this former German white goods giant is now a subsidiary of a Turkish firm. For Arçelik, acquisitions, joint ventures and strategic alliances are a quiet affair, thus allowing it to leverage the branding that is already in place.

Ghoshal (1987) on Arçelik

Ghoshal (1987) integrated a number of theories and thoughts on global business strategy into one cohesive framework. There are three aspects to his framework: (a) achieving efficiency; (b) managing risks; and (c) fostering innovation and learning.

Again, Arçelik has managed to be successful on all of these fronts. In order to achieve efficiency and, thereby, competitive advantage, a firm must know when to standardize and when to tailor the firm's value chain. While there are clear-cut cost advantages to full integration and standardization, this is not always possible to realize. In particular, the global white goods sector is characterized by a myriad of consumer preferences due to distinct national preferences for cooking style, residential structure (size of home, etc.) and climate. Arçelik has been able to encompass both extremes through diversified branding. In less developed markets, where standardization is possible, Arçelik has chosen to purchase locally popular, economical and technologically simple brands (the local pyramid in Fig. 4). However, in more advanced markets, a certain level of differentiation is required as consumers are more sophisticated and require a higher-quality good. Thus, Arçelik has endeavored to acquire globally popular, more expensive and technologically advanced brands (the global pyramid in Fig. 4).

The company has also been successful in managing risks despite Turkey's chronic economic volatility. With a strong background and experience in risk management in Turkey, Arçelik was able to easily understand and penetrate risky foreign markets such as Uzbekistan and Azerbaijan. Armed with this knowledge, it was fairly easy to penetrate markets seen as less traditionally risky, such as Germany and the UK. However, there are other types of risks (i.e., competitive and resource risks) in the more advanced markets. Had Arçelik entered those markets without being aware of the competitive risk, it would have had a difficult time competing against more established multinationals. However, by entering those markets under the guise of

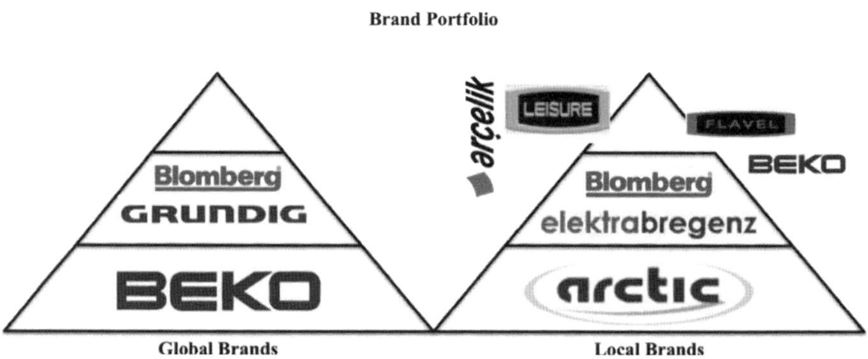

Fig. 4. Arçelik's brand portfolio.

"one of us", Arçelik was able to overcome both competitive and resource risks that exist in more advanced nations.

Lastly, by entering different markets in the world, including Europe and the Asia Pacific, Arçelik has learned how to innovate continuously. Innovation is key to the success of any global company. Arçelik has, in a very short period of time, learned from its experiences, thrived through internationalization and effectively competed head-to-head with firms that have been around for much longer, while enjoying a monopolistic position in its home country.

Discussion Questions

1. The "thrust and parry" concept came out in the 1980s. Do you think that this can still be applied to today's world or has the nature of competition evolved significantly? What are some examples?

2. Can the concept of "loose bricks" be likened to the Blue Ocean idea? Discuss the similarities and differences.

3. The "Californization of need" seems similar to the notion of standardization. How is it different from the standardization argument, and do you agree with it?

4. If firms were to arrange strategic alliances on a 50/50 basis, would they continue to function and achieve their objectives more easily or with more difficulty?

5. Can firms really ever effectively manage risk? If so, how can they effectively manage the four risks mentioned by Ghoshal (1987)?

6. Which of the above three approaches — Hamel and Prahalad (1985), Ohmae (1989) and Ghoshal (1987) — do you find most effective in explaining the case of Arçelik? Why?

CHAPTER 8

Developing and Extending Analytical Models

Chapter Guideline

The concept of global business strategy is quite difficult to grasp because of its complex and multi-dimensional nature. Even after the plethora of business literature written on global business strategy, there is still little consensus and much room for further development. In this chapter, we will look at the works of scholars who have attempted to provide overarching analytical frameworks in order to help scholars, managers and students gain a better understanding of global business strategy.

Summary of Previous Models

After studying various business models, we have elevated our analysis to the global level by looking at prominent scholars who have attempted to analyze global business strategy from various perspectives. As illuminating as their works have been, we could also see that there are still many loopholes and missing variables that have not been accounted for. Even Ghoshal's (1987) synthesis is still not clear enough and does not provide a systematic framework to analyze the degree of globalization.

8.1 Configuration-Coordination Model

We now come back to Porter once again in order to gain an overarching perspective on global competition and strategy. The starting point of Porter's analysis is the fact that previous literature has only given a partial view of how global business strategy should be conceived (Porter 1986). The purpose is to explore international competition under the context of competitive strategy. The key question that needs to be answered is how a firm's activity in one country affects or is affected by what is going on in other countries.

Patterns of International Competition

Two important concepts, "multidomestic" and "global", are introduced for modeling global strategy. These terms set the two opposing continuums that describe the pattern of international competition, depending on the industry. A multidomestic industry, as the name suggests, is an industry in which competition in one country is independent from competition in other countries. The competitive advantage of a firm, therefore, is specific to the country because an advantage in one nation largely does not transfer into another nation. An appropriate example would be the packaged foods industry, which is characterized by a myriad of consumer tastes and preferences. Global industries, on the other hand, are the polar opposite of multidomestic industries, since competitive advantage in one nation has a significant impact on the other nation. The commercial aircraft industry is a good example, where economies of scale and product standardization are the key ingredients for success. The distinction between these two types of industries has profound implications. Understanding the determinants of industry structure, therefore, is the most important idea.

Causes of Globalization

Then what makes an industry global? An industry becomes global when there is competitive advantage to be derived from integrating activities across many different countries. In order to specify what integrating activities means, the value chain is introduced (see Fig. 1).

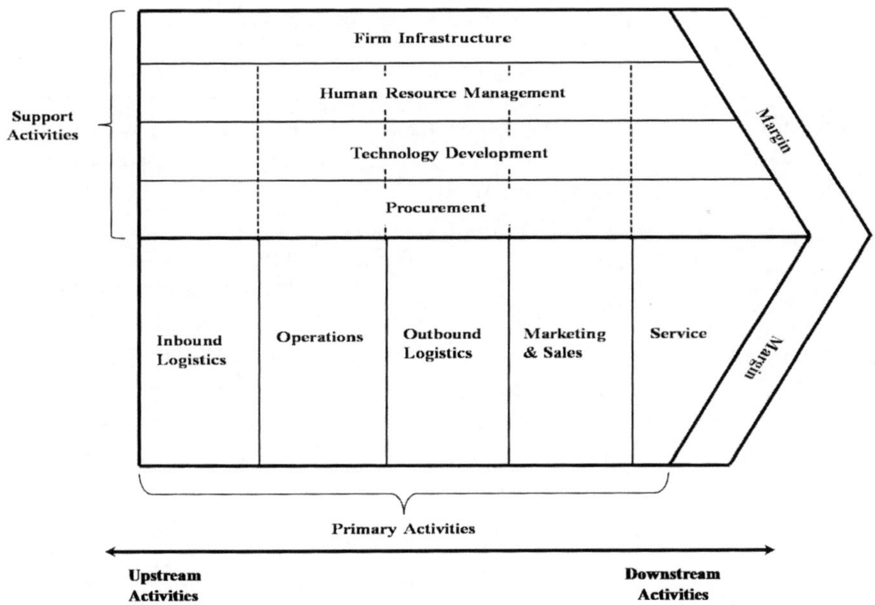

Fig. 1. The value chain.[1]

The important point here is the distinction between upstream and downstream activities. Competitive advantage in downstream activities is largely derived from performing country-specific activities, while advantages in upstream and support activities are generally those that can be derived from one or a few source countries. The heart of global strategy is to perform these activities in a global context to maximize the firm's competitive advantage. But how does a firm achieve this feat? What kinds of tools are available? Here, an important basis for a framework emerges which Porter (1986) calls *configuration* and *coordination*. Configuration refers to the location in the world where each activity in the value chain is performed, while coordination refers to how similar activities performed in different countries are coordinated with each other. Table 1 illustrates several examples that help the reader grasp this configuration-coordination (C-C) concept.

[1] Porter (1986), p. 24.

Table 1. Configuration and coordination issues by category of activity.[2]

Value activity	Configuration issue	Coordination issue
Operations	Location of production facilities for components and end products	Allocation of production tasks among dispersed facilities Networking of international plants Transfer of process technology and production know-how among plants
Marketing and Sales	Product line selection Country selection Location of preparation of advertising materials	Commonality of brand name worldwide Coordination of sales to multinational accounts Similarity of channels and product positioning worldwide Coordination of pricing in different countries
Service	Location of the service organization	Similarity of service standards and procedures worldwide
Technology Development	Number and location of R&D centers	Allocation of research tasks among dispersed R&D centers Interchange among R&D centers Development of products responsive to market needs in many countries Sequences of product introductions around the world
Procurement	Location of the purchasing function	Location and management of suppliers in different countries Transfer of knowledge about input markets Coordination of purchases of common items

[2] *Ibid.*, p. 26.

As we can see from Table 1, various parts of the global value chain can be configured and coordinated in order to enhance the competitive advantage of a firm. With this understanding, Porter (1986) defines global strategy as one in which a firm acquires competitive advantage through configuration and/or coordination among dispersed activities. This concept can be summarized into a simple yet powerful analytical framework, as illustrated in Fig. 2.

As depicted on the right-hand side of Fig. 2, Toyota has concentrated all of its production facilities in one location while coordinating other activities that must be performed near the consumers. GM, on the other hand, chose the polar opposite route and decided to take a country-centered strategy with separate brand names and production facilities for each market the company wishes to operate in. As the arrows indicate, all automobile firms are moving towards what Porter (1986) sees as the final stage (the upper right-hand corner) in order to maximize the benefits derived from internationally coordinating and geographically concentrating different activities in the value chain.

Then, the question arises, when should firms concentrate their activities globally and/or coordinate dispersed activities? A firm should concentrate its activities when there are economies of scale, a proprietary learning curve, a comparative advantage of one or a few

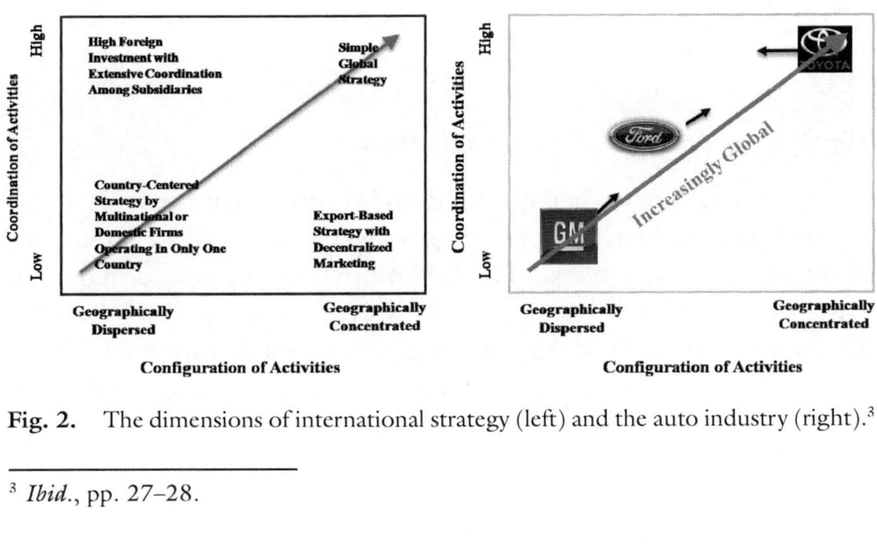

Fig. 2. The dimensions of international strategy (left) and the auto industry (right).[3]

[3] *Ibid.*, pp. 27–28.

locations for performing the activity, and/or advantages of co-locating linked activities such as R&D and production. In other words, when locating linked or similar activities in one spot generates synergies, the advantages of concentration outweigh those of dispersion. On the other hand, dispersion of activities is more favorable when customer needs are different according to the location and/or communications and transportation conditions. Coordinating these geographically dispersed activities may lead to numerous advantages such as an increased knowledge base, local responsiveness and the ability to exploit favorable local conditions (such as the exchange rate and tax incentives).

Configuration/Coordination and the Pattern of International Competition

The activities from which a firm can derive competitive advantage depend on the industry and countries. For example, as mentioned before, the commercial aircraft industry is characterized by immense competitive advantage derived from concentrating R&D and production activities. Also, in the film industry, a firm is more likely to derive competitive advantage from coordinating its various activities in countries with similar languages and cultures. The important message here is that the specifics of how to coordinate/configure the various activities within a firm's value chain depend on the structure of the industry in which the firm operates.

The Process of Industry Globalization

Industries move from being multidomestic to global for several reasons. Exogenous variables such as general technological advancement, buyer needs, government policy or country infrastructure may have major influences. For example, when buyer needs become homogenized for electronic products, having global outreach and economies of scale gives crucial advantages to firms that possess such capabilities. When such influences become strong enough, an industry becomes global because of the immense benefits that can be reaped from going global. IBM for computers, Boeing for aircrafts and Honda for motorcycles are good examples.

Global Platform

The term "global platform" is another way of describing how individual countries should no longer be regarded as stand-alone entities. Rather, individual countries should be regarded as components of the whole picture. This distinction is important because it is a significant deviation from the traditional concept of comparative advantage, which views a nation's factor endowment as the ultimate source of advantage. While the traditional view of factor endowment is still valid, it needs to be defined broadly and incorporated into the term "global platform". This platform includes not only these traditional elements, but also demand sophistication as well as the appropriate technical personnel, infrastructure and local operating environment (such as competition and rivalry). The importance of traditional determinants such as low-cost labor and abundant resources is decreasing; while more complex drivers, such as those listed in the previous sentence, are becoming far more significant. Therefore, in deciding whether to operate in a country or not, the traditional perception of a nation's factor endowment is insufficient and must incorporate a more rigorous and comprehensive view which sees individual countries as part of a larger entity.

Strategic Implications of Globalization

In light of the above analysis, it is evident that when an industry goes global, firms must rethink the way they formulate strategy. Traditionally, the focus has been on how to adapt to the conditions of certain locations and optimize a firm's operations accordingly. However, from the above analysis, we can see that the issue has an additional dimension, namely how to link and coordinate activities performed in individual countries in order to derive the maximum

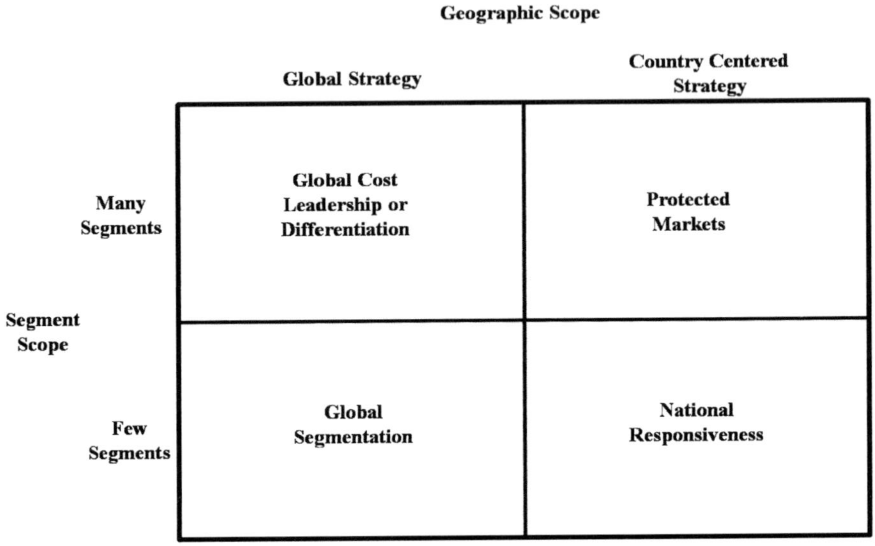

Fig. 3. Strategic alternatives in a global industry.[4]

advantage from a global industry. Figure 3 depicts the strategic choices that firms can make in a global industry.

The following gives a more specific explanation for each category:

- *Global Cost Leadership or Differentiation* — A firm's strategic choices are defined either by cost leadership or differentiation. These choices are realized through coordination and/or configuration of its activities by selling a wide array of products to consumers in many countries.
- *Global Segmentation* — This is a strategy in which a firm caters to a specific segment in many countries. A good example is the luxury car market (such as Mercedes), which is a homogenized segment in various countries.
- *Protected Markets* — Firms can shelter themselves from global competition by finding markets that are protected by the national

[4] *Ibid.*, p. 46.

government. Because the market is protected, a firm can produce a wide array of goods regardless of competition.

- *National Responsiveness* — Firms can choose to cater to a particular nation's needs, even though the industry itself is global. Unusual customer needs, for instance, can create a feasible condition for this kind of approach.

The four strategic choices elaborated above reflect obvious trade-offs. However, each is often not mutually exclusive from one another, as many firms pursue one or more strategies simultaneously. This point will be further elaborated as the chapter progresses.

Analysis

As always, Porter (1986) presents us with a sweeping picture of a highly complex phenomenon. In essence, Porter's analysis is based on his fundamental grasp of competition: advantages are derived from low cost or differentiation, and industry is the most important unit of analysis. Because each industry has a different structural composition, some industries become global while others remain multidomestic. From this theoretical foundation, Porter asserts that a firm should employ a global strategy when the benefits derived from coordinating and configuring its value chain activities over a wide array of countries are substantial. The costs and benefits of a global strategy mostly depend on the industry structure and the level of advantage that can be derived from a different mix of global coordination and configuration. Porter goes on to analyze the various implications this foundation has for firm activities in the global business strategic context.

Porter's contribution is significant in two ways. First, Porter fuses his value chain framework with globalization in order to provide a functional-level analysis of global strategy. This is significant because, realistically, a firm has differing degrees of globalization in each of its value chain activities. Second, Porter's analysis provides us with important insights as to why an industry globalizes and how a firm's function can be dispersed in various countries to maximize the benefits of globalization. However, even this seemingly flawless analysis contains some problems, as will be seen in the following sections.

8.2 Three-Dimensional Global Model

Moon (1994) critically reviews Porter's (1986) framework and presents an enhanced framework. The starting point of Moon's criticism is the issue of configuration in Porter's framework (see Fig. 2). According to Porter's model, a purely global strategy requires geographical concentration and a high level of coordination. In terms of configuration, a more geographically concentrated configuration implies a more global strategy and geographic dispersion leads to a weak global strategy.

This logic is highly problematic if we apply this to the service industry. Consider two airline companies, American Airlines and Eastern Airways. American Airlines is an international company with 635 fleets and 161 destinations. It coordinates its various activities in geographically diverse areas. Eastern Airways, on the other hand, is a regional airline based in the UK with 29 fleets and 18 destinations. It has a high level of coordination along very limited geographic locations. In terms of Porter's (1986) framework, these two firms can be depicted as in Fig. 4.

Clearly, there is something wrong with Fig. 4, as American Airlines is depicted as less global compared to Eastern Airways. Figure 4 would look more appropriate if "Geographically Concentrated" and "Geographically Dispersed" were switched. This begs the question, why did Porter make such a mistake? The first reason is Porter's overemphasis on economies of scale. As he lucidly argued, global industries have increased scale benefits, mostly due to homogenization of demand, which means that concentrating production activity in one location is more advantageous. However, with technological innovation and flexible manufacturing processes, firms can benefit more from coordinating their dispersed production activities. Secondly, Porter's framework is too specific to the Japanese automakers' experience in the 1970s. After their success with the so-called "purely

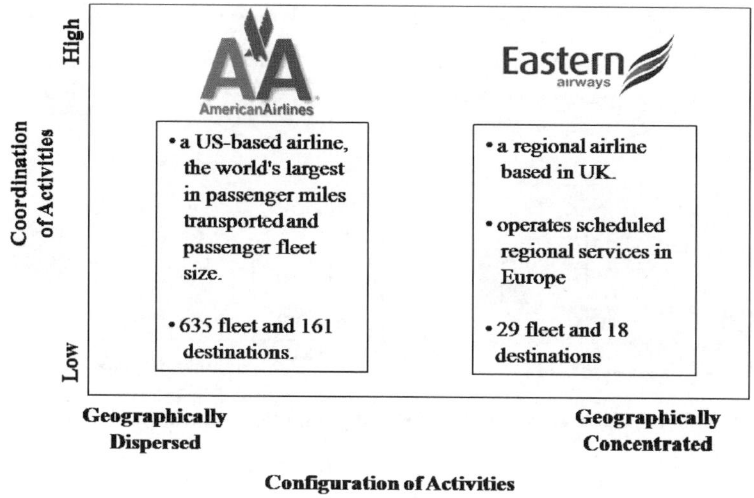

Fig. 4. American Airlines and Eastern Airways according to Porter's (1986) framework.

global strategy", they are now moving towards dispersing their activities over many different countries. Therefore, one can see that Porter's framework may be useful for analyzing a specific global strategy at a specific time, but does not truly capture the evolving nature of global industries.

A New Framework of Global Strategy

Therefore, Moon (1994) proposes a framework that separates the upstream and downstream activities. There are two different paths toward a purely global strategy: a production-seeking global strategy and a market-seeking global strategy (see Fig. 5).

Note that the horizontal axes have been replaced with "number of countries", and the vertical axes with "production coordination" and "marketing coordination". By separating the marketing side and production side, this framework gives a more precise picture for understanding the exact globalization path of different firms. Also, by choosing the number of countries, instead of configuration, we can now more specifically measure the degree of dispersion of a global firm.

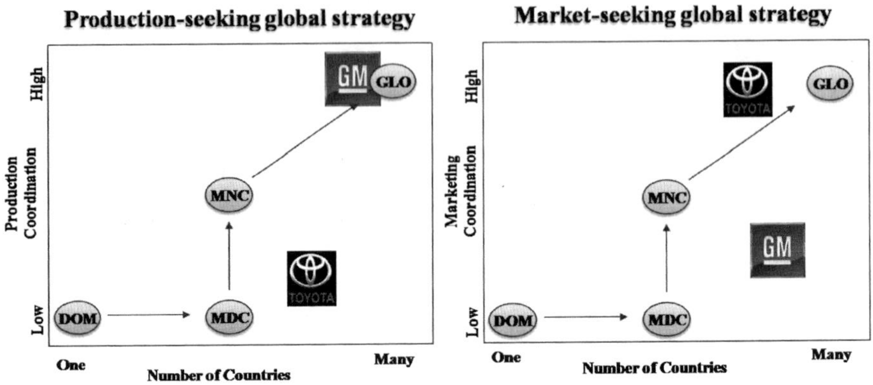

Fig. 5. Production-seeking global strategy vs. market-seeking global strategy.[5]

Here, we can see that the two major automakers, GM and Toyota, have taken very different paths in terms of global strategy. Instead of a singular framework in which GM is deemed less global than Toyota, we can see that they have simply taken different routes toward the same end. While GM disperses its production activities in many countries, Toyota concentrates its production activities in relatively fewer locations. In terms of marketing, Toyota coordinates activities in many countries, while GM — although it has markets in many countries — maintains a relatively lower level of coordination. In essence, global strategy does not have to take one singular path. Toyota decided to focus more on penetrating global markets, while GM's strategy was more focused on using global resources efficiently.

Three-Dimensional Framework and Patterns of International Expansion

When we put all the above information together, a new 3D framework for understanding global strategy emerges (see Fig. 6).

With this figure, we can now map the global expansionary path and the final destination. The two auto giants took different

[5] Moon (1994).

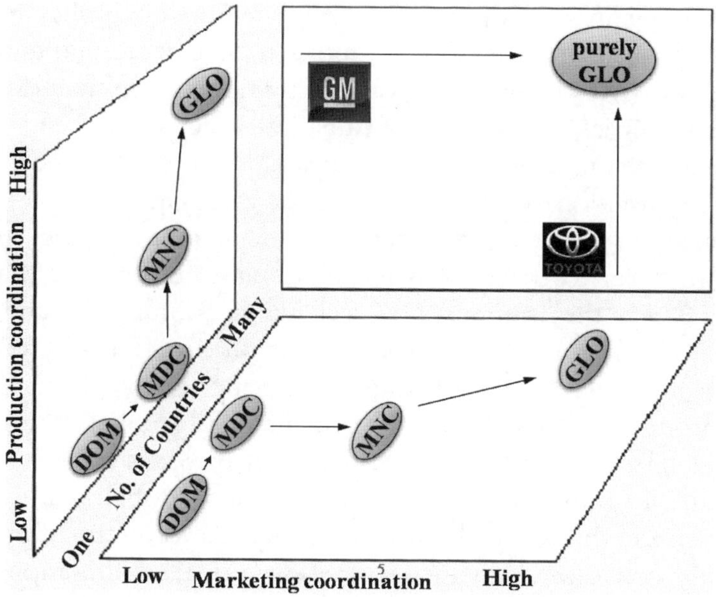

Fig. 6. Global expansion paths.[6]

expansionary paths: GM focused more on production coordination, and Toyota on marketing coordination. However, the final destination should be the same: a purely global strategy, which consists of both high production coordination and high marketing coordination. Thus, in order for GM to become a more global firm, it must increase its marketing coordination, while Toyota needs to expand its production coordination. The essential message here is that neither firm is more global than the other. The two firms are just ***differently global*** as they are each focused on different aspects in their journey to reach the final stage.

A general implication for global strategy can be derived from this framework. All firms start out as purely domestic (DOM) competitors and then move on to become multidomestic (MDC) players. A company can reach this level through increasing either production

[6] *Ibid.*

or marketing in several countries. After a firm establishes itself in several countries, it will seek to move to become a multinational corporation (MNC) through coordinating the activities it performs in various countries. When this coordination is heightened and expansion reaches into many more countries, the firm then becomes a global corporation (GLO). However, at this stage there is still an imbalance between the two activities, depending on the strategy focus. In order to correct this imbalance and become purely global (purely GLO), the firm must now seek higher coordination and international expansion in the activity that it previously neglected. GM needs a higher level of marketing coordination, while Toyota needs more production coordination, to attain a purely global strategy.

This framework is significant in that it provides a concrete and quantifiable framework to track a firm's globalization path. Furthermore, this analysis gives conceptual clarity to the often overused and convoluted distinction among global, multinational and multidomestic firms. One can now easily understand the degree and specific direction that firms take in order to take advantage of globalization.

Analysis

This section provided an enhanced analytical framework for understanding the complex and often misunderstood concept of globalization. While many indices of globalization and transnationality are available, they are usually biased in one way or another. The new 3D framework presented in this section provides the means to analyze globalization in an easy yet comprehensive manner.

An important point that readers should recognize is the fact that the number of countries is used as an indicator in this case. While this is clearly an enhancement from Porter's (1986) framework, a technical problem still remains. For example, if firm A has two production facilities located in China and two located in the US while firm B has one production facility each in Belgium, the Netherlands, Sweden and Finland, firm B can be considered more global than firm A. However, when one considers the physical distance, the story becomes quite different, as China and the US are quite far away from each other while those four European countries are very much clustered around each other. This could potentially be an area of further study to adjust the 3D framework according to physical distance.

8.3 DDC Model

Moon and Kim (2008) further advance the previous model set forth by Moon (1994), and provide a rigorous quantitative methodology that can be readily applied to analyze the degree of globalization of multiple firms in an industry.

The two authors start off by criticizing the various existing frameworks. First, the integration-responsiveness framework by Prahalad and Doz (1987) is flawed (at least in its original format) because it fails to provide a comprehensive framework that encompasses both production and marketing. Next, Porter's configuration-coordination framework (1986) suffers from a similar bias, since it is only suitable to analyze the manufacturing industry. When the service industry is analyzed through this lens, the framework clearly loses its explanatory power (refer to Fig. 4).

As this analysis shows, there are several problems with the prior frameworks as they are either flawed or biased towards one side (see Table 2). Therefore, what is needed is a comprehensive framework that encompasses production, marketing and the number of countries in which both these activities are coordinated. With such a theoretical foundation, one can determine a more precise degree and path of a firm's globalization.

Functional Division

Porter (1986) was the first scholar to bring the globalization analysis down to the functional level through the value chain, which is the right place to start. However, he failed to consider that different firms configure and coordinate their activities in a wide variety of patterns.

Table 2. Comprehensive comparison of existing models and a new model.[7]

	Configuration-coordination model	Integration-responsiveness model	Extended model		
	Porter (1986)	Prahalad and Doz (1987)	Harzing (2000)	Moon (1994)	DDC model
Diversification					
P	Configuration	•	•	Number of countries	Production diversification
M	•	Responsiveness	Responsiveness	Number of countries	Marketing diversification
D^1	•	•	•	•	○
Coordination					
P	•	Integration	Interdependence	Production coordination	Production coordination
M	Coordination	•	•	Marketing coordination	Marketing coordination
D^2	•	•	•	○	○
Functional division	•	•	•	•	○

Note: P, production; M, marketing; D^1, division of the production number of countries and the marketing number of countries; D^2, division of the production coordination and the marketing coordination; •, missing; ○, included.

[7] Moon and Kim (2008).

Unlike what Porter thinks, there are various paths available in terms of dispersing a firm's value chain activities. Therefore, in order to map the complex and diverse nature of a firm's globalization path, a different framework is needed that focuses on the functional division of the value chain, not the firm itself.

Different Paths of Functional Activities in Global Expansion

Then, how do we map the globalization strategy of a variety of firms that take different paths from each other? Furthermore, if firms disperse their value activities differently from each other, how can we map this in a comprehensive framework? The key to the answer is to first clarify the terms "multidomestic" and "global". While many scholars have discussed these two concepts, most have been biased towards one or the other and failed to take a balanced view.

What clearly emerges from synthesizing the various viewpoints is the need for a functional division within the firm's value chain activities. Firms with a core competence in the production functions will tend to take a more *global strategy*, while firms with advantages in marketing activities will take a more *multidomestic strategy*. Now that the functional division and terminologies are clarified, we can proceed to look at the dynamic diversification-coordination (DDC) model, which shows a firm's globalization path according to the functional division (Fig. 7).

What we can see from this model is a two-way path to becoming a transnational corporation: global and multidomestic. Firms with a production focus will take the global path, while firms with a marketing focus will take the multidomestic path. Both activities require coordination and diversification, but production will lean more towards coordination while marketing will lean more towards diversification, at least in the first two stages. However, in the final stage, both production and marketing will be widely diversified and highly coordinated to take full advantage of a transnational strategy.

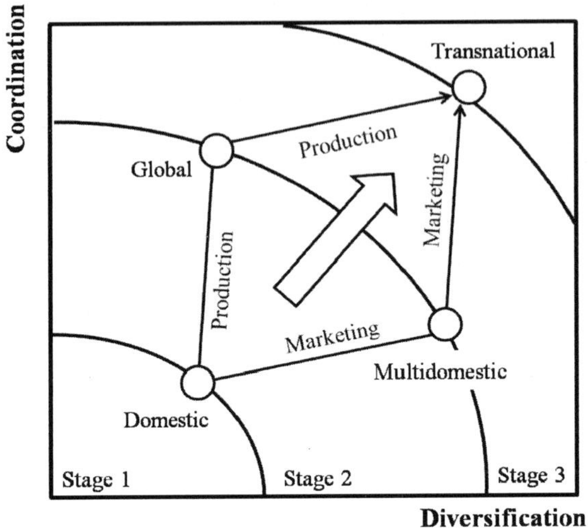

Fig. 7. DDC model.[8]

Empirical Analysis

While this section does not give a full presentation of the empirical analysis based on the DDC model, it is still important to note the two hypotheses proven:

- *Hypothesis 1* — There is a division of functions in the process of global expansion.
- *Hypothesis 2* — Firms take a global strategy for the production function, while they implement a multidomestic strategy for the marketing function.

By verifying the above two hypotheses, one can gain a better understanding of a firm's globalization path. This approach has contributed to the existing literature in two major ways. Firstly, it shifted the unit of analysis down to the functional level and therefore added analytical rigor to the field. Next, the DDC framework showed a more specific

[8] *Ibid.*

methodology to quantify and map the globalization path of various firms. Instead of fixing the analysis on one side or the other, this new framework can account for the wide array of firms that exist within the same global industry.[9]

Analysis

What we have seen is a clear progression and improvement from model to model, with each one improving and correcting the previous model's flaws and imperfections. So, have we reached the ultimate power of explanation with the most updated model? This question can only be answered with repeated application of the model to a variety of firms and industries. While the concepts of production and marketing do indeed cover almost all of a firm's functions, successful application of the model to a multitude of industry types has yet to be conducted. Until then, improvements on Porter's original work (1986) remain largely theoretical.

Finally, should we infer that all firms have the goal or dream of reaching the transnational stage? Assuming that transnational is the best strategy for all firms may be a little imperious. Thus, if firms are to halt their progress on the DDC model, should we assume that they have faltered and failed on their path? Can they then be deemed as unsuccessful ventures? The DDC model is a useful tool for the analysis of a firm's progression, but should be used with caution when analyzing different positions of firms in different industries.

Case Study 1: Hyundai Motor Company[10]

The Hyundai Motor Company is a division of the Hyundai Kia Automotive Group and is South Korea's largest, and the world's fifth largest, automaker in terms of units sold per year.[11] However, it has

---

[9] For more discussion and empirical tests, see Moon and Kim (2008).

[10] Information for this case study is abstracted from the Hyundai Motor Company official website (worldwide.hyundai.com) and Kim and Moon (2006).

[11] *Business Trends Asia* (2007).

not always played a significant role on the global stage in terms of automobile development and manufacturing. During the firm's humble beginnings, it was forced to rely on licensed technology (mostly from Japan) and was largely considered a peripheral, low-cost manufacturer. However, over time the company has built up its strengths and has recently become the world's fifth largest automaker. We can apply the models explained in this chapter to analyze the long-term evolution of the firm's development path. We will begin with Porter's (1986) configuration-coordination model, then utilize Moon's (1994) extension of Porter's model and finally apply the DDC model (Moon and Kim 2008).

Before we formally analyze Hyundai's global strategy, we need to know a little background information on its history. Hyundai Motor Company was established in 1967, and in 1968 it produced two models — the Cortina and the Granada (with Ford branding) — for sale in the South Korean market. In 1975, the firm produced its first Hyundai-branded car, the Pony, for the Korean market. At this point, the firm produced and sold its automobiles only in South Korea, but hired foreign expertise to improve the quality and design of its cars (Italian firms for design, Japanese engineers for engines, and British experts for R&D).

In 1976, the firm started to export its cars to Ecuador and Benelux countries, and entered the US market in 1986. The firm then opened a production plant in Canada, which unfortunately closed down in 1993, and established a design center in the US in 1990. Despite the initial failure in expanding production overseas, Hyundai opened another production plant in India in 1996 and then went on to open production plants in the US as well as R&D centers in Germany and the US. Following these initial successes, Hyundai Motor Company has spread out across the globe for production, R&D and sales (see Table 3).

Now that we have a clearer understanding of the timeline and order of Hyundai's development since its founding, we are in a better position to document the firm's growth through the use of the analytical models. We will begin with Porter's (1986) configuration-coordination model.

Table 3. Hyundai Motor Company's assets worldwide.[12]

Region	Country	Significant assets
North America	US	R&D center, production plant and regional office
Eastern Europe	Czech Republic	Overseas subsidiary and production plant
	Russia	Regional HQ and production plant
	Slovenia	Regional office
Western Europe	Italy & UK	Overseas subsidiaries
	Germany	R&D center and overseas subsidiary
Asia-Pacific	Australia, Bangladesh & Brunei	Overseas subsidiaries
	China	Overseas subsidiary, production plant and regional office
	Malaysia	Regional HQ and production plant
	Fiji, French Polynesia & Guam	Overseas subsidiaries
	India	Production plant
	Taiwan	Regional office
	Japan	R&D center

Figure 8 shows a basic example of Porter's C-C model. Using this framework, we can map Hyundai's development over the course of its history (see Fig. 9).

According to Porter's C-C model, Hyundai would have begun in the bottom right-hand corner, as it started out as a purely domestic automaker and operated only in the South Korean market. Therefore, its configuration of activities was concentrated and coordination of its activities was quite low. However, over time, although Hyundai remained geographically concentrated in only South Korea, it did begin to widen its corporate outreach through exports and therefore began to coordinate a wider array of activities worldwide.

[12] Hyundai Motor Company website (worldwide.hyundai.com).

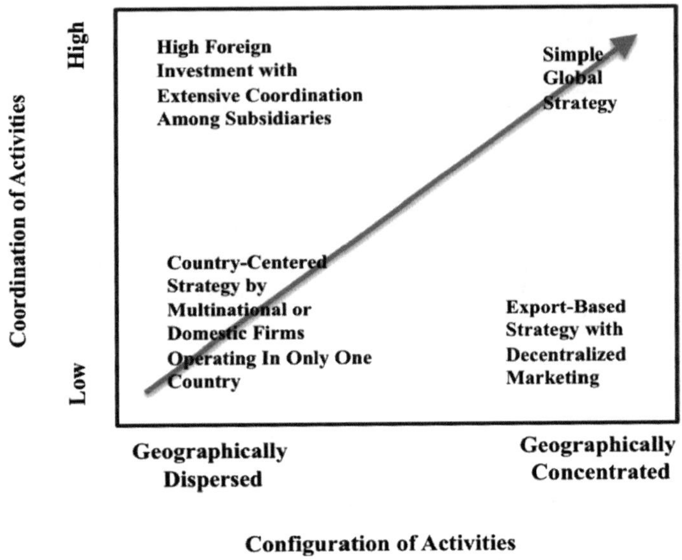

Fig. 8. Configuration-coordination model.[13]

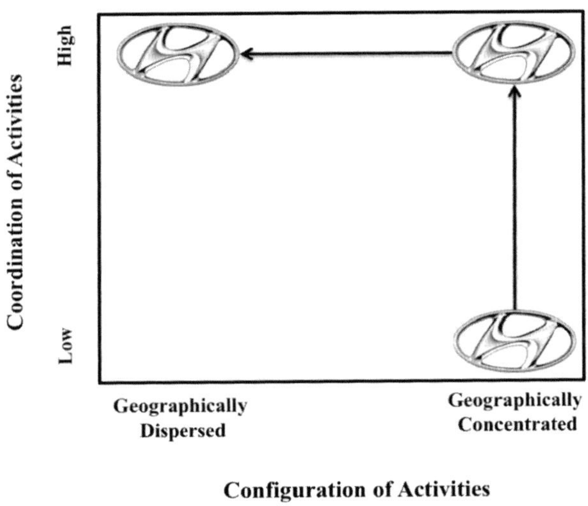

Fig. 9. Hyundai Motor Company's historical development.

[13] Porter (1986), p. 27.

Fast forward to recent years, and we can see a sprawling global conglomerate with a strong global outreach and brand name. Hyundai Motor Company has a geographically dispersed configuration of activities comprised of regional headquarters, regional offices, production plants and R&D facilities in numerous countries across a number of regions. The firm also has a high level of coordination of activities, with a large number of subsidiaries scattered across the globe that maintain a high level of interaction with the central headquarters in South Korea. Thus, according to Porter (1986), Hyundai managed to obtain the ultimate global positioning (as indicated by the top right-hand corner) in the middle of its development phase and has since moved away from that position to the status of a less globalized firm (as indicated by the top left-hand corner). In order to clarify this position, let's now look at Moon's (1994) extension to Porter's model.

As highlighted previously, Moon (1994) argues that Porter (1986) made a fundamental error in labeling his axes in the configuration and coordination model, which Hyundai Motor Company's progression may confirm. Although it has been traditionally argued that Hyundai has focused more on a production-seeking global strategy, using Moon's altered framework, it can be argued that Hyundai Motor Company has in fact focused more on a market-seeking global strategy. This can be confirmed when looking at the number of production facilities Hyundai holds compared to the number and dispersion of its regional HQs, regional offices and overseas subsidiaries. Figures 10 and 11 are graphical illustrations of Hyundai's production-seeking global strategy and market-seeking global strategy, respectively.

When we compare Figs. 10 and 11 with Fig. 6, we can see that, in terms of a production-seeking global strategy, Hyundai has not yet reached the global stage and can be more accurately described as a multinational with the potential to become a global firm. However, in terms of a market-seeking global strategy, Hyundai is indeed a global firm and has followed the path of shifting from a domestic firm to a multinational firm to global firm status. This can be depicted more succinctly from a 3D perspective, as in Fig. 12. Thus, using this

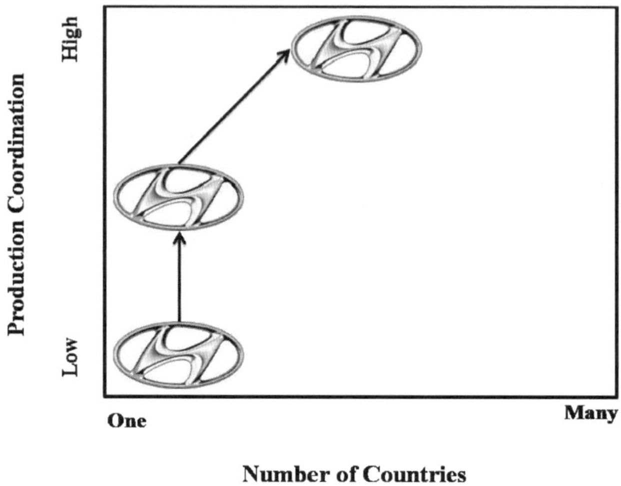

Fig. 10. Hyundai Motor Company's production-seeking global strategy.

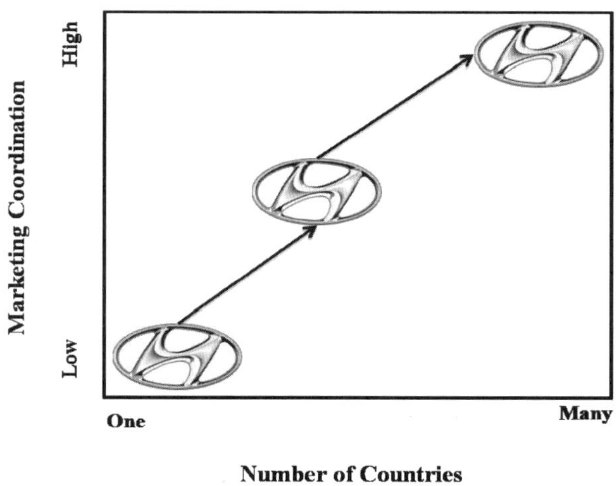

Fig. 11. Hyundai Motor Company's market-seeking global strategy.

extension of Porter's (1986) model, we can see that in terms of production Hyundai has yet to move into a global position, although it has achieved global status from a marketing perspective. Once the firm moves into a global stance in production, Hyundai will then

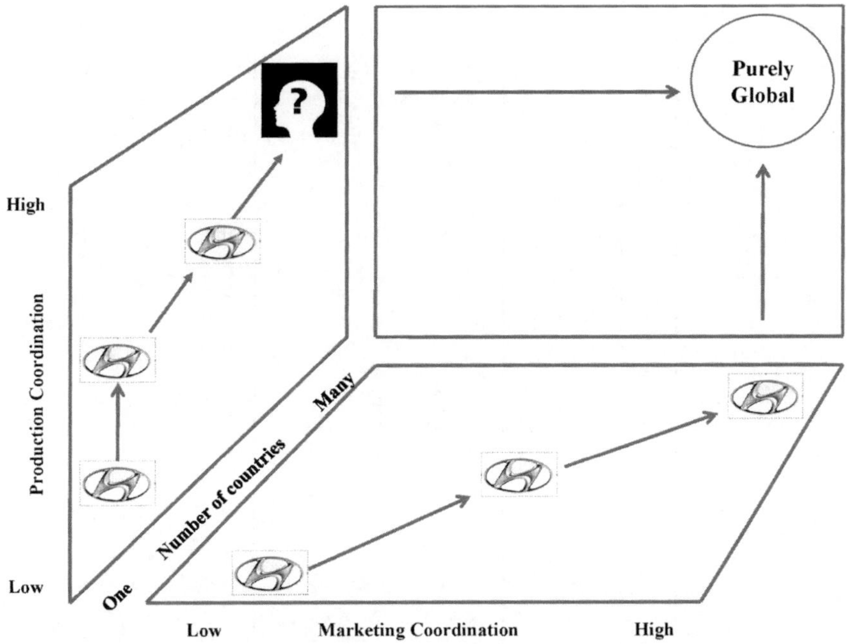

Fig. 12. 3D perspective of Hyundai Motor Company's global strategy.

have to deal with how to amalgamate the production and marketing aspects of its operation in order to transform into a purely global firm.

Moon and Kim (2008) further extended the 3D model to the DDC model, as explained in Sec. 8.3. An empirical analysis using the DDC model provides us with a much more accurate analysis of Hyundai's global strategy. Table 4 below shows that the DDC model (far right column of Table 2) is the most effective model in fully utilizing the variables of production, marketing, diversification and coordination, compared with other models which utilize the variables only partially. Finally, Fig. 13 illustrates the empirical data for the DDC model to show the relative position of the major automakers.[14]

The results show that Hyundai Motor Company does indeed, as suspected, have a lower level of transnationality from a production

[14] For full empirical result, see Kim and Moon (2006).

Table 4. Variables for measuring global expansion.[15]

			UNCTAD (1995, 2002)		Extended model		
	C-C model (Porter 1986)	I-R model (Prahalad and Doz 1987)	TNI	NSI	Moon (1994)	Harzing (2000)	Contractor *et al.* (2003)
Production	•	Integration	FATA FETE	•	Production coordination	Interdependence	FETE
Marketing	Coordination	•	FSTS	•	Marketing coordination	•	FSTS
Diversification	Configuration	Responsiveness	•	Number of countries	Number of countries	Responsiveness	FOTO
Coordination	○	○	•	•	○	•	•

Note: FATA, foreign assets as a percentage of total assets; FSTS, foreign sales as a percentage of total sales; FETE, number of foreign employees to total number of employees; FOTO, number of foreign offices to total number of offices; TNI, Transnationality Index; NSI, Network Spread Index; •, missing; ○, included.

[15] Extracted from Kim and Moon (2006).

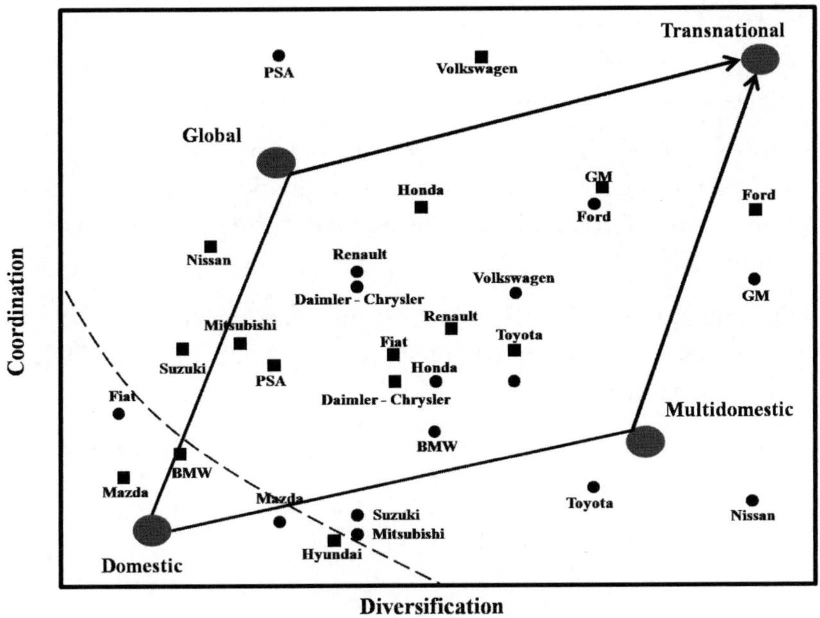

Fig. 13. Integrated scatter diagram.[16]

aspect than from a marketing aspect. Thus, we can conclude that Hyundai does need to shift its focus towards a more global level of production. Once Hyundai reaches a global level of marketing and production functions together, its focus will be the integration of the two in order to achieve a purely global or transnational business strategy.

Discussion Questions

1. In his C-C model, Porter (1986) classified the top right-hand corner as being a global strategy. How would you classify the other three corners using Porter's definitions in Fig. 2?

---

[16] Kim and Moon (2006).

2. Porter (1986) made an error in classifying the axes in his C-C model. What other weaknesses do you note? What, then, are the strengths of the model? Discuss.

3. Moon (1994) divides his model into two sections: production and marketing. Is this the only way to divide the firm's strategies? Can you think of a third or more vital strategic path that a firm might follow?

4. Do you agree with Moon (1994) that production and marketing strategies must be coordinated before being able to become a truly global firm? Why or why not?

5. Do all firms want or need to be transnational? Why or why not?

6. According the DDC model, what specific suggestions can you provide for Hyundai Motor Company? Discuss.

CHAPTER 9

The Grand Debate Over Standardization Strategy

Chapter Guideline

We now turn to the debate between standardization and differentiation. Globalization has two paradoxical effects, as firms increasingly standardize to meet homogeneous tastes while also differentiate to meet the individual needs of consumers in different locations. So what is the answer? The simple answer would be to say it depends, but this response, although impeccably logical, does not leave us with useful insight. Furthermore, this kind of simplification leaves us little room to explore the pros and cons of this exciting debate. This chapter will look at some prominent scholars who have tried to provide us with some answers on this topic.

Summary of Previous Models

So far, we have looked at the various concepts of business strategy and what it means to elevate these concepts to a global level. In the previous chapter, we looked at some analytical frameworks that could provide a shortcut to understanding the real world. Now, we turn our eyes to the nature of the phenomenon itself and try to answer the classic question of whether to standardize or differentiate. Through this chapter, we will gain a firm understanding of this polemic debate and use it as a platform to add another piece to the puzzle.

9.1 The Grand Thesis: The World Is Flat?

Thomas Friedman's *The World Is Flat* (2005) became an instant bestseller, and raised critical acclaim as well as sharp criticisms. The core message of the book is that globalization has leveled the competitive playing field between developed and developing economies. He attributes this trend mainly to various technological advances in computer and information technology, which grant access to technology and information to anyone with a laptop and an Internet connection. This transformed global landscape is dubbed "Globalization 3.0", in which individuals from the peripheries (emerging economies) are now a tour de force in the globalization story. Friedman metaphorically describes this leveled playing field as a "flat world". However, as sensational as this concept was in 2005, Friedman was not the first one to come up with this term. A flat world was prophesized in 1983 by the eminent business and economics scholar, Theodore Levitt.

Living in the Republic of Technology

The starting point of Levitt's (1983) article is the dissemination of technology, which has led to the inclusion of previously untapped areas into the global economic system. Through the spread of technology, the world is integrating into singularity, and this has led to the emergence of a homogeneous market base at an unprecedented scale. Thus, the term "Republic of Technology" aptly represents this global trend in which the world surges towards singularity, since technology is the main driving force.

In order to articulate his point further, Levitt (1983) distinguishes between the two terms "global corporation" and "multinational corporation". A multinational corporation operates in many different countries, but differentiates its strategies according to the market in which it operates; while a global corporation has a multinational outreach, but provides all markets with a standardized product. Levitt's conclusion is that the world is increasingly gravitating towards being in favor of the latter.

Vindication of the Model T

One may counter Levitt (1983) and assert that national dissimilarities are indeed still very real, and that many firms differentiate according to markets and reap great success. Levitt does not deny that there are several strategies which individual firms can adopt in order to gain global commercial success. However, the aggregate trend that the world is moving towards is definitely towards increased standardization and homogenized taste. Consider Ford's Model T, the first mass-produced automobile. The Model T demonstrates that, despite individual differences and preferences, the customer's ultimate wants can be boiled down to low-cost and high-quality goods.

Expanding this logic to the global scale, we can see why so many Japanese automobile companies (with highly standardized products) were able to garner massive success in the world market. Of course, Japanese automobile companies lost some market positions because they did not differentiate according to local markets. However, overall, the formula for the Japanese success boils down to two simple variables: low cost and high quality. Thus, a company that can take full advantage of this kind of context is one that is an expert in one great truth (a global company) rather than one that knows a lot about many different things (a multinational company). Levitt's (1983) famous analogy, the fox and the hedgehog, aptly portrays this relationship in which the fox — who knows a lot about many things — represents a multinational, while the hedgehog — who knows everything about one great thing — represents a global company.

The Remaining Differences and Accepting the Inevitable

According to Levitt (1983), the remaining national differences are mainly a reflection of people's misguided beliefs. Multinationals erroneously assume that they must differentiate in order to succeed, while customers also believe that their tastes are fixed. But when customers are presented with low-cost and high-quality goods, the national barrier and remaining differences can actually be nullified. The only problem is that both marketers and customers alike do not understand this fact. The implication here is that truly successful firms are those that can actually go beyond this mode of thought, boldly pursue standardization and move on to become global companies. Despite all the differences and seemingly insurmountable barriers, the overarching common denominator is that consumers desire low-cost and high-quality goods, and standardization is the key to providing these timeless values.

The Earth Is Flat

Now made even more famous by Thomas Friedman (2005), this term succinctly portrays Levitt's (1983) message. The world is still round, and many national differences persist and will continue to exist in the future. However, the key is to treat the world as flat, and focus on creating a consumer and then keeping it. Rather than assuming a static view of customer preference, truly successful companies will actually mold their customers into liking them. Furthermore, the current technological and institutional developments are becoming increasingly favorable to this trend. Developments such as the rapid dissemination of IT technology, drastic improvements in transportation in terms of both technology and cost, and reduced trade barriers through the World Trade Organization (WTO) and numerous regional trade agreements (RTAs) all support the general gravitation towards a flatter world.

Analysis

It is quite interesting to look back at Levitt's (1983) article, a few decades after it was written. The question really boils down to this: is the world becoming more similar or different? Differences are still prevalent and a large portion of the world's population is still left out of the global economic system. As we will see in the following sections, many scholars have criticized Levitt from various perspectives. In this sense, Levitt's prophecy may not have been entirely accurate. However, what is undeniable is the general trend or direction that the forces of globalization are steering this world towards.

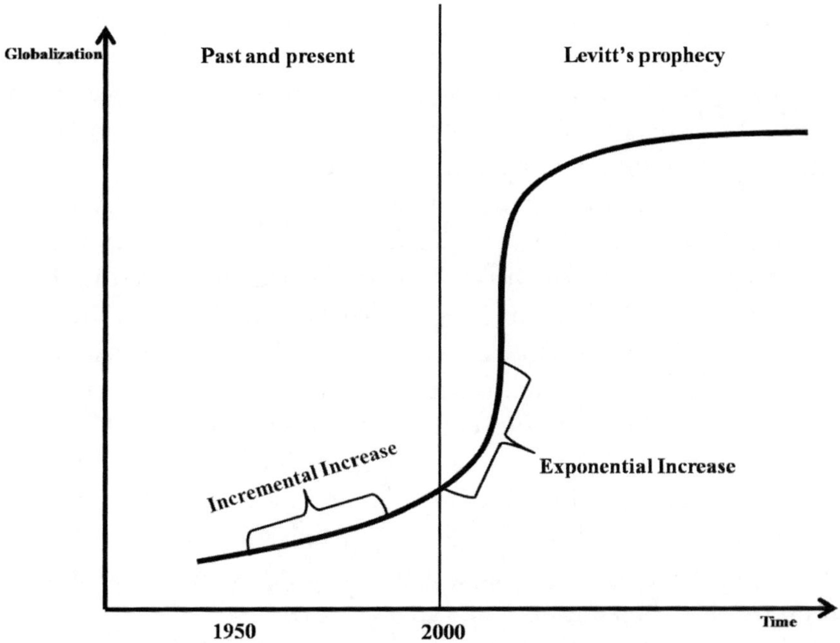

Fig. 1. Levitt's (1983) prophecy in Saffo's (2007) S-curve.

Let us go back to Saffo's (2007) S-curve that we discussed in Chap. 6 and illustrate Levitt's (1983) prophetic analysis in this analytical framework (see Fig. 1).

According to Saffo (2007), change comes in an S-curve pattern in which change starts slowly and incrementally before suddenly exploding. Figure 1 maps a hypothetical globalization S-curve. The 1940s and 1950s saw the end of the Second World War and the inception of the Bretton Woods system. From the 1960s to 1980s, the world slowly headed towards economic integration through multilateral frameworks such as the General Agreement on Tariffs and Trade (GATT). The 1990s were marked by the sudden disintegration of the Soviet Union and former communist economies. The current decade is characterized by increased regional and bilateral trade agreements as well as the increasing influence of the WTO. An effective forecaster must predict the inflection point before it actually hits, and Levitt's

1983 article can be understood as he forecast the inflection point in Fig. 1. Whether or not the world economic system will hit this inflection point between "incremental increase" and "exponential increase" is one of the most central questions in many academic disciplines, including international business.

Regardless of whether or not Levitt's (1983) prophecy materializes anytime soon, many subsequent scholars have been in line with Levitt's prophetic message that the world is heading towards a flatter and homogenized platform. Porter (1986) and Prahalad and Doz (1987), for instance, characterized global industries as those having low responsiveness and high integration. In a global industry, a firm's competitive position in one country is significantly affected by its position in other countries. Commercial aircrafts, TV sets, semiconductors, copiers, automobiles and watches are appropriate examples under this category. Accordingly, a firm must integrate its activities on a worldwide basis to capture the linkages among countries to maximize scale benefits and cost advantages.

Morrison (1990) refined this logic and delved deeper into the specifics. He concluded that global industries are those that have intense levels of international competition, which leads to the marketing of standardized products worldwide. Therefore, industry competitors usually have a presence in all key international markets and promote high levels of international trade. More recently, Isenberg (2008), in his analysis of start-up companies, asserted that successful entrepreneurs must not be overwhelmed by the prevailing national differences. He urged that only those who boldly ride the wave of globalization through a global strategy can achieve a sustainable competitive advantage. As can be seen from this extensive list of follow-ups, many scholars do believe (of course, to varying degrees) that the world is heading towards the direction in which Levitt envisioned in his 1983 article.

9.2 Antithesis: The World Is Spiky?

Now, we will take a look at the antithesis to Levitt's (1983) hypothesis: the differentiation story. Douglas and Wind (1987) assert that global standardization is merely one of a number of strategies which may be successful in international markets. Rather than viewing globalization as a unilateral process in which standardization overrides all strategies, Douglas and Wind paint a much more complex and diverse picture whereby both standardization and differentiation become more pronounced due to globalization. As the two scholars are both marketing specialists, their article is heavily focused on the marketing aspect of firms. The authors contend that increasing global integration has taken place and that a global perspective in marketing strategy is highly crucial. However, this does not mean that marketing strategy must follow a singular formula of standardization. In fact, global products and brands are appropriate for only certain market segments, while others need a more differentiated approach.

The Big Debate: Global Standardization versus Differentiation

The biggest debate in international marketing strategy has been between implementing a uniform worldwide strategy and adapting to specific local market conditions. Proponents of standardization argue that implementing a uniform strategy creates international synergies, maximizing a firm's global competitive advantage. Others, however, have argued that a uniform global strategy could lead to a crucial mistake of neglecting some important market segments. Douglas and Wind (1987) conclude that uniform standardization is not only dangerous for a firm's competitive advantage, but also downright impossible at times because of external barriers such as government regulation. In order to articulate this argument further, the three underlying assumptions of Levitt's (1983) global standardization philosophy are refuted one by one.

- *Homogenization of the World Wants* — As Ohmae (1989) aptly put it, "Californization of needs" integrates the global population into a single set of demands. How true is this? Not so true, according to Douglas and Wind (1987). They point out that there is a lack of empirical evidence to support this claim. Moreover, many companies actually adopt unique, tailored approaches in individual markets. Coca-Cola, the epitome of a global company, actually markets many products that are customized to local tastes, such as Aquarius (cold canned coffee) in Japan. Another reason why this assumption is flawed is because of the growing body of evidence which indicates significant differences within countries. In other words, what Levitt (1983) and other standardization proponents argue for homogenization of needs is in fact limited to a very specific population segment in multiple countries. In every country, there are certain pockets of global consumers, but the majority of them are out of this standardization story.

- *Universal Preference for Low Price at Acceptable Quality* — Can we view low price and high quality as universal values that override all other differentiators? Douglas and Wind (1987) disagree, based on three counterarguments. First, low price positioning is a vulnerable strategy that is unsustainable in the long run. New technological innovations, for example, can quickly nullify such an advantage. Second, there is a severe lack of evidence to support the universal preference theory. Price-sensitive segments have existed universally, but there is no clear indication that they are on the rise due to increased globalization. Finally, standardized low-price products in one country can mean a high price in others. A US$10 pair of shoes in the US is a decent deal, but the same standard-priced product would be very expensive in Ghana. Therefore, without differentiation, standardized low-price products can fail to tap into many global segments.
- *Economies of Scale of Production and Marketing* — Integration of firm activities can lead to significant economies of scale, as firms can reduce the average production cost per unit. This logic, however, neglects three factors. Firstly, flexible factory automation allows economies of scale to be achieved in much lower levels of

output. Secondly, the cost of production is not a major component of total cost. Marketing costs, for example, can become even more substantial than production costs. Lastly, market strategy should be based on various components such as brand name and advertising.

Requisite Conditions for Global Standardization

Douglas and Wind's (1987) point is not that standardization is a completely invalid strategy, but that it can only be successful under certain exogenous conditions as outlined below:

- *Existence of Global Market Segments* — Simply put, without demand for standardized goods, supply cannot be sustained. In industrial markets, where differentiation of goods is rather insignificant (e.g., cement), standardization would be a good choice. However, industries that are highly sensitive to local tastes (e.g., food) need to be differentiated. A global segment for consumption is a prerequisite for global standardization.
- *Synergies Associated with Global Standardization* — Standardizing a product leads to numerous synergistic benefits because an action in one country can enhance the performance in another. For example, if a company develops a detergent suitable for the Japanese market, then it will probably boost the product's success in similar countries such as Korea. These kinds of synergistic benefits must exist for global standardization to be a viable choice.
- *Availability of an International Communication and Distribution Infrastructure* — Without a convenient worldwide distribution system and communications network, standardization cannot succeed. Technological innovations in both of these areas have made global standardization a more feasible choice, but there are still significant barriers.

Operational Constraints to Effective Implementation of a Standardization Strategy

Achieving globalization is not difficult, but it does come at a cost. This section outlines the external and internal constraints pointed out by Douglas and Wind (1987).

- *External Constraints* — Four external constraints inhibit firms from pursuing a global strategy. Firstly, government and trade restrictions, such as tariffs and quotas, severely limit a firm's ability to standardize globally. For example, high tariffs force firms to differentiate their pricing and thus uniform pricing becomes an impossible option. Secondly, marketing infrastructure, such as available media outlets, may differ from country to country. A standardized marketing approach, therefore, becomes undesirable. Thirdly, differences in availability and cost of resources may force a firm to change its product design or component. For example, a global paper manufacturer must modify or replace its wood fiber content when producing in countries where wood is scarce. Lastly, competition structures are also different among countries. In certain countries, lower-end products are at the heart of competition; while in others, higher-end products are more important. Therefore, adopting a singular competitive strategy will ultimately lead to failure.
- *Internal Constraints* — There are two noticeable internal constraints for a global strategy. First, if a firm had no prior global operation whatsoever, it can adopt a standardized approach without much internal trouble. However, this is not the case for most firms, as they already have pre-existing global operations which need to be restructured to fit a standardized strategy. Dislocating the firm's previous global commitment such as joint ventures or partnerships requires significant costs, which could have a severe adverse effect on the firm. Second, local management motivation and attitudes could pose another problem, as standardization requires centralized planning and diminished authority of previously autonomous entities within the firm. This

has a very high potential for internal conflict, which can lead to significant losses for the firm.

A Framework for Classifying Global Strategy Options

Douglas and Wind (1987) conclude that global standardization is only feasible when certain conditions (both internal and external) are met. Rather than viewing global standardization as the optimum strategic choice, Douglas and Wind emphasize that it is one out of many choices available. Therefore, instead of viewing the choice as either standardization or differentiation, the appropriate way to look at it is a mixture between the two extremes. Figure 2 illustrates the possible strategic mixes available for a company.

As Fig. 2 illustrates, no firm can actually pursue a purely differentiated or standardized strategy. Depending on the category, location

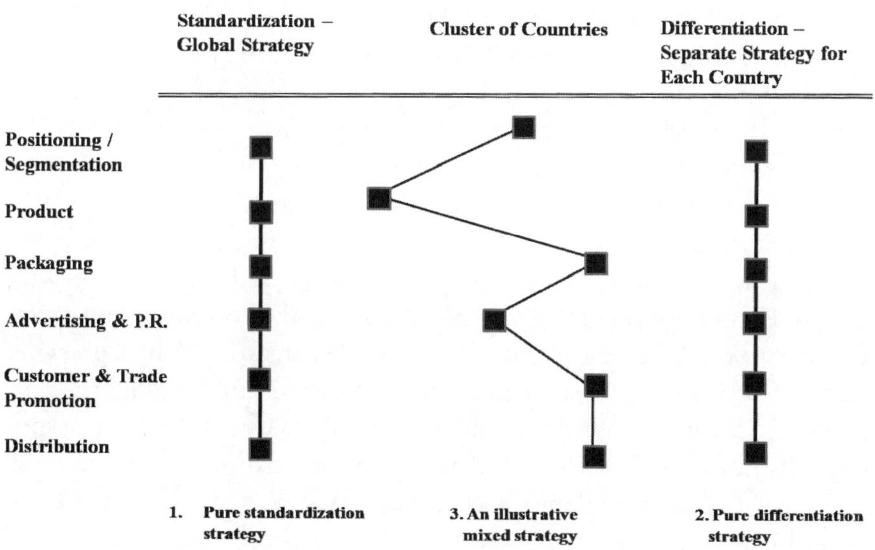

Fig. 2. The standardization-differentiation continuum.[1]

[1] Douglas and Wind (1987).

and industry, firms will take various mixes of the two elements to optimize their operation.

The core message of Douglas and Wind (1987) is that standardization is not a silver bullet in the world of globalization, but a viable option only under very specific circumstances. Furthermore, in most cases, the optimal strategy requires an appropriate mixture of both extremes because national dissimilarities in many perspectives pervade in reality. Therefore, firms are destined to run into major obstacles if they devise and implement their strategies without considering the vast discrepancy between the standardization theory and reality.

Analysis

Douglas and Wind (1987) convincingly countered Levitt's (1983) argument, and many scholars have followed this antithesis from various angles and perspectives. Rugman and Verbeke (2004), for example, asserted that very few multinational enterprises have the ability to sell standardized products and services around the world, thereby refuting the type of globalization originally advocated by Levitt. After an empirical analysis of the largest 500 international firms in the world, they confirmed that most firms are not "global",[2] but are rather regional companies with the majority of their presence in the triad (Europe, Japan and North America) region. Similarly, Garvin and Levesque (2008) argued that a multi-unit enterprise, which is characterized by a geographically dispersed organization with a high level of autonomy, is the norm among the top 500 companies. Furthermore, Ghemawat and Hout (2008) insisted that a growing number of firms from emerging economies are building their global positions through a focused and vertical business. These firms spot opportunities to pull apart and reconfigure existing value chains in order to deploy capital more efficiently. An even stronger assertion came from Greenwald and Kahn (2005), as they argued that global

[2] Rugman and Verbeke (2004) defined "global" as having sales of 20% or more in each of the three parts of the triad — namely, North America (or NAFTA), the European Union and Asia — but less than 50% in any one region of the triad.

consumer demand is still highly segregated since separate local environments are still characterized, in both obvious and subtle ways, by different tastes, different government rules, different business practices and different cultural norms. Thus, the authors proclaimed that all strategies are essentially local.

It is true that, in some cases, differences have become even more pronounced and many firms are adopting ever more eclectic strategies. However, one must pause to think whether Douglas and Wind's (1987) article is truly an antithesis to Levitt (1983). While the authors' intention may have been something close to it, it seems that standardization and differentiation are actually different sides of the same coin. What this means is that, rather than viewing standardization or differentiation as an end point, it would be more appropriate to view these two concepts as different paths to reach a certain final point. Recall Moon and Kim's (2008) dynamic diversification-coordination (DDC) model, which we discussed back in the previous chapter (Fig. 3).

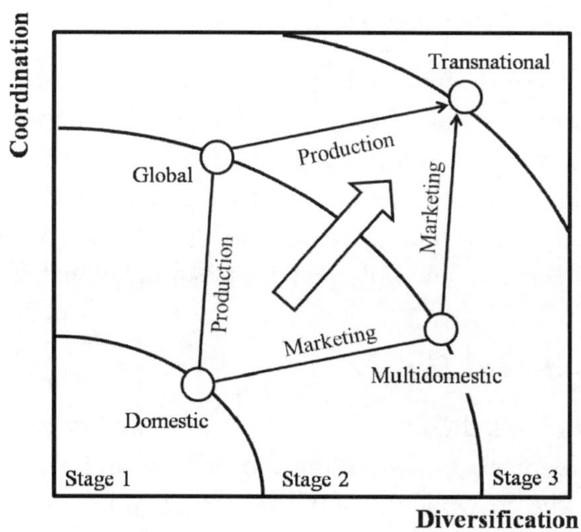

Fig. 3. Moon and Kim's DDC model.[3]

[3] Moon and Kim (2008).

Using Fig. 3, we can actually visualize Levitt's (1983) thesis being on the global path and Douglas and Wind's (1987) thesis being on the multidomestic path. The point is that the two apparently conflicting theories may simply just be describing different paths to the same final destination.

9.3 Another Antithesis: The World Is Not Flat

Ghemawat's (2007) article, "Why the world isn't flat", presents an antithesis to Thomas Friedman's famous *New York Times* article and subsequent book, *The World Is Flat* (2005). The crux of Ghemawat's argument is that globalization and standardization proponents are simply wrong and that they have overblown the globalization myth. While many assume that the world is heading towards an integrated and connected world, the truth is that only a fraction of the global population is in this globalized world while the overwhelming majority is still out of the loop.

The Ten-Percent Presumption

The fraction of those involved in the globalized world, according to Ghemawat (2007), is only about 10% of the world's population. A large majority of the world is still not engaged in activities that fall under the category of "globalization". Representative globalization indicators such as immigration, investments, patents and phone call revenues all hover around the 10% mark. The only exception is trade, which is around 20%.

A Strong National Defense

The reason behind these surprisingly low numbers is the prevailing nationalist and protectionist sentiments which still define the world. Even Infosys, the crown jewel of the Indian IT industry and Friedman's (2005) favorite example, is not exempt from this archaic paradigm. To be sure, Infosys does serve many American clients halfway across the globe through a wired world. However, this is not just because the boundaries are becoming nullified, but also because a large part of

Infosys investment is actually American capital. The national origin of the capital investment is one of the main reasons why Infosys caters to the US market. Expanding on this conjecture, Ghemawat (2007) also points out that most investments are intra-regional and largely domestic. The so-called "free flow of global capital" is an overblown myth which neglects the reality that, even today, an overwhelming majority of fixed capital is from domestic or regional sources.

Turning Back the Clock

Ghemawat (2007) does not deny that there has been some progress towards what globalization proponents call an integrated world. However, the proportion of this phenomenon is severely overblown in most literature and this trend has the potential of being reversed. In times of economic crisis or large calamities, countries tend to turn to protectionist barriers, which may undo the little integration that has occurred across the world. In other words, unlike globalization proponents who argue that worldwide integration is an inevitable and powerful force, Ghemawat points out that it is very fragile and has overwhelming potential to be dismantled. The current economic crisis of 2008–2009 is a good testbed to see whether Ghemawat's warning will become a reality.

Analysis

Samuel Huntington, in his controversial book, *The Clash of Civilizations and the Remaking of World Order* (1996), recognized the globalized elites as those in the "Davos culture". This culture, according to Huntington, is shared by the few who believe in the pursuit of global mass consumption under the leadership of elite corporations, media moguls and bankers. Furthermore, constituents of those who identify with this Davos culture are the ones who follow the global standardization trend and are the core consumers and proponents of global standardization. Thus, the global culture, or Davos culture, is only a limited phenomenon shared by a small portion of the global population. Ghemawat's (2007) analysis is on a similar yet even more critical line, as he poses the possibility of this limited globalization to actually unwind. Therefore, what we accept as a given fact may not be so solid after all. Given the current financial crisis that is touching all corners of the world, it is unfortunately the perfect time to test Ghemawat's theory of the possible rise of economic nationalism and reversal of globalization.

However, there are other possibilities. The so-called "Davos culture" few may be powerful and wealthy enough to hold together the current level of global connectivity and perhaps even increase it. Through their influence and with governmental cooperation, it may be entirely possible to make globalization a truly global trend and, moreover, one that has a positive effect on all those lives it touches. Too idealistic? Perhaps, but being too idealistic may be what the world needs rather than focusing on the more gloomy outlooks provided by Ghemawat (2007) and other such scholars. That is not to suggest that Ghemawat's theory should be entirely discounted. However, we need to recall an old saying: "Always plan for the best, but prepare for the worst."

Case Study 1: Amore Pacific Goes to France[4]

When people think of the economic strengths of South Korea (hereinafter "Korea"), shipbuilding, automobiles, steel and IT are probably the immediate words that come into their minds. However, there is one Korean company which has made significant strides in an industry that Western companies have traditionally dominated: the cosmetics industry. Amore Pacific is Korea's leading high-end cosmetics brand, which became immensely successful among the growing middle-to-upper-class segment of Korean women. Amore Pacific's spectacular rise from being a humble, local niche player to a global cosmetics powerhouse is a success story, and one that

[4] Information for this case study is abstracted from the Amore Pacific website (www.amorepacific.com), *The New York Times* (2005b) and the DHC website (www.dhccare.com).

demonstrates the power of a carefully thought-out global standardization strategy.

The exponential rate of economic growth from the 1960s transformed the war-devastated Korea from one of the poorest nations in the world to the 13th largest trading nation in the world. The Korean population's concern quickly gravitated from basic survival necessities to more advanced utilities such as aesthetic beauty. Amore Pacific developed its products using ingredients long tried and tested by Korean women, who are very sophisticated consumers of cosmetic products. These ingredients are viewed as being completely natural and highly beneficial to enhancing women's beauty, namely green tea, Korean red ginseng and bamboo. In terms of product range, Amore Pacific focused on using these three key ingredients in items such as anti-aging cream, cleansers and moisturizers as well as in the cosmetics lines. The results were fabulous, and Amore Pacific became a household name in Korea.

However, the firm's success did not stop in Korea. Amore Pacific's formula for success — high-quality cosmetic products with natural ingredients — had a strong appeal to other Asian consumers who had similar tastes. Its reputation began to spread among the Asian countries, in particular Japan, which is renowned for its sophisticated cosmetics industry. Before long, Amore Pacific products were competing with the likes of Shiseido and SK-II (a Procter & Gamble brand) of Japan. Thus, products developed initially only for the Korean market could be applied in the exact same form throughout the Asian market, particularly Japan and then China. However, this may not seem unusual, as it is not uncommon for regional markets to share similarities in tastes and therefore demands. The real test would come when launching Amore Pacific in the Western markets such as Europe and the US.

Amore Pacific has since launched its products on a global scale and has garnered success through a series of very interesting developments. Amore Pacific has realized what other Asian cosmetics firms have not, that is, all women essentially pursue the same values when it comes to cosmetic products. Women want effective anti-aging and cleansing properties using the most natural and resultant ingredients.

Thus, Amore Pacific was able to market its products — which were created in Korea for Koreans — to women in the US and even in Europe, where the cosmetics market is known for being particularly sophisticated and difficult in which to gain a foothold. In fact, the company was even able to play up the "Asianess" of the products' ingredients as a developing trend in the well-being concept of Asian products via ancient knowledge of natural ingredients. Elevating a previously local product to the regional and finally to the global level, Amore Pacific is now a formidable global force in the global cosmetics industry.

Most recently, due to the launch of its perfume line, Amore Pacific has become the fourth-largest cosmetics firm in France, which is the world's most competitive market. Thus, as Levitt (1983) pointed out, as markets become more homogenized, the potential for massive growth, through the development of an appropriate standardized product, increases exponentially. However, the case of Amore Pacific is a little counterintuitive. While Levitt focuses on low-cost and high-quality products being the most likely candidates for standardization, Amore Pacific's products cater to those interested in high cost and high quality. Therefore, Amore Pacific is a good example not only of product standardization, but also of the ability to homogenize a luxury product in the global arena.

In a similar vein, Japan has witnessed the rise of one of its skincare leaders. The Daigaku Honyaku Center (DHC), established in 1972, is a Japanese firm manufacturing cosmetics. Similar to Amore Pacific, the company has built a strong reputation in Japan as a skincare company that utilizes the natural benefits provided by a recognizable yet unsophisticated raw material. In contrast to Amore Pacific, DHC started out using a key ingredient that was more recognizable to the Western customers than to the Asian customers — olives.

Intuitively, one could assume that Japanese consumers may have been reluctant to try olive-based products, since olives are not a familiar ingredient for Japanese consumers. Furthermore, Douglas and Wind (1987) would have us believe that access to Japanese consumers would be challenging given the discrepancy in taste between the Japanese and Western consumers. Familiarity and security are two friends that are difficult to part, and people across the globe tend to prefer products with ingredients that they are familiar with. However, due to a Japanese desire to emulate Western ideals, Japanese women were quick to try the product.

The product was a huge success, and DHC quickly became a household name throughout Japan and later in Korea and China as well. DHC skincare products, although manufactured in Japan, have been able to seamlessly integrate themselves into the Western cosmetics market. Western women consider olives to have amazing restorative powers, and thus the product instantly appealed to consumers in the US and Europe alike. Furthermore, there has been a growing trend in the West related to the use of Asian products. Although the olive is a Western ingredient, Western consumers may feel that the Japanese aspect of the product merely adds to, rather than detracts from, its appeal (see Fig. 4).

The Amore Pacific case and the DHC case both represent a high level of standardization, although the starting points were significantly different. There seems to be a desire by both sides of the globe to assimilate one another to a certain extent. Thus, the standardization comes from a meeting point somewhere in the middle of the spectrum rather than from the extreme point on one side or another, as the term "standardization" seems to suggest, as shown in Fig. 4. Perhaps, then, we can conclude that standardization is merely the desired meeting point of aspects of differentiation, which would certainly integrate both Levitt's (1983) and Friedman's (2005) supposition of "the world is flat" with Douglas and Wind's (1987) theory of "the world is spiky".

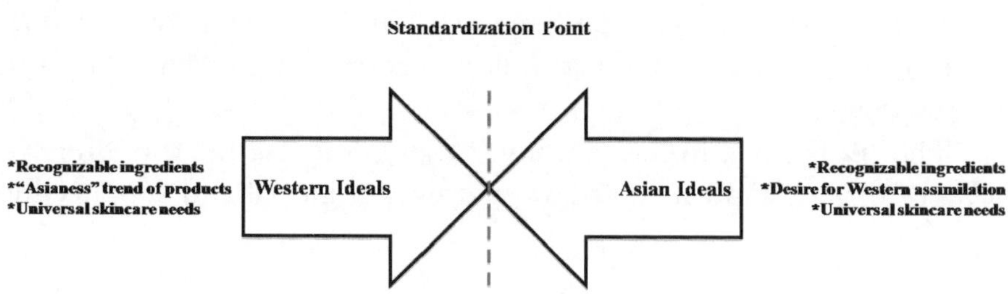

Fig. 4. The standardization point.

Case Study 2: Mythical Standards[5]

The Golden Arches are noted as the epitome of globalization, homogenization and standardization. Of course, we are talking about McDonald's, the (in)famous American fast food chain that has developed into a global empire. However, is McDonald's really that standardized? Can a product as personal as food be completely standardized? Douglas and Wind (1987) would answer to the contrary, while Levitt (1983) would be more than happy to use McDonald's as a representative case for his argument.

McDonald's was a local firm that focused on producing goods that catered strictly to American tastes. However, the concept of the restaurant was appealing on a global scale. The concept included hot, tasty and inexpensive food that could be delivered to the consumer in the least amount of time. As successful as the concept was, the product itself was proving difficult to sell. McDonald's was hugely lucrative in America, but less so in Europe and least of all in Asia. The logical reason was that different tastes exist in those regional and even individual markets.

Let's take a look at the Bulgogi Burger. This is an item that is specifically geared towards the Korean market and is not available in neighboring Japan or China. The Bulgogi Burger is not available in Japan, as the Japanese prefer their localized version of the Teriyaki Burger. In Italy, where people are picky about their cheese, the burger patty is draped in Parmigiano-Reggiano, not just your regular run-of-the-mill cheddar cheese slice. In Germany and Switzerland, both countries famous for beer, one can purchase a nice cold glass of local brew along with a McDonald's burger. In the Middle East, all of the meat must follow *halal* requirements (Muslim dietary laws); while in Israel, the products must follow *kosher* requirements (Jewish dietary laws).

The Bulgogi Burger, among others, represents the highest level of differentiation. It shows that even a global and supposedly

---

[5] Information for this case study is abstracted from the McDonald's official website (www.mcdonalds.com).

standardized firm, such as McDonald's, must cater to unique tastes on a country-by-country, regional or even religious basis. Therefore, the McDonald's story may confirm Douglas and Wind's (1987) hypothesis. However, despite McDonald's differentiation, core products such as the Big Mac, Double Cheeseburger and McChicken Sandwich, which define McDonald's, are still massively popular all over the world. The local and regional versions constitute a smaller proportion of the menus that McDonald's offers to its customers.

Another point that must be raised is the difference in appropriate strategy based on the functional-level division. While product standardization and differentiation remain separate concepts, it seems that marketing strategy, for the most part, needs to be thought of in terms of differentiation. Take a look at the examples provided below[6]:

- In 2002, Umbro, the UK sports manufacturer, had to withdraw its new trainers (sneakers) called the Zyklon. The firm received complaints from many organizations and individuals, as it was the name of the gas used by the Nazi regime to murder millions of Jews in concentration camps.
- Staff at the African port of Stevadores saw the internationally recognized symbol for "fragile" (i.e., broken wine glass) and presumed it was a box of broken glass. Rather than wasting space by keeping the boxes, they threw them all into the sea!
- Irish Mist (an alcoholic drink), Mist Stick (a curling iron from Clairol) and Silver Mist (Rolls Royce car) all flopped in Germany. *Mist* in German means "dung/manure". Fancy a glass of Irish dung?
- Managers at one American company were startled when they discovered that the brand name of the cooking oil they were marketing in a Latin American country translated into Spanish as "Jackass Oil".

---

[6] All examples are extracted from Kwintessential ("Cross cultural business blunders").

- American Motors tried to market its new car, the Matador, based on the image of courage and strength. However, in Puerto Rico, the name means "killer" and so the car was not popular on the hazardous roads in the country.
- A golf ball manufacturing company packaged golf balls in packs of four for convenient purchase in Japan. Unfortunately, the pronunciation of the word "four" in Japanese sounds like the word "death" and items packaged in fours are unpopular.

The above examples are amusing, but they also raise the question whether to standardize or not on a global scale. Thus, as mentioned previously, production and marketing strategies may require different paths and should not be simultaneously standardized.

Discussion Questions

1. Do you agree with Levitt's (1983) theorization of global versus multinational firms? Do global firms always have the advantage? Discuss.
2. Levitt (1983) used the analogy of a hedgehog and a fox. Can you think of firms that represent the fox well and firms that represent the hedgehog well?
3. Do you agree with Douglas and Wind's (1987) requisites for global standardization? Can you think of others that may be required for globalization?
4. Are standardization and differentiation just two sides of the same coin? Can both lead the firm to the same outcome? Discuss.
5. Do you agree that the 10% supposition is representative of an under-globalized world with the potential to become even less so? Why or why not?
6. Do you agree that McDonald's is pursuing a certain level of differentiation or is it merely an anomaly in a sea of standardization? Discuss.

CHAPTER 10

All Together Now...

Chapter Guideline

Standardization or differentiation? Globalization or localization? These dichotomies seem to be inherently conflicting. The debate over standardization has left us with more questions than answers. What is the appropriate strategy in an international setting? Can these apparently contradictory terms be reconciled to create a more comprehensive framework to understand the complex nature of global strategy? Yes, they can. The previous chapter highlighted the points of debate, and this chapter will provide some answers to the questions that linger in our minds.

Summary of Previous Models

We are now at the penultimate chapter of our long journey in the world of global business strategy. Based on a conceptual grasp of business strategy, we have delved deep into the issues pertaining to elevating business strategy to the global level. The result was a series of analyses by scholars who are seemingly contradictory, but convincing in their own right. Now, we look at some scholars who have tried to fuse all the existing studies to create a truly overarching view of understanding the complex and multidimensional nature of global business strategy.

10.1 Global Strategy: The Context

"To globalize or not to globalize: that is the question". This modified version of Hamlet's soliloquy used to be the most important question in international business during the 1970s and 1980s. Consequently, many studies have tried to shed light on this question, and many scholars have presented evidence that a global strategy or increasing the degree of globalization leads to better firm performance (Vernon 1971; Grant 1987; Daniels and Bracker 1989; Geringer *et al.* 1989).

Globalization, of course, is not a panacea for all the problems that a firm faces. This is a very important point to note, as globalization can just as easily detract from profitability as it can contribute to it, since going global requires incurring significant costs. Kim, Hwang and Burgers (1989), for example, empirically demonstrated that most firms that pursued international diversification into related and supporting sectors were able to achieve success, while others that attempted to internationalize into unrelated sectors were not so successful. However, what has also become apparent is that globalization provides amazing opportunities and firms must globalize in order to maintain or advance their competitiveness. Therefore, the question of "to globalize or not to globalize" has now evolved into "how to globalize most effectively". In this sense, Yip (1989) provides a detailed yet succinct analysis of whether and how to globalize firm strategy. The key point of Yip's analysis is illustrated in Fig. 1, which he calls "total global strategy".

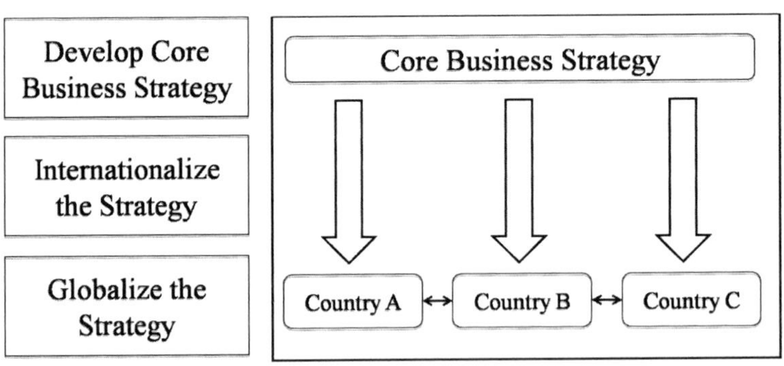

Fig. 1. Total global strategy.[1]

[1] Yip (1989).

Following Fig. 1, we can see that formulating a global strategy requires three concrete steps:

- *Developing a Core Business Strategy* — Every competitive firm possesses some kind of core, firm-specific advantage. This concept is similar to what Porter described as "strategic fits". This element is a necessary condition for firms to go global.
- *Internationalizing the Strategy* — This is when a firm elevates its firm-specific advantage to the global arena. This stage requires coordinating and configuring the firm's value chain activities according to the global setting.
- *Globalizing the Strategy* — The final stage is to generate synergies from linking dispersed activities. The numerous activities performed in various locations all combine to create a strong global strategic fit.

Therefore, the exogenous variables (industry globalization drivers) and endogenous variables (organization's ability to implement a global strategy and resources of business) all converge into setting global strategy levers. By considering these variables, we can assess the costs/benefits of implementing a global strategy.

What Is Global Strategy?

Yip (1989) distinguishes between a multidomestic strategy and a pure global strategy, and explains their implications on five dimensions.

- *Market Participation* — In a multidomestic strategy, countries are selected based purely on their market potential. However, in a global strategy, countries are selected based not only on their market potential, but also on their impact on the overall strategy.
- *Product Offering* — Products are tailored to match local tastes and needs in a multidomestic strategy. On the contrary, a purely

global strategy offers fully standardized products regardless of the market.

- *Location of Value-Added Activities* — All activities occur in each country in a multidomestic strategy. However, a global strategy requires a fully integrated and dispersed value activity that takes full advantage of differences among countries.
- *Marketing Approach* — In a multidomestic strategy, just like product offering, marketing is completely customized for individual countries. However, global marketing requires a uniform approach regardless of countries.
- *Competitive Moves* — A multidomestic strategy does not have to consider its impact on competition in other countries. However, global strategy managers must always keep in mind that a decision made in one location has an impact on another location.

Benefits of Global Strategy

So what are the advantages of global strategy? Yip (1989) provides the following answers:

- *Cost Reductions* — A company can increase the benefits from economies of scale by pooling production or other activities on a global scale. The second benefit is exploiting low factor costs in different countries. Third is exploiting flexibility, such as operating in multiple locations depending on the economic situation in each country.
- *Improved Quality of Products and Programs* — Firms with global strategies can focus on a few standardized products and programs. They can concentrate their resources to increase the quality of these selected few.
- *Enhanced Customer Preference* — Global availability, serviceability and recognition can enhance customer preference. Global suppliers,

such as fast food companies and credit card companies, can provide a multinational customer with a standard product around the world and gain from worldwide familiarity.

- *Increased Competitive Leverage* — A global strategy provides more opportunities for offense and defense. As Hamel and Prahalad (1985) described, a firm can gain a wider array of weapons in its strategic armory through globalizing its operations.

Drawbacks of Global Strategy

However, all is not rosy as there are clear tradeoffs in pursuing a global strategy.

- *Increased Coordination Costs* — A firm must incur substantial costs in terms of implementing appropriate mechanisms, at least in the initial phase of globalization.
- *Customer Preference Tradeoff* — As Douglas and Wind (1987) pointed out, standardized products may not be able to satisfy all customer tastes and may lead to losses in certain markets.
- *Lower Responsiveness* — Since a global strategy requires homogeneous marketing regardless of location, firms may be slow to react to changing local needs.

Finding the Balance

Considering these strengths and weaknesses of global strategy, the most crucial decision that firms have to make is *to what degree* a firm should globalize. Of course, this decision must be based on careful consideration of various factors. Yip (1989) discusses this balance through the framework shown in Fig. 2.

As we can see from this framework, certain industries have a high potential for globalization while others do not. Consider business A versus business D. While they are both operating in the same industry, the less globalized business A is outperforming the overglobalized

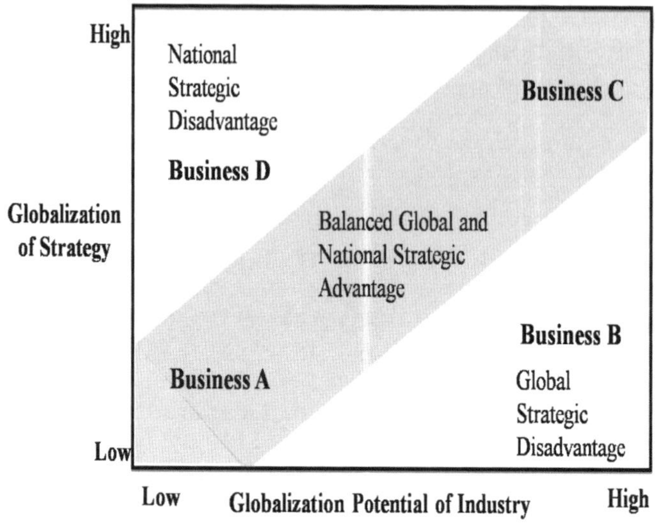

Fig. 2. Globalization potential of industry versus globalization of strategy.[2]

business D. On the other hand, in an industry of high globalization potential, the more globalized business C is performing better than the less globalized business B.

Industry Globalization Drivers

If the globalization potential differs from industry to industry, what drives these differences? Yip (1989) identifies four broad categories of drivers: market, cost, governmental and competitive.

- *Market Drivers* — Homogeneous customer needs, global customers, global channels and transferable marketing fall under this category. A homogeneous customer base leads to a global customer who is willing to buy the same product in multiple locations. This homogenization allows for uniform marketing, since customers now react similarly to the standardized product.

---

[2] *Ibid.*

Global channels of distribution link these market drivers to the producers.

- *Cost Drivers* — Obvious cost drivers are economies of scale and scope, since a global outreach allows firms to increase both of these elements. Another cost driver is enhanced sourcing efficiency from global outreach. Logistics also become more convenient and cheaper because the sales value relative to transportation cost increases.
- *Governmental Drivers* — These include government actions such as favorable trade policies, compatible technical standards and common marketing regulations. Government globalization drivers depend on the rules set by national governments and affect the use of all global strategy levers.
- *Competitive Drivers* — When a firm's activities are distributed among countries, a competitor's market share in one country affects its competitive position in another country. This is similar to Porter's discussion of the nature of global competition. Yip (1989) describes further possibilities for firms to actually enhance the globalization potential of an industry through interactions of national differences and competitors' moves.

Considering these complex variables that decide whether or not a firm should globalize, Yip (1989) concludes that successful international strategies have varying shades and degrees. First, a firm must have a clear understanding of the industry in which it operates. As shown in Fig. 2, overglobalization can actually lead to a strategic disadvantage depending on the drivers present in an industry. Next, global strategies require a significant level of initial fixed cost. Although a firm may reap tremendous benefits after these costs are installed, a firm must have the muscle to incur the initial short-term disadvantage. Lastly, an organization's culture, structure and people may not be suited for a global strategy. Firms from highly ethnocentric backgrounds may have difficulty implementing global strategies due to insufficient human resources.

Analysis

Yip's (1989) analysis presents a new look at the age-old debate between global and multidomestic strategies. In the previous chapter, we saw scholars such as Levitt (1983), Douglas and Wind (1987), and Ghemawat (2007) argue for or against the globalization of firm strategy. Yip succinctly summarizes the pros and cons of both strategies, and concludes that it is not a question of selecting one or the other, but of attaining the appropriate balance between the two depending on the various exogenous and endogenous variables present. Yip's article essentially provides us with many answers to the questions that we may have had from the previous chapter. However, as is always true in the world of academia, Yip has also left us with more questions that need to be addressed.

One point that must be raised is Yip's (1989) framework of total global strategy (see Fig. 1). The idea here is that a firm develops its core business strategy in its domestic market, internationalizes the strategy and then moves on to globalize it through integrating the strategy in various countries. As logical as this may sound, this framework is quite inadequate to explain global strategy from the Asian perspective. Firms from the US and Europe may have taken this route, as they developed a significant advantage from their domestic markets and then elevated their strategies to the global arena. This method was plausible for Western firms because they did not face any significant challenges from outside forces during their initial internationalization phases. Moreover, the global economic system evolved heavily in their favor and they did not need to modify their core business strategies too much in order to internationalize and then globalize.

However, when we look at the evolution of non-Western firms or latecomers, a different picture emerges. Because these firms cannot enjoy the various advantages that most Western firms had, non-Western firms must simultaneously modify their core business strategies as they internationalize. Therefore, in order to explain the non-Western evolution of global strategy, Fig. 1 must be slightly modified as depicted in Fig. 3.

While the visual difference is merely one-sided arrows replaced with two-sided arrows, the implications are profound. Western firms

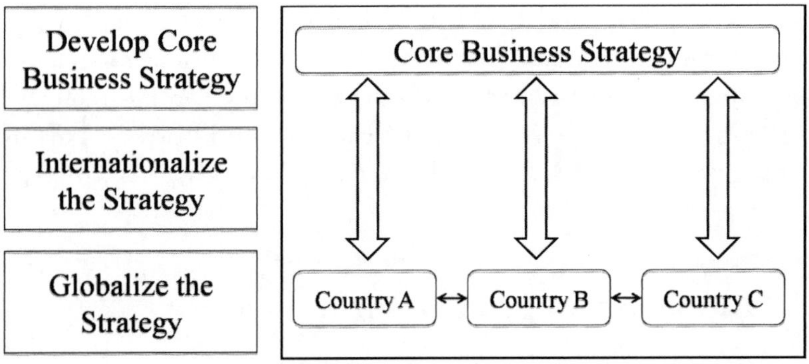

Fig. 3. Total global strategy for emerging multinational companies.

simply duplicate their success in their domestic markets on the global stage, while non-Western firms dynamically formulate their global strategy during their processes of globalization. This novel feature of latecomers has recently caught the attention of many scholars (Bartlett and Ghoshal 2000; Mathews 2002; Bonaglia *et al.* 2007; Ghemawat and Hout 2008; Khanna and Palepu 2006).

This distinction is crucial because it becomes very important in explaining how emerging multinational corporations (EMNCs) from developing countries have been aggressively adopting international strategies in recent years. Since EMNCs start off in a more integrated global economy, they must simultaneously formulate their core strategy while they face global competition. This may seem disadvantageous at first glance, but latecomers do have certain advantages which they can exploit. As Bartlett and Ghoshal (2000) noted, EMNCs can quickly emulate the more established global players and then sidestep them to produce a plus-alpha to their added value. For example, in mature industries such as the white goods industry, many corporations from emerging markets have acquired global competitiveness in a very short period of time and added their plus-alpha to create a "cheap and chic" line of white goods to global consumers (Bonaglia *et al.* 2007).

Some scholars have even proposed the "born global" model, which describes small- and medium-sized start-ups that go global in the very early stage (first or second year) of their inception. Born globals are defined as those that, from inception, pursue a vision of becoming global and often globalize their business rapidly without an earlier long-term domestic or internationalization period (Luostarinen and Gabrielsson 2004; Oviatt and McDougall 1994). Therefore, the dynamic strategies of EMNCs and born globals in the new integrated global economy leave us with another very interesting topic for further discussion.

10.2 Global Strategy: The Firm

If Yip (1989) presented us with an overarching view of the globalization phenomenon, it is now time to zoom in our lenses and look at how the firm itself should be managed within this context. Bartlett and Ghoshal (1989), in their seminal work, presented a detailed look at the organizational model that firms should follow in this increasingly globalized world.

However, before we look at the firm itself, it is important to clarify the differences in terminology. While Yip's analysis was based on "multidomestic versus global", Bartlett and Ghoshal use the term "transnational" to describe the new organizational model. This typological difference is important and Table 1 summarizes the categorization.

The key difference between the terms "international" and "transnational" is that assets and capabilities are dispersed yet interdependent for a transnational strategy. In other words, a transnational has all the strengths of a multinational (local responsiveness, etc.) combined with those of a global company (standardization, scale economies, etc.). A transnational does not simply centralize or decentralize, but makes selective and complex decisions which allow the organization to exploit the maximum benefit from both ends of the spectrum.

What emerges is a very different type of organization that can truly maximize the full benefits of global operations. It takes the best of everything and forges a formidable advantage against other firms. The interaction between subsidiaries and the headquarters is not one-sided but efficiently dynamic, as a perfectly integrated yet diversified organization interacts extensively to take advantage of the various differences that exist among locations.

Table 1. Organizational characteristics of the transnational.[3]

Organizational characteristics	Multinational	Global	International	Transnational
Configuration of assets and capabilities	Decentralized and nationally self-sufficient	Centralized and globally scaled	Sources of core competence centralized, others decentralized	Dispersed, interdependent, and specialized
Role of overseas operations	Sensing and exploiting local opportunities	Implementing parent company strategies	Adapting and leveraging parent company competencies	Differentiated contributions by national units to integrate worldwide operations
Development and diffusion of knowledge	Knowledge developed and retained within each unit	Knowledge developed and retained at the center	Knowledge developed at the center and transferred to overseas unit	Knowledge developed jointly and shared worldwide

Building and Managing the Transnational

However, as attractive as the above proposition sounds, not many can actually achieve such a complex feat. Building and managing a transnational is not an easy task, as it requires dealing with several delicate challenges. The three main sources of difficulties come from balancing diverse perspectives and capabilities within an organization, developing flexible coordination processes, and unifying diverse elements within the organization under a shared vision (see Table 2 for an overview).

- *Balancing Perspectives and Capabilities* — As we can see from Table 2, a transnational firm's competitiveness is derived from dispersed and interdependent assets and resources. Therefore, managers must be able to aggregate diverse perspectives and

[3] Bartlett and Ghoshal (1989).

Table 2. Building and managing the transnational.[4]

Strategic capability	Organizational characteristics	Management tasks
Global competitiveness	Dispersed and interdependent assets and resources	Legitimizing diverse perspectives and capabilities
Multinational flexibility	Differential and specialized subsidiary roles	Developing multiple and flexible coordination processes
Worldwide learning	Joint development and worldwide sharing of knowledge	Building shared vision and individual commitment

capabilities without having one segment of the organization dominate the other.

- *Developing Flexible Coordination Processes* — Since a transnational firm requires increased integration between departments and nations, the organization takes on a much more multidimensional and complex landscape. In order to manage this properly, the transnational firm must consider three issues: (a) flow of parts, components and finished goods; (b) flow of funds, skills and other scarce resources among units; and (c) flow of intelligence, ideas and knowledge.
- *Unifying the Organization through Vision and Co-option* — All firms need to instill their employees with a common vision to direct the diverse resources toward one strategic direction. This becomes especially important when managing a complex organizational structure embedded in a transnational firm.

Analysis

The key contribution of Bartlett and Ghoshal (1989) is the conceptualization of an ideal firm that can exploit the maximum benefits of

[4] *Ibid.*

globalization. The transnational organization, like a chameleon, is a new kind of animal that can be highly standardized yet responsive at the same time. By introducing the organizational characteristics of different firms, the two authors have provided a typological categorization that can be used to distinguish firms according to their degree of internationalization.

However, in order to truly understand the implication, it is necessary to analyze these typologies from an all-encompassing framework (see Fig. 4). When we see Bartlett and Ghoshal's (1989) typologies according to this framework, several questions immediately emerge. The first one is the authors' basic idea that a firm evolves from domestic → multinational → global → international → transnational. As we can see from Fig. 4, the authors' idea becomes problematic because it would mean that a firm evolves to the lower right-hand corner (multinational), moves to the upper left (global),

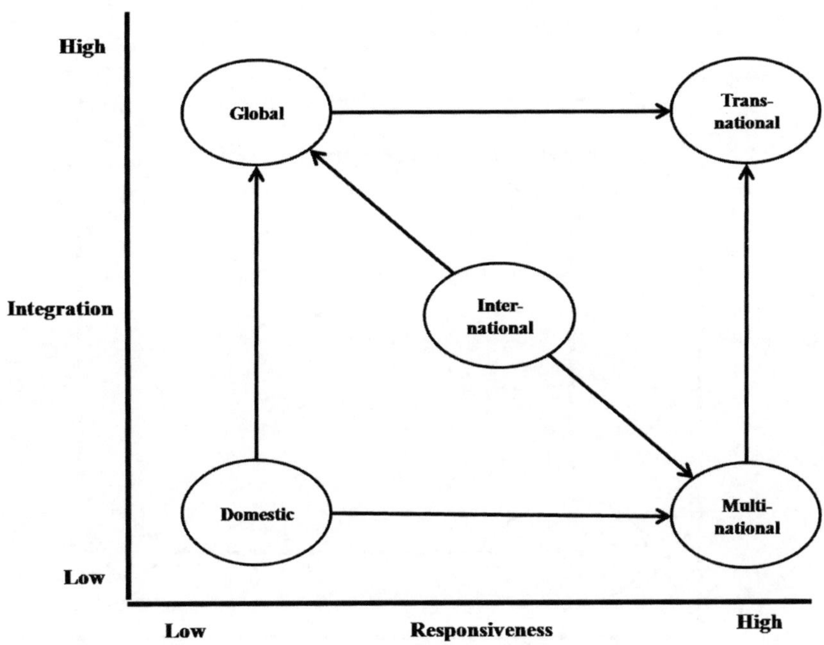

Fig. 4. Domestic, multinational, global, international and transnational: the I-R framework.

comes to the center (international) and then mysteriously jumps to the final upper right-hand corner (transnational). This point is crucial because the authors assume that a firm that used to have a federation of decentralized and nationally self-sufficient units will centralize its operation and then decentralize again. This seems highly complicated and inefficient, even intuitively.

A better way to look at the evolution of firms is to think of multinational and global as different paths to reach the final stage (transnational), rather than viewing global as a more evolved form of multinational. Furthermore, rather than using the term "multinational", it is typologically more precise to use the term "multidomestic" since we are discussing individual markets. Therefore, when we correct this flaw, we can see that a more organized and sensible framework emerges (see Fig. 5).

What we can see is that the ultimate goal is transnational, which is characterized by high levels of integration and responsiveness.

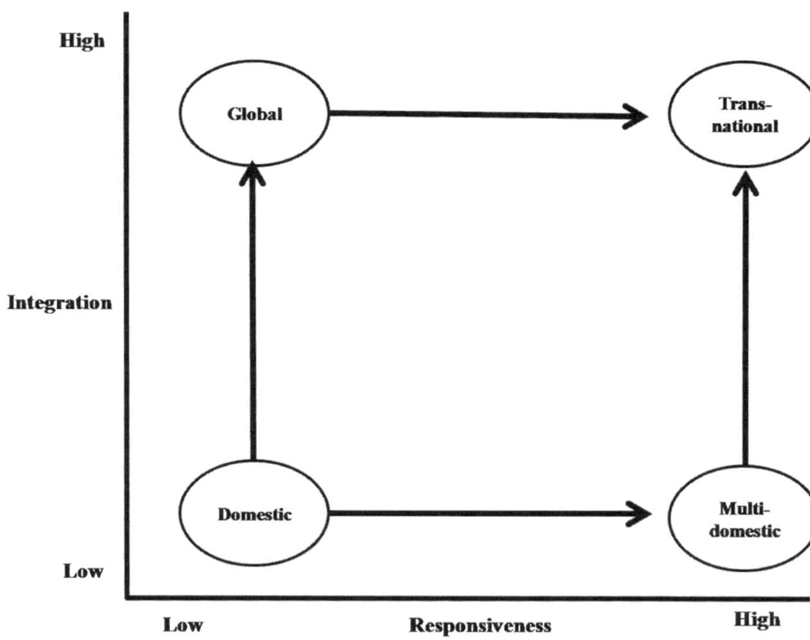

Fig. 5. Modified framework.

The path to reach that goal can be achieved either through standardizing aggressively (global) or developing a high responsiveness to individual markets (multidomestic). Afterwards, in order to reach a transnational stage, companies in the global stage can gradually increase their responsiveness while multidomestic companies can integrate their previously decentralized units to reach the purely global stage.

10.3 Global Strategy: The Manager

If we liken this chapter to a plane journey through the world of globalization, we can say that Yip (1989) presented us with a detailed flight map, while Bartlett and Ghoshal (1989) analyzed the optimal jet plane that we need to successfully navigate through this volatile world. Now, Kedia and Mukherji (1999) provide a detailed account of the requirements of the pilot who can fly the jet through the world of globalization.

It is apparent from our previous discussion that a firm which can exploit the full benefits of globalization is different from the organizations of the past. Therefore, the people who manage this multidimensional and intricately integrated organization must have a different mindset as well.

Changing Orientation of Managers

In the past, manager training was mainly focused on "hard" issues such as cost reduction, manufacturing and budget allocation. However, these hard issues can no longer remain the most important sources of competitiveness, as most valid competitors are increasingly competent in these basic factors. Therefore, the orientation is now changing to "soft" issues such as values, culture, vision, leadership style, innovation and risks. The issues that global managers must deal with are far more eclectic and complex in scope, and require a different mindset than that of the past. This shift in mindset is illustrated in Fig. 6. The important point to note in Fig. 6 is that this framework suggests a holistic orientation. Rather than focusing on hard or soft

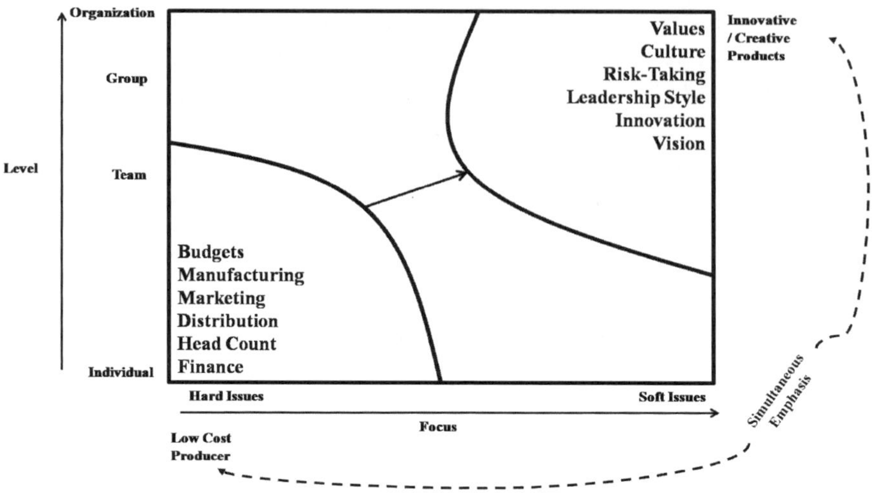

Fig. 6. Changing orientation of global managers.[5]

issues, a global manager must do both and balance the two aspects to the firm's best advantage.

Framework to Develop a Global Perspective

Now that we have an understanding of the shifting orientation, we must look at the necessary tools for achieving this shift. Kedia and Mukherji (1999) suggest that a global mindset is required to achieve this holistic orientation. In addition, two distinct aspects — knowledge and skills — need to be cultivated for this kind of mindset. The overall relationship is defined in Fig. 7.

Knowledge for a Global Mindset

A global manager must be equipped with socio-political, economic and cultural perspectives. These requisites give a global manager

[5] Kedia and Mukherji (1999) [adapted from Tichy 1992].

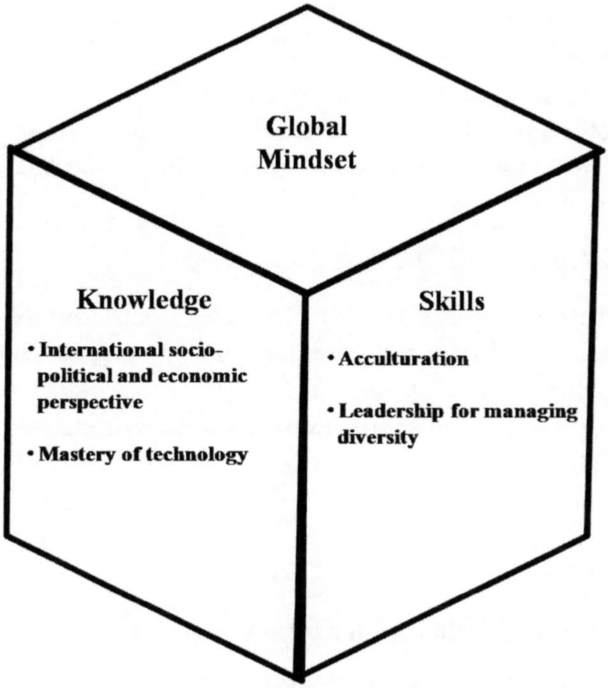

Fig. 7. Developing a global perspective.[6]

a firm grasp of how various global issues affect the firm's operations. Mastery of technology is also important because it has revolutionized various aspects of a firm's operation including manufacturing, processes and services. The impact that a technological development has is clearly exponential, especially when compared with the past.

Skills for a Global Mindset

If knowledge is the building block of a global mindset, skills allow the manager to execute his or her knowledge in the field.

---

[6] *Ibid.*

Acculturation, which refers to the process of becoming privy to other cultures through constant interaction, is crucial because of the multicultural nature of global operations. Acculturation, therefore, enables managers to map out this seemingly unmanageable task because it familiarizes managers in dealing with this complex issue on a daily basis.

Development of a Global Mindset

As the above discussion set us with the end goal, now we must look at how to reach it. Kedia and Mukherji (1999) suggest four concrete actions that can help: (a) foreign travel; (b) teams made up of people from diverse backgrounds; (c) training; and (d) transfers to foreign locations. The point of these measures is that exposure to diverse working conditions and constant training are all-crucial to achieving a global mindset.

The Changing Mindset of Managers

In this section, Kedia and Mukherji (1999) trace how managerial mindsets have evolved throughout history and present a typological framework to understand this evolution. Table 3 outlines the changes in managerial perspectives, according to the evolution of firm strategy from ethnocentrism to geocentricism, as a firm evolves from international to transnational.

Table 3. Changing managerial perspectives.[7]

Mindset	Outlook	Strategy
Ethnocentrism: Home Country Perspective	Centralized/Controlled	International
Polycentrism/Regiocentrism: Host Country Perspective	Decentralized/Autonomous	Multinational
Geocentrism: Global Perspective	Networked/Interdependent	Transnational

[7] *Ibid.*

Table 4. The four mindsets and global perspectives.[8]

Mindset	Defender	Explorer	Controller	Integrator
Level of Global Perspective	None	Surface level	Intermediate level	Deep level
Global Identify				
Self	Maintain self-sufficiency	Define differences	Redefine self	Integrate
Others	Acknowledge	Explore	Control	Leverage diversity

Managerial Mindsets

Next, we must take a look at the typological distinctions of different mindsets and how they are evolving. Four categories are constructed in Table 4: (a) defender; (b) explorer; (c) controller; and (d) integrator. Each category has a different mindset on global perspective and identity.

- *Defender* — This is the traditional managerial mindset that was predominant before the wave of globalization. A defender maintains a world in which all outsiders are potential competitors and threats to its position. Therefore, a defender frequently asks for protection from foreign competition.
- *Explorer* — An explorer is more open to foreign opportunities, but is still cautious of allowing them into its own organization. Managers with this kind of mindset typically occupy a dominant position in the domestic market, but have a weak presence outside.
- *Controller* — Managers in this category are more open and globalized than managers in the former two categories, and are willing to take more daring approaches in going abroad. However, the mentality is still dominated by control and is not fond of bestowing foreign subsidiaries with significant autonomy or decision-making

[8] *Ibid.*

power. Firms with these kinds of managers may have a significant international presence, but will still prefer to retain much of the central decision-making authority in headquarters.

- *Integrator* — This describes the ideal mentality of global management, as it integrates and leverages diversity. An integrator has the ability to organize and manage a complex web of multidimensional and multicultural operations, and enjoys the full benefits of globalization. Overall, managers in this category possess a much more flexible, dynamic and coordinated mindset.

Strategizing and Integrating Globally

A global manager requires specific skills that are necessary for integrating, coordinating and leveraging (see Fig. 8). While each of the three actors in Fig. 8 has its specific field (specialization), all must keep a global perspective in mind at all times (integration), as represented by the rectangular box in the middle. More specifically,

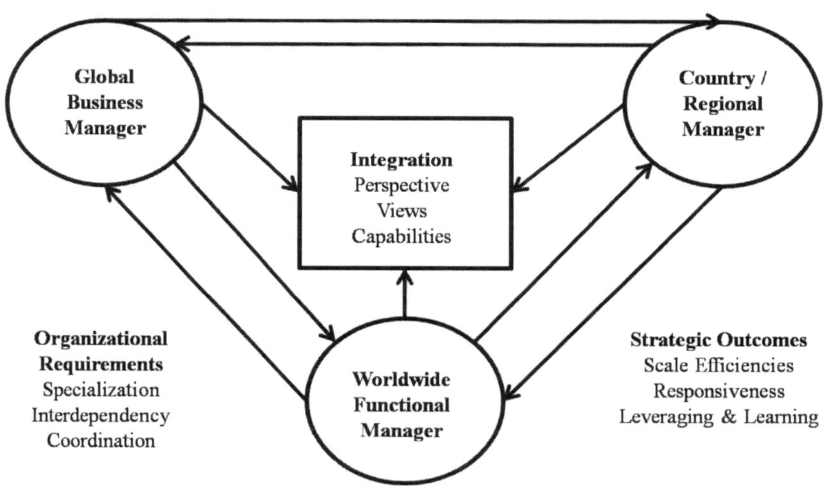

Fig. 8. Integrating and strategizing globally.[9]

[9] *Ibid.* [adapted from Bartlett and Ghoshal 1992].

a global business manager is responsible for the coordination of the whole operation, whereas a country manager is responsible for local responsiveness. In terms of the integration-responsiveness (I-R) framework, a global business manager integrates while a country manager responds. The worldwide functional manager oversees the interaction between the two in order to ensure that the organization as a whole is moving towards a singular vision. The dynamics among these three actors demonstrate that no matter which function an individual performs in a transnational organization, he or she must be constantly aware that his or her action affects others and the organization as a whole.

Analysis

Perlmutter (1969) systematically categorized different types of worker attitudes and explained the various obstacles that prevented workers from acquiring a multicultural and globalized outlook. Perlmutter identified three distinct types of worker orientation (which can be loosely interpreted as attitude, perspective or outlook): (a) ethnocentric; (b) polycentric; and (c) geocentric. As the names aptly convey, the degree of global orientation increases from ethnocentric to geocentric. What Kedia and Mukherji (1999) describe as the ideal worker is a further refinement and extension of Perlmutter's geocentric concept.

Human resources have always been key to a firm's success, and will become increasingly so. This is why so many firms take great care in choosing the right people for the organization. In this sense, Kedia and Mukherji (1999) provide a very interesting and useful insight into what kind of person is suited to lead a transnational organization: a coordinator with an open mind and the ability to integrate complex tasks and elements into a shared direction. It is without a doubt that the profiles of desirable employees are rapidly shifting and will shift even further in the future. Traditional workers' attitudes (especially preferred by Asian companies) such as diligence and subservience are becoming less desirable, while creativity and multicultural sensitivity are becoming much more valuable.

Asian companies, especially those with a strong collectivist culture and a vertical hierarchy structure, have difficulty accepting the need for a geocentric attitude. Unlike Western European nations or the United States, which are mostly multiracial and multicultural nations, Asian countries such as Japan, Korea and China are largely homogeneous in terms of their composition. Homogeneity leads to ethnic nationalism, which also influences the corporate culture to be rather ethnocentric. While recent efforts by Japanese and Korean multinationals have been geared towards adopting geocentric company goals and hiring more geocentric employees, there is still a long way to go in terms of achieving a truly geocentric corporate culture because of the deeply ingrained ethnocentric practices and culture.

Another point that needs to be made regarding human resources is the need for strategic training. In the past, many assumed that formulating, implementing and understanding strategy could only be done by a gifted, elite few. Therefore, the managerial structure was highly vertical, like in the military, in which top executives would unilaterally issue orders down to the bottom and require them to execute. It is unsurprising, therefore, that many corporate titles, such as Chief Executive Officer, have their roots in the military ranking system. However, this kind of vertical organizational measure is no longer desirable and could impede the adoption of a geocentric corporate culture. In an era of rapid globalization and an increased need for a nimble yet multidimensional organizational structure, a vertical organizational dynamic will only lead to rigidity and failure. What is needed then is for all employees, from bottom to top, to have a firm grasp of the strategic direction that the company is heading towards. In order to achieve this feat, it is crucial to abandon the traditional, elitist attitude on strategy.

But how do we achieve this? The most important step would be to provide concrete training in utilizing and understanding analytical frameworks. Frameworks, unlike theories, are highly applicable and can be easily understood. While some business managers lament the fact that business frameworks are abstract and unrealistic, this is based on a shallow understanding of the power of analytical frameworks. Frameworks are shortcuts to understanding real-world phenomena and, by having employees who possess a solid understanding of various frameworks, firms can mobilize their employees toward a desirable strategic direction with relative ease.

Case Study 1: Chinese Lenovo Goes Global[10]

Headlines over the past few years have undoubtedly highlighted the ambitions of many large Chinese firms that are pursuing an aggressive internationalization drive. In recent years, we have seen the China National Offshore Oil Corporation make an incredibly gutsy, albeit failed, bid of US$19.6 billion for the US-based Unocal; we have heard of scores of buyouts, takeovers and mergers orchestrated by Chinese companies; and firms such as Huawei and Haier are beginning to make names for themselves abroad. Although we have yet to see a truly global Chinese firm emerge from the formerly centralized economy, one firm stands out from the rest of the crowd: Lenovo. As you read this, you may be fondly looking over at your laptop computer sitting on top of your desk or thinking about the one in your bag at your feet. Why? Because it may just be a Lenovo laptop.

Lenovo was founded in 1984 by a group of 11 Chinese engineers and was originally known as Legend Group Ltd. It started out as a fairly small domestic PC manufacturing firm. While maintaining its roots and original goal, the firm has since grown into the largest PC manufacturing firm in China and the fourth-largest PC manufacturer in the world after Hewlett-Packard and Dell of the US and Acer of Taiwan. In such a short time, the company has undergone a tremendous evolution and it is interesting to look at this evolution from the perspectives afforded by Yip (1989), Bartlett and Ghoshal (1989), and Kedia and Mukherji (1999).

Yip (1989) stated that a firm's goal is to move from being multidomestic to global. There are five areas in which a firm should desire to become global: market participation, product offering, location of value-added activities, marketing approach and competitive moves.

---

[10] Information for this case study is abstracted from the Lenovo official website (www.lenovo.com), *BusinessWeek* (2008) and *International Herald Tribune* (2008).

In terms of market participation, Lenovo has seemingly moved away from a multidomestic strategy. The company intentionally moves into markets not just for their market potential, but also for their wider-reaching strategic impacts. Lenovo, as a Chinese firm, understands that in order to become a global firm, it cannot be identified solely as a Chinese firm. Thus, having a presence in more developed and highly globalized areas such as the US, Europe and Singapore is essential to Lenovo's overall strategy. We can therefore identify Lenovo as being more global in this aspect.

Lenovo's product offering is fairly standardized. The firm offers two types of products, laptops and desktops, which are subdivided into ThinkPads and IdeaPads. While ThinkPads are more suitable for business or commercial purposes, IdeaPads are better used as personal computers. Each computer is, of course, engineered to a very high standard. However, designs, colors and options are fairly limited, which is why we believe that its product offering is more standardized than tailored to local tastes. Therefore, we can also assume that Lenovo has a more global mold from this viewpoint.

The locations of value-added activities are multidomestic when independent of each other and global when fully integrated and dispersed. Lenovo has developed a business model that it dubs "worldsourcing". Essentially, the firm's ideas, operations and resources are literally borderless. It does not have a global headquarters, but rather has instituted a distributed management structure that places operational hubs around the world. These hubs interact fully with each other in a multi-way communication format. So rather than seeing the typical hub-and-spoke setup that most firms have, Lenovo has a spider-web network through which resources can flow easily. Thus, according to Yip (1989), Lenovo has a global strategy in its location of value-added activities.

With regards to the marketing approach, a multidomestic strategy would provide a more customized marketing approach for each country, whereas a global strategy would provide a uniform marketing approach. Lenovo pursues a very uniform marketing approach, which is evident from its official website. Lenovo does not change its marketing approach for each country, except for the language in which the product is marketed. Therefore, Lenovo's marketing approach is also based on a global strategy.

Lastly, we must look at Lenovo's competitive moves. Lenovo is a highly integrated firm that relies on "world-sourcing" as its business model. This means that every aspect of Lenovo's operations is integrated to a high degree and operations affect each other directly. Lenovo benefits from this high level of integration, making the company's strategy fairly global.

Therefore, according to Yip's (1989) framework, Lenovo can be identified as one of the first Chinese firms to truly go global in all aspects of its strategic endeavors. However, Yip's framework does not inform us of how Lenovo has achieved this level of globalization. Using the I-R framework, we can note that Lenovo is placed in the upper left-hand corner with a high level of integration and a low level of responsiveness (see Fig. 9). Now we must ask whether the ultimate point should really be in that upper left-hand corner.

According to Bartlett and Ghoshal (1989), a firm's ultimate move is to become a transnational firm. More specifically, they imply that the firm's total assets and capabilities must be dispersed yet interdependent. The firm should possess the strengths of a multinational as well as a global firm. For example, having a high level of local responsiveness while simultaneously possessing the strengths of a global firm shows a high level of integration. This requires a much more complex configuration of activities for the firm.

Again utilizing the I-R framework, we can follow Bartlett and Ghoshal's (1989) logic when explaining the development of a firm. In the upper right-hand corner lies the transnational. A transnational demonstrates a high level of integration coupled with a high level of responsiveness. Having already applied the I-R framework to Yip's (1989) interpretation of a firm, we know that Lenovo lies in the upper left-hand side of the framework. Thus, we can determine that Lenovo can be classified as a global firm (see Fig. 9). However, a point of contention may be how Lenovo actually reached the global position. Was the firm able to bypass the multinational stage through its 2005 acquisition of IBM's ThinkPad division? Anyhow, Lenovo has yet to become a truly transnational firm.

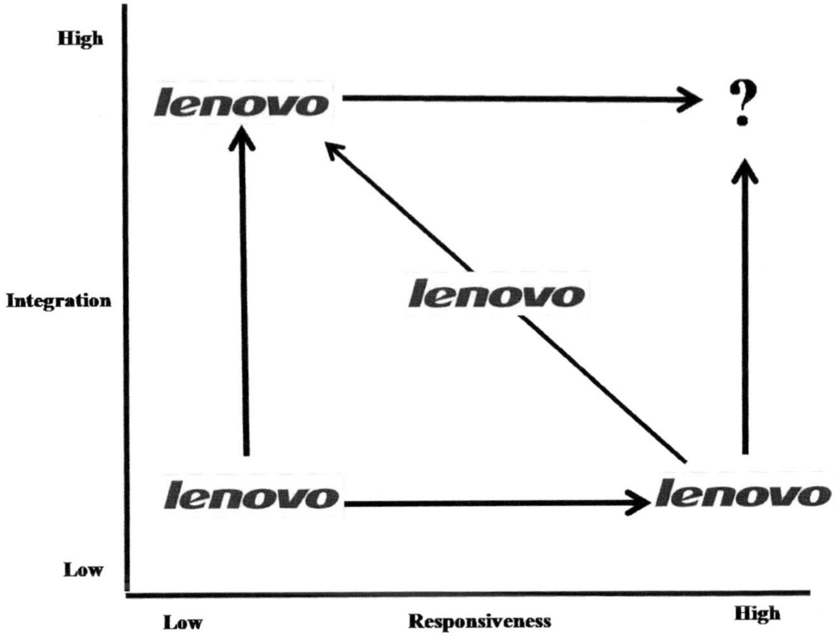

Fig. 9. Lenovo's position in relation to organizational characteristics of domestic, multinational, global, international and transnational types.

Kedia and Mukherji (1999) offer a viewpoint from a management perspective on how to reach the final stage of transnationalism. They argue that management of days gone by was overly focused on hard issues such as cost reduction, manufacturing and budget allocation. Today, soft issues such as firm values, culture, vision and leadership are often more important than hard issues. However, changing from one focus to another is not the issue. Rather, finding the balance is the most important aspect for an efficient management.

Kedia and Mukherji (1999) identify four different types of managers: the defender, the explorer, the controller and the integrator. Sticking with our I-R framework, we can place these four types into the framework in order to analyze current positions and future management strategy (see Fig. 10). The defender can be placed in the lower left-hand (domestic) corner due to its emphasis on the domestic market and fear of the international market.

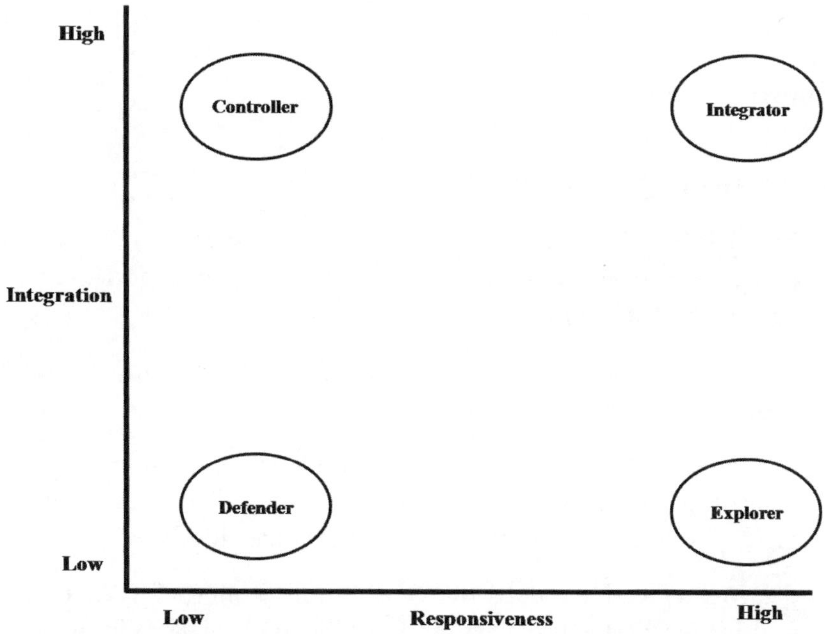

Fig. 10. Management styles from an I-R framework perspective.

The explorer can be placed in the lower right-hand (multidomestic) corner due to its acknowledgment of the importance of foreign opportunities and its initial parlay into foreign markets. The controller can be placed in the upper left-hand (global) corner, as it is willing to take a far more coordinated approach to going abroad. Finally, the integrator can be classified as a transnational manager (upper right-hand corner), as the integrator is able to integrate and leverage diversity, which is very different from the other management styles.

According to Fig. 10, Lenovo is located in the upper left-hand corner (i.e., controller). Lenovo's strategy could be successful, partly because in 2005 the company acquired the personal computer division of IBM, which is a well-established and internationally experienced company. If Lenovo had not purchased the division of IBM, the company might have gone through all the necessary international business and cultural experiences. The purchase of a renowned global company, or an alliance with it, may be a fast route to becoming a global company for a latecomer, such as Lenovo.

Discussion Questions

1. Yip (1989) talks of five global strategy levers. Are any of the five elements now obsolete or can you think of an additional lever to add to the list? Explain.
2. Do you agree with Yip's (1989) benefits and drawbacks of having a global strategy? Why or why not?
3. Bartlett and Ghoshal (1989) offer an explanation of terminology regarding multinational, global, international and transnational firms. Do you agree with the definitions provided?
4. Previously, we have used the term "multidomestic". Where does multidomestic fit into Bartlett and Ghoshal's (1989) framework?
5. According to Bartlett and Ghoshal (1989), the final destination is not global but transnational. Do you agree with this perspective? Discuss.
6. In your opinion, is Lenovo a multinational, global, international or transnational firm? Explain your choice.

CHAPTER 11

Dynamic Perspectives on Globalization

Chapter Guideline

In this final chapter, we will look at the critical relationship between the external environment and the firm itself. Are firms prisoners of the given environment or can they proactively change it? This is a critical question that must be examined because much of the existing literature is focused on explaining how firms can succeed in a given environment. This chapter will present cutting-edge views on this critical issue so that we can gain a firm grasp of the link between the exogenous and endogenous variables that determine the world of global business strategy.

Summary of Previous Models

Our long journey into the world of global business strategy is now approaching the end as we come to the final chapter. Hopefully, the reader has been able to grasp a firm understanding of the cutting-edge issues of global business strategy. While we have seen many scholars' viewpoints on numerous subjects, one common denominator that runs through all of them has been the unilateral focus on either the endogenous or exogenous variables of business strategy. Controllable variables and uncontrollable variables have been looked at in great detail, but the link between the two groups has yet to be analyzed. This chapter will discuss the possibility of how firms can influence the exogenous variables and change the very environment in which they operate. The answer to this question may leave us with profound implications as to how we should perceive and execute global business strategy.

11.1 Controlling the Uncontrollable

Are we prisoners or masters of our destinies? This is a question which many scholars have pondered upon. Before the advent of scientific thinking and enlightenment, human beings were generally overwhelmed by the seemingly insurmountable power of nature and held a deterministic view of human destiny. However, passing the Enlightenment and Renaissance periods, human beings started to develop a more proactive mindset under the premise that humans are masters of their own destinies. Indeed, the human conception of the link between the endogenous and exogenous variables of life has significantly evolved throughout history. As Machiavelli, the great Renaissance thinker, once wrote: "God is not willing to do everything, and thus take away our free will and that share of glory which belongs to us" (Machiavelli 1532, reprinted 2003, p. 82).

The discipline of international business is no exception to this general trend, and many scholars have pondered on whether strategic decisions can actually shape the business environment we operate in. Surprisingly, a majority of scholars and managers assume a deterministic view and regard the business environment as fixed. This is quite surprising, considering the modern and forward-looking nature of international business as a discipline. The root of this trend lies in the inherent volatility and effervescent nature of international business. Because myriads of variables interact on a daily basis to constantly create new and unfamiliar situations, scholars and managers have come to believe that business environments are essentially uncontrollable.

However, business is largely a human phenomenon, and we are all components of this apparently uncontrollable phenomenon. If the fundamental constituent unit of business is humans, it is also reasonable to argue that human will has the power to change the fundamentals of the phenomena we observe in international business.

Of course, this is not to deny the immovable fact that business is significantly affected by uncontrollable variables such as weather, climate, terrain and so on. However, unlike natural science, the *raison d'être* of social science is to derive general implications and prescriptions to provide shortcuts to understanding the real world. Social science should not only concern itself with learning a theory, but also provide a concrete guideline to translate the theory into practice.

As DeRond and Thietart (2007) noted, strategic management would seem pointless in a deterministic universe where yesterday's events dictate today's. Managers make strategic choices because they believe these will influence the course of events. They must also believe their choices to be freely made in principle, even if they often remain subject to various constraints. However, the causation between strategic choice and outcome seems nebulous at best. Some have even argued that in the case of small- and medium-sized enterprises, because of their small size, they are unable to induce much change through strategic choices and are largely bound to exogenous and endogenous constraints (Harvie and Lee 2002; Kirby and Watson 2003; Fogel *et al.* 2006).

Varadarajan, Clark and Pride (1992) take a deeper look into the power of strategic choice versus environmental determinism. The authors conclude that the most successful marketers can proactively create a favorable environment.

Environmental Determinism versus Strategic Choice

According to Varadarajan *et al.* (1992), the following are some representative analytical tools and frameworks derived from a deterministic view of business:

- *Product Life Cycle (PLC)* — Ever since Vernon introduced this concept in 1966, it has been one of the most important tools in marketing analysis.[1] The key to this concept is a stage model that maps the introduction, growth, maturity and decline of an

[1] See Vernon (1966) for further explanation.

industry, product or brand. This essentially leaves marketers with a passive role of managing the brand, product or industry based on the cycle which it goes through.

- *Matrix Approaches to Product Portfolio Analysis and Planning* — The matrix approach is a very useful analytical tool that organizes the strategic objectives and direction in a readily comprehensible framework. For example, the Boston Consulting Group's growth-share matrix designates the optimal strategic movement based on given market conditions. Similar to the PLC concept, the matrix approach assumes that market conditions are essentially uncontrollable, as its purpose is to map out the consequences of certain strategic choices within the confines of given constraints.
- *Profit Impact of Market Strategy (PIMS)* — This approach aggregates and analyzes historical data from thousands of small business units to answer the question, "What strategy pursued under what conditions produces what results?" This is a useful tool, as analysts and strategic planners can look back at past performances in order to devise appropriate future strategies. However, similar to the previous tools, it derives its assumptions from previous market conditions, which renders the analysis to be static.
- *The Industrial Organization Economics Approach* — Porter's *Competitive Strategy* (1980) is the epitome of this school of thought. This approach focuses on structural determinants of an industry that induce firm actions, which then lead to enhanced performance. Firm performance, therefore, is a function of structural elements such as threat of competitors and barriers to entry. Although Porter emphasized the power of firms to change the industrial structure to their advantage, many subsequent adherents of Porter's thoughts omitted this critical point and focused more on the deterministic aspects of his work.

The above discussion demonstrates how many adhere to the deterministic view of business strategy. However, some scholars and managers have challenged the conventional view with innovative strategic tools, which we will look at next.

Strategies to Influence Demand

- *Primary Demand Stimulation* — Demand can be divided into primary and secondary demands. Primary demand refers to the absolute size of the demand, while secondary demand refers to the share. Therefore, primary demand stimulation focuses on enlarging the market itself. Rather than passively waiting for the market growth to fluctuate, this method attempts to proactively control the market growth.
- *Product Evolutionary Cycle (PEC)* — Clearly named as an antithesis to the product life cycle (PLC) concept, the PEC does not define a sequence of cycles. Instead, the PEC only defines a beginning and an end, and believes that everything within these two extremes is controllable.
- *Strategic Self-Renewal* — This is designed as an antithesis to the matrix approach and is based on the premise that managerial action can actually influence the environment. Rather than looking at the past as fixed, this approach regards past market conditions as malleable and focuses on how managerial decisions could have altered the given environment.
- *Stimulational Marketing* — This is a very unique approach that attempts to create demand where there is none. For example, Akio Morita, the legendary CEO of Sony Corporation, explained that when Sony first came up with its first pocket-sized transistor radio in 1957, the item did not actually fit in most pockets. Instead of giving up, however, Morita decided to equip Sony salesmen with shirts with slightly oversized pockets to convey to potential buyers that the product was indeed pocket-sized.
- *Mandatory Consumption Stimulation* — Firms can promote consumption through inducing regulatory and legislative changes. For example, smoke detector manufacturers have stimulated

mandatory consumption after making lawmakers understand the importance of their products in fire safety.

Strategies for Macro-environmental Change

- *Issues Management* — Issues management refers to identifying and managing issues that might affect the firm's operations. For example, firms with an environmentally unfriendly image can change this public perception through advertising and corporate social responsibility (CSR) activities.
- *Corporate Political Activity* — Commonly known as lobbying, firms can actively induce politicians to alter regulations and public policies to be more favorable to the firm's operations.
- *Mega-Marketing Strategies* — Firms can strategically coordinate their economic, political and public relations activities in order to create a favorable operating environment. Mega-marketing strategies incorporate various tools to comprehensively manage and eliminate barriers that inhibit the firm's activities.
- *New Game Strategies* — Similar to the Blue Ocean concept, this strategy creates new demand in populations that were previously untapped through satisfying a whole new set of customer needs.

While many of the above tools have been the source of political controversy, they are available for firms to shape their own destinies rather than to react passively in a given environment.

Analysis

Bourgeois (1984) noted that if we were to follow the deterministic view of strategic management, we might as well resign ourselves to succumbing to the matrix of deterministic forces presented by environmental, technical and human forces which impinge on the freedom of choice. At best, management becomes a computational exercise; at worst, it becomes a reactive waiting game, exploiting contingencies only as they arise through political forces. This is especially problematic because the very purpose of strategy is to distinguish one's firm from its competitors.

Therefore, the strategic decisions managers make cannot be assumed to be the product of deterministic forces in their environments. Any such assumption would eliminate the very need for management as a discipline because it implies that the strategy of an organization follows, more or less automatically, a technical appreciation of its environmental situation. In essence, strategic management itself, according to Bourgeois (1984), cannot exist when confined within the boundaries of environmental determinism. Of course, this must not be misconstrued as neglecting the importance of environmental constraints. As a matter of fact, being overly confident in the power of humans could be equally misleading. As Hrebiniak and Joyce (1985) explain, strategic choice and environmental determinism are not mutually exclusive concepts, but are rather two separate independent variables that can be positioned on two separate continua to develop a typology of organizational adaptation.

The truth is that excessive faith in one idea or the other will never lead to the optimal outcome. The "golden mean", or *zhong yong* (中庸) in Chinese, is always an important perspective that we should keep in mind. For example, if a strategist adopts an overly deterministic view, he or she may be limiting himself or herself into mediocre achievements at best. On the other hand, if a strategist becomes overly ambitious and believes he or she can override any constraint through strategy, then he or she will jeopardize his or her organization through reckless decisions. Somewhere in the middle, we may find the "golden mean" to strategic management.

For scholars, this lesson can be applied to academic endeavors. For example, many young scholars are eager to incorporate bold and creative ideas in their academic pursuits. However, in many cases, they fail to obtain substantial progress because they forget that new ideas must be grounded on a thorough understanding of past studies. New ideas without a solid foundation are more than likely to end up being incoherent and incomprehensible. Other students suffer from the polar opposite problem, as they become overly prudent and limit themselves to previous studies. Any meaningful scholarly work must advance the state-of-the-art knowledge, even if its contribution is marginal. The key, therefore, is to do both and keep a healthy balance without overly swaying towards one side. For this purpose, keeping the following formula in mind will help students achieve the difficult task of contributing to academia:

$$\Delta + \alpha = \square + ?$$

This seemingly cryptic formula summarizes the secret to inducing proactive change based on a solid understanding of the past. Δ represents the past, accumulated knowledge which scholars must acquire through meticulous and extensive research. This provides a solid foundation for extending the frontiers of academia. α is the additional scholarly contribution to the existing body of knowledge. This represents the portion of the proactive change that we can induce through our ability. The combination of the two leaves us with $\square$, which represents the more complete body of knowledge that is derived by fusing the existing knowledge with our contribution. In any case, one cannot stand without the other, and all young scholars must note that both elements — the past and the future — must be present to truly make meaningful contributions. However, nothing is perfect as there are always further extensions that could be made by ourselves or by someone else, as represented by ?. This is a room for students and scholars to take constructive criticisms and further improve on their findings. Keeping this simple formula in mind will help us organize and understand our position as scholars in terms of how to make meaningful contributions to the academic discipline.

11.2 Standardization: Key to Success?

The rise of emerging markets is one of the most exciting topics in international business today. From the strategic management perspective, the big debate is centered on the appropriate strategy in entering these markets. Should multinationals simply elevate their existing strategies into these new arenas or should they customize their strategies to fit the specific market conditions in emerging markets? Khanna and Palepu (2006) noted that successful companies develop strategies for doing business in emerging markets that are different from those they use at home and often find novel ways of implementing them. However, scholars such as Springer and Czinkota (1999) urged that Western firms might find it beneficial to pursue a strategy of actually altering the emerging market environment step by step in order to move it closer to a functioning market economy. Rather than tailoring corporate strategy according to each market (as Khanna and Palepu prescribed), successful firms are those that change the market itself in order to create a favorable operating environment. So, what is the appropriate way to success in the emerging market?

A case in point for this section is the Central and Eastern European (CEE) region, which has emerged as an exciting new market with soaring consumer demands and rapid deregulation. The Czech Republic, Hungary, Poland, Slovakia and Slovenia rapidly transformed from a centrally planned economy to a liberal market democracy after the fall of the Iron Curtain. Their incorporation into the European Union (EU) also augmented their market attractiveness. Unsurprisingly, many international firms rushed in to gain a foothold in this arena because of the potentially lucrative payoff. However, the fundamental dilemma for many of these firms has been whether to differentiate or standardize their marketing foray into the CEE region. Intuitively, because the CEE region is a distinct market sphere with different consumer tastes, income levels and other elements, a strong case can be made for customization. However, a surprising number of firms in various industries have adopted the opposite strategy, i.e., a standardized approach in the CEE region. As Arnold, Chadraba and Springer (2001) concluded, although the CEE region is currently in a transition period (albeit a rapid one), the region will ultimately converge to the standards of industrialized Western European countries. Springer and Czinkota (1999) went further to state that a successful transformation of the formerly planned economies to vibrant market economies requires the development of a market orientation. This means that international firms have not only the opportunity, but the obligation, to help restructure society and business processes in order to improve the standard of living in the CEE region.

Schuh (2000) presents the reasons behind why large multinationals have adopted a standardized approach in entering the CEE region. The main analytical framework utilized by the author is illustrated schematically in Fig. 1.

As can be seen in this framework, both external and internal factors affect the decision of whether or not to standardize a marketing program. Furthermore, a marketing manager's variety of tools to decide on the degree of standardization is illustrated inside the square box in the center of Fig. 1. Based on this framework, Schuh (2000)

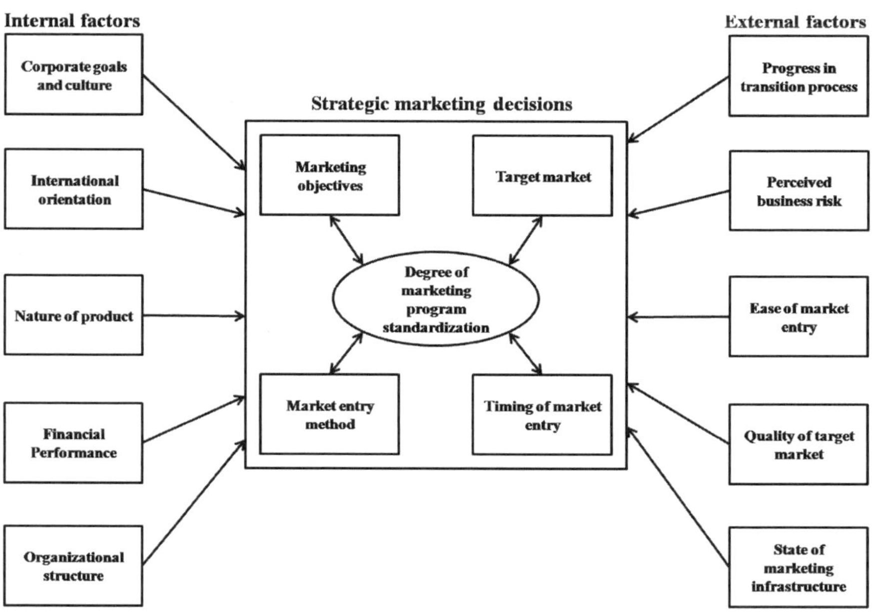

Fig. 1. Framework for determining international marketing program standardization.[2]

[2] Schuh (2000).

analyzed eight prominent companies that entered the CEE region: 3M, Royal Philips Electronics, McDonald's, Ogilvy & Mather, BBAG, Argana AG, Felix Austria and Henkel CEE.

The key findings indicate that out of the eight companies, six have pursued a highly standardized marketing program while the other two implemented a dual strategy of offering both localized and globally standardized products. This is a very interesting finding, considering the fact that all these companies operate in different industries.

How was this possible? The common reasoning behind this is that, within the price-sensitive and mostly low-income CEE countries, there exists a relatively affluent middle- to high-income segment that yearns for a global lifestyle similar to the standards of advanced Western nations. In this sense, these companies were able to exploit that market segment through their global brand image, which satisfies the global product standard and lifestyle that this segment wishes to consume. Furthermore, by integrating the marketing operation into a globally standardized one, these companies opted to reduce the coordination costs which could arise with an overly customized approach.

Of course, certain differentiating aspects such as labeling content, instructions and product mixes (e.g., McDonald's offers a different version of the local cuisine) are present. However, even this slight degree of customization is confined to marginal aspects. The overwhelming trend exhibited by multinationals operating in the CEE market is to standardize the basic platform and modify the periphery.

These case studies are very interesting, as intuitive thinking would favor localization when marketing in this region. However, when analyzed with a comprehensive framework as in Fig. 1, the reasons for standardization can be easily understood. Another important point is these corporations' expectation that customer preferences will evolve over time and will converge to the global standard. An increasing average income in the CEE region will promote further integration with the rest of Europe, which will then lead to increased homogenization of customer needs. Most importantly, the corporations not only anticipate, but accelerate, this process through their strategic choice.

Analysis

Schuh's (2000) analysis presents a very vivid picture of international companies operating in the CEE region. The implications are quite profound, as most of these firms are pursuing a globally standardized operation rather than a regionalized or localized one. A more general lesson can be derived from Schuh's article. The classic debate between customization and standardization has sparked numerous offshoots in academia, and many scholars have had heated discussions on this subject. As we have seen from Chap. 9, the debate is polarized between Levitt's (1983) position (standardization) and Douglas and Wind's (1987) position (customization), while Bartlett and Ghoshal (1989) proposed a transnational solution as a synthesis. Schuh's study adds an interesting perspective to this classic debate, by observing a fairly standardized strategy in much differentiated markets. This is an interesting observation, which will be further looked at in the next section.

Another interesting aspect of the CEE region is the infiltration of firms from emerging economies — emerging multinational corporations (EMNCs) such as those from China, Turkey and Russia. These firms not only have the capability of providing products of global standards, but they also have the ability to promote cost-competitive goods to cater to the lower-income segments which the established corporations are reluctant to do. Case Study 2, which analyzes Arçelik's thrust into the CEE region, will present a more detailed look into this phenomenon.

11.3 The World Is Not Flat ... But You Can Flatten It!

So far, we have analyzed the various arguments surrounding the standardization vs. customization debate using Levitt (1983), Douglas and Wind (1987), and Bartlett and Ghoshal (1989) as fulcrums of different perspectives. But what is the most appropriate global strategy? Despite the extensive discussion, the debate rages on and hence we are left with often confusing and overlapping prescriptions.

Recent terms such as "glocal" (Robertson 1995), "regionalization" (Rugman 2000), "metanational" (Doz *et al.* 2001) and "multi-unit enterprise" (Garvin and Levesque 2008) add to the already complex landscape of this age-old debate.

All of the above analyses in fact share a common limitation that reduces their explanatory power: they adopt a static view of internationalization. While previous attempts have done remarkably well in terms of depicting a certain moment in time, not many have been able to accurately convey the dynamic and constantly evolving nature of internationalization. However, as we have seen in previous sections, the various forces that determine our settings are not set in stone. Rather, these forces can change, especially depending on our strategic choices.

Moon (2005) presents a different picture to this debate by adopting a dynamic perspective. Moon starts off by reviewing the various assumptions of the standardization proponents based on Levitt's 1983 article. The main assumptions of standardization are (a) converging consumer tastes; (b) consumer willingness to sacrifice personal preferences for lower prices; and (c) increase in economies of scale.

Douglas and Wind (1987) countered these three assumptions by asserting that (a) differences are significant and often increasing among consumers in different nations; (b) low price does not override preferences and cannot be a basis for sustainable competitive advantage; (c) technological developments such as a flexible factory and automation nullify the benefits from economies of scale; (d) the cost of production is only one component of the total cost; and (e) the marketing mix must be considered in the total picture.

Bartlett and Ghoshal (1989) reconciled these two conflicting views, and asserted that the appropriate strategy depends on the conditions and industry in which the firm operates — hence, the birth of the famous integration-responsiveness (I-R) framework, which we have already discussed extensively in Chap. 10. Depending on the industry, a firm can customize some of its activities while centralizing (or standardizing) others. However, it can be argued that, although industry differences are relevant, it would be more appropriate to look at the firm level rather than the industry level since some firms (even in the same industry) have differing levels of standardization.

While it is inevitable that firms are affected by industry forces, this does not mean that firms must remain prisoners of the industry structure. Just because the industry is not conducive for standardization, it does not mean that firms cannot pursue a standardized approach. In other words, the real issue is neither to choose one of the two extremes nor to compromise the two, but how to increase the degree of standardization by enhancing the product value. We also need to clearly distinguish product standardization from that of other marketing mix elements. Coca-Cola, for example, may have different promotion and distribution strategies across borders, but the product itself is highly standardized. As a matter of fact, Coca-Cola has discontinued many of the products that it used to promote for local responsiveness. Coca-Cola BlāK, which was promoted largely in the CEE region, was discontinued in 2008, as was Coca-Cola C2 which was designed for Japanese consumers.

Consider the difference between a hamburger and kimchi. Both products are squarely located in the foods industry, which is traditionally considered to be a multidomestic industry. A hamburger is a highly global item that is consumed by billions of consumers all around the world. Kimchi, on the other hand, is a highly local product that caters to a uniquely Korean preference for fermented vegetables fused with high doses of garlic, red pepper and fish extracts. This logic is mapped in Fig. 2.

Why is this so? Is the hamburger an inherently superior food to kimchi? Far from it; the health benefits of kimchi have been very well documented, while the various malaise caused by hamburgers have been shockingly presented in numerous documentaries such as *Super Size Me*. The answer is quite simple, as the hamburger provides a more convenient and comprehensive option at a much lower price than kimchi does. While the hamburger was originally an American staple, it rapidly gained prominence as a global food item due to its superior value in terms of low cost and good quality.

Therefore, the real issue is not to choose between standardization and customization or to compromise the two. The primary concern

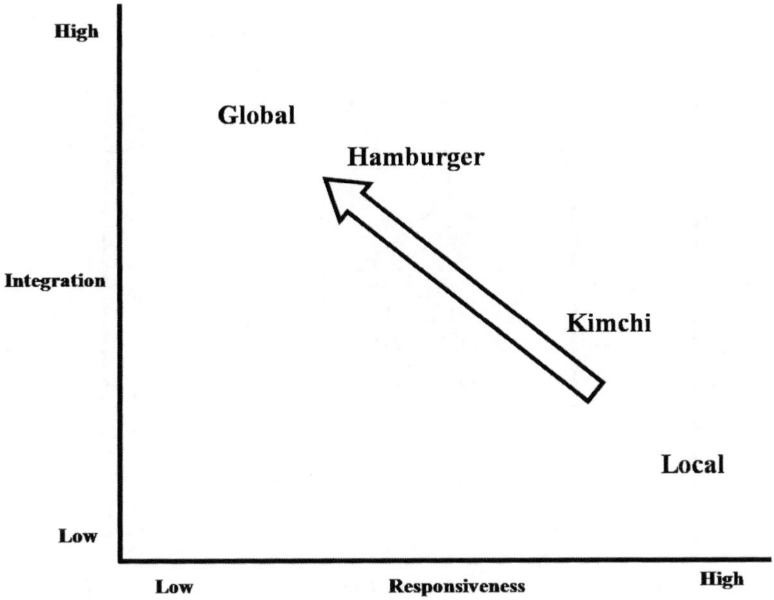

Fig. 2. Different strategic positioning.[3]

should be how to increase the degree of standardization. A truly successful firm does not choose one or the other, but boldly elevates the country-specific strategy to a global level through standardization. Thus, the firm can raise the timeless values of low cost and high quality to a degree which can override national preferences and dissimilarities. One need not look any further than at the millions of Koreans, who are well known for their unyielding love for kimchi, consuming Big Macs and Whoppers. If we ask any of these Korean consumers, "Do you like hamburgers more than kimchi?", the overwhelming majority will answer "no". But why, then, do they flock to McDonald's and Burger King for a quick lunch? Simply because the utility generated from the high quality and low cost of hamburgers, as well as the convenience in terms of time and location, overrides the national preference for kimchi (see Fig. 3).

[3] Moon (2005).

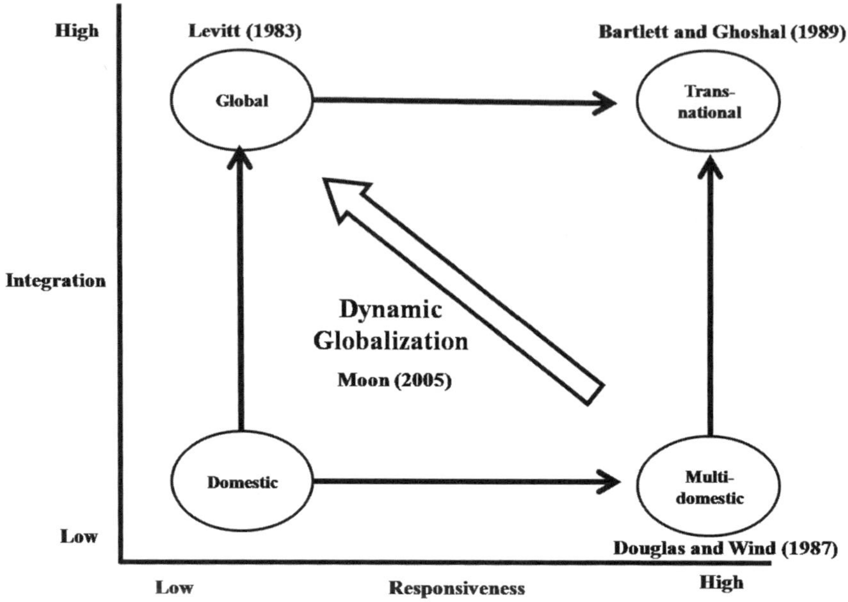

Fig. 3. Types of international strategies.[4]

As we can see in Fig. 3, the appropriate approach is to elevate a multidomestic or even domestic strategy to the global level. This brings us to the last and most important point, as the fundamental premise of all debates so far has been static and has assumed the market conditions to be fixed. However, the reality is dynamic and, rather than simply treating the world as flat, individuals and corporations have the power to actually flatten it. Therefore, instead of dwelling on old certainties, it is important for firms to create new possibilities to induce changes that are more conducive to their operations.

The world's most successful global products such as Coca-Cola, the McDonald's hamburger and Levi's jeans have all followed this formula of elevating a national- or local-level product to the global level. McDonald's has achieved worldwide success providing high economic value through its products based on a highly integrated and

---

[4] *Ibid.*

standardized formula. While the difference in national preferences for food is an important prevailing force, McDonald's has been able to override the desire for non-economic factors by offering high economic factors, namely high-quality and low-cost goods, as well as convenience of time and location. Therefore, the real focus is not to choose between standardization and customization, but to boldly elevate the country-specific strategy to a global level through enhancing economic value. Thus, the firm can raise the timeless and universal values of low cost and high quality to a degree which can override the local preferences and dissimilarities.

Analysis

The last section of this book leaves us with an important topic for thought: how are we to view this ever-changing world? Most academic disciplines have had their fair share of debate on this common topic. Some emphasize the increasing differences among different cultural, societal and economic groupings; while others perceive a converging and integrating world. In international relations, Huntington's (1996) "clash of civilizations" hypothesis versus Fukuyama's (1992) "end of history" represent this dichotomy. Huntington argues that the world is heading towards the next great conflict whereby the battle lines will be marked by cultural differences. On the other hand, Fukuyama insists that we are witnessing a general convergence into a Western-style free market democracy, which will lead to the "end of history" as we know it. In linguistics, Noam Chomsky (1976) suggests that a streak of common pattern among all languages can be found, which he dubs "universal grammar"; while others believe that universal grammar is a limited phenomenon which only shows part of the story. In the world of international business, Douglas and Wind (1987) versus Levitt (1983) form two opposing pillars, as has been explained extensively in the preceding sections.

On a more general level, globalization generates two apparently paradoxical trends that have confounded many observers. On one side, globalization integrates the world into singularity; while simultaneously accentuating the prevailing differences among national, cultural and societal groups on the other side. The debate between standardization versus customization and all the related discussions are derived from these two opposing phenomena. However, at least in the realm of international business, the fundamental question that we should never forget is how to maximize profit or, put differently, how to sell what to whom. The best answer for both questions is to find more important similarities and come up with ways to flatten other differences to your best advantage.

Case Study 1: Globalizing China[5]

This chapter offers a number of methods and ways by which a firm can proactively stimulate business and alter the macro-environment in which it functions. Thus, firms are not necessarily passive entities subject to the uncontrollable forces of their environments, but can be proactive and influence the very environment in which they operate to their advantage. This is schematically represented in Fig. 4.

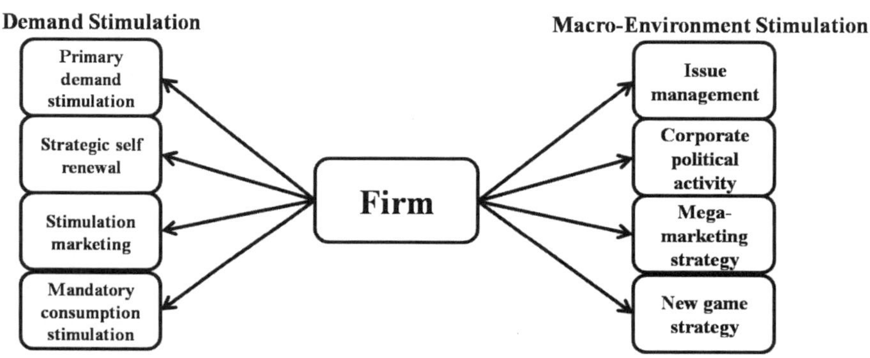

Fig. 4. Firm influence over environment.

[5] Information for this case study is abstracted from the Air China official website (www.airchina.com), Euromonitor International (2004) and the Sinopec official website (english.sinopec.com).

In previous case studies, we have presented particular firms and their experiences through a variety of frameworks and theories. However, for this case study, we are going to focus on the experiences of a number of firms from or operating in a particular country, namely China. Why China? China is a country where firms have been forced to shape the environment in which they function. Were they to allow their environment to control their destinies, Chinese firms would have remained as niche, domestic players. China offers us a unique opportunity to study firms that develop and expand in new and exciting ways to incorporate the Chinese market into global business, thereby expanding their scope of business.

Let's first look at Air China in the context of primary demand stimulation, which can increase one's market share using tools such as product promotion. When Air China first started out, it was a little-known, mostly domestic airline company. However, over the years it has managed to grow into a major airline that now owns 176 Boeing and Airbus planes and flies to 22 countries and districts, and 36 international and 70 domestic cities.

The main reason for Air China's remarkable growth has been the stimulation of consumer demand, both domestically and internationally, through product/service promotion. Firstly, Air China negotiated with the Chinese government to become the only air carrier authorized to fly national leaders to its numerous destinations as well as transport foreign dignitaries and government leaders to China. Furthermore, Air China was one of the first airlines to develop regional hubs in Chengdu, Shanghai and Guangzhou, rather than simply focusing on Beijing, thus extending its reach around China. The firm also attached great importance on cooperating with foreign airlines and has signed code-sharing agreements with 11 domestic and foreign airlines, thus allowing the firm to offer domestic and foreign customers more convenient flight options. Most recently, in 2008, Air China became the sole airline partner of the Beijing Olympic Games. Air China knew it had to actively expand its own market through various promotions in order to avoid being classed as a low-level domestic-only service.

For another example, think back to Chap. 1 and recall the case study regarding Starbucks in China from a stimulational marketing perspective. China is renowned for its tea-drinking culture, yet the coffee-drinking culture has spread to China. Starbucks has opened more than 90 outlets around the country, and is set to open even more in the future. But just how did Starbucks create and expand demand? Firstly, it appealed to the adventurous, open-minded, young and affluent, urban consumers. Those consumers already looked up to Western lifestyles, and were eager to try goods and services that gave them the utility of a sophisticated and modern outlook. Starbucks was able to reinforce this idea by further appealing to returnees. A huge number of Chinese students have been returning from Western countries over the past years. Many of these students lived abroad for an extended period of time and have returned with a Westernized consumer preference, and have been able to reinforce it with their high salaries and fashionable Western lifestyles. Lastly, Starbucks has tapped into the foreign expatriate communities and Western tourists, people who are generally big coffee drinkers.

In terms of issues management, China undoubtedly needs further development, particularly in terms of corporate social responsibility (CSR). The country's terrible environmental record reflects this, and a 2008 World Bank survey claims that 20 out of the top 30 worst polluted cities in the world lie in China. However, there are a few "bright spots" amidst the darkness that are attempting to convey a sense of CSR through a variety of activities and, thus, alter the public's perception. One such firm is China's Sinopec, which is a semi-national petroleum and chemical corporation. In recent years, it has dedicated time and resources to energy conservation efforts. In particular, great effort has been made in a large number of energy-saving projects such as coal replacing oil, gas replacing oil, electric power grid modification, water-flooding adjustment and remaining heat utilization. Remarkable achievements have been made in energy conservation. Overall, the firm has upgraded equipments in its bid to preserve China's environment. This move has improved the company's public image around China and the world.

We have looked at a few firms, both Chinese firms and a foreign firm operating in China, and applied only a few environmental stimulation factors discussed in Fig. 4. However, it has been empirically demonstrated that a firm can alter its environment rather than be altered by its environment. Furthermore, applying all factors to one firm would have been redundant and, in most cases, not all aspects of one's environment need to be altered. Instead, those who are dissatisfied with their environment find it preferable to change one or two key factors rather than their entire environment. Remember, the point is not to throw out the proverbial business environment "baby" with the strategic bathwater, but to add a hot or cold touch to enhance the "baby's" environment.

Case Study 2: Back to Turkey's Arçelik[6]

If you recall, we have already looked at a superb case study involving Arçelik, and have highlighted the uniqueness of the firm and its growth pattern. We are going back to look once more at the same Turkish white goods firm, but from a slightly different perspective.

In Sec. 11.2 of this chapter, eight firms in the CEE region were analyzed in order to discover whether the firms used a standardized or differentiated marketing program for this particular region. Counterintuitively, it was discovered that six of the eight firms used a highly standardized marketing program, while the remaining two implemented a dual-strategy marketing program. Arçelik is another firm that has recently endeavored to enter the CEE region, and it is noteworthy to analyze how Arçelik has proceeded in this environment.

As mentioned in the previous case study, Arçelik has experienced rapid international growth. Through a variety of investments, acquisitions and strategic alliances, Arçelik achieved a 23% revenue growth in 2007 alone and international sales have increased by 14% per annum on average during the past 5 years. While Arçelik has been

[6] Information for this case study is abstracted from the Arçelik official website (www.arcelik.com.tr/english) and *appliance DESIGN* (2002).

looking to expand into more advanced economies, it has not ignored the underdeveloped potential market that exists in the nearby CEE region, and is thus turning not only westwards but also eastwards.

With a GDP of around US$272.881 billion (PPP) (41st in the world) and a GDP per capita of US$12,698 (64th in the world) estimated for 2008 by the IMF, Romania is an upper-middle-income economy and has been part of the European Union since January 1, 2007. This newly prospering nation offers a unique challenge for firms such as Arçelik. After the communist regime collapsed in late 1989 following the Romanian Revolution, the country experienced a decade of economic instability and decline, led in part by an obsolete industrial base and a lack of structural reform. It is, therefore, only since early 2000 that the nation has experienced any lasting form of stability. This is quite representative of the CEE region and provides a unique environment, as there is an emerging upper-middle-income band but there still exists a significant lower-income band within the population.

After analyzing the unique environment of the CEE countries, and in particular Romania, Arçelik decided to opt for a dual marketing strategy in order to satisfy both kinds of consumers:

- those who want a high-quality product, with a recognizable name brand, and do not mind paying extra for such a product in order to emulate a more Westernized lifestyle; and
- those who want a reliable-quality product, with a reliable name brand, at a reasonable price.

Thus, Arçelik first entered Romania, targeting the first type of consumers. Using its global brand Beko, Arçelik signaled a standardized, global message to the upper-middle-income Romanian customers. Beko was able to garner success in Romania and has become an established, trusted and desirable brand.

However, Arçelik still needed to cater to the second type of consumers. Building a low-cost trusted brand in Romania would take the firm a considerable amount of time, funds and effort, all of which

Arçelik's management wished to avoid. Especially since low-cost, local white goods providers have a remarkable ability to capture distinct local preferences, Arçelik, without the clout of a Western multinational or the advantage of a local firm, would have been left astray. Arçelik's strategy, then, was to set its sights on Arctic. The Arctic brand was the most powerful name in Romania with 96% brand awareness and was the market leader with a market share exceeding 30%. In 2002, Arçelik acquired Arctic, and continued the tradition of catering to the lower-income population of Romania.

Looking once more at Fig. 1 in Sec. 11.2, we can see that Arçelik carefully considered its marketing objectives, target market, market entry mode and the timing of market entry when deciding on the degree of marketing program standardization. In particular, the range of consumers that exist in this type of emerging economy and the possibilities for gaining a larger market share had a great influence on Arçelik's decision to expand into the market using both a standardized and customized approach.

Case Study 3: Tea and Hamburgers Go Global?[7]

Green tea has been around for a long time and its origins can be traced, in Chinese literature, as far back as 5,000 years ago. According to some Chinese legends, it dates back to approximately 2737 B.C., but a number of theories suggest an even more historic origin. Some claim that a man called Shien Non Shei discovered the plant, tasted a leaf from it and found it to be fantastic. He then decided to mix it with water and make a drink out of it, and further thought that the drink had medicinal qualities. However, another story goes that Emperor Shen Nung came upon the tea when a leaf from the plant fell into a cup of hot water he was drinking at the time. Whatever your

[7] Information for this case study is abstracted from the Tata Tea official website (www.tatatea.com), the Zhejiang Tea Import and Export Company official website (www.chinagreentea.com), the Dr. Lee's TeaForHealth official website (www.teaforhealth.com) and Stradley (2004).

belief of its origin, green tea has been used in China as a healthy, medicinal drink for thousands of years.

Therefore, we can assume that green tea began its product life as a highly localized and customized product. Making a cup of green tea was regarded as a distinct Chinese art form. The appropriate utensils had to be used, the water temperature had to be monitored, and the leaves themselves were not processed but had to be mixed with water and then strained. The Chinese went about making their green tea, and we can assume it was an arduous process. The process, however, was one that managed to spread throughout the Northeast Asian region, as drinking green tea also became a highly popular pastime in both Korea and Japan. As these nations are somewhat similar in culture and values, we can assume that the product itself maintained a high degree of regionalization and customization.

However, over the years, the methodology behind brewing a cup of green tea has become a much simpler process, largely due to a desire to sell the product further afield than the Asian market. Thus, the simplification of the product has allowed it to essentially go global. In order to simplify it, the level of local responsiveness has been decreased dramatically, thus making it more appealing to Western customers. Figure 5 represents this in that the tea industry has moved from a multidomestic strategy, which includes a high level of local responsiveness and a low level of global integration, to a global strategy, which is representative of a high level of global integration and a low level of local responsiveness.

Most recently, Tata Tea, an Indian tea company, realized the potential of green tea in the global market. Therefore, Tata Tea began a joint venture with Zhejiang Tea Import and Export Company in China. Their goal was to bring high-quality green tea at a low price and in a recognizable manner to the global consumer. Thus, the two firms have shifted their strategic positioning from multidomestic to global by introducing a more standardized product, i.e., the (green) tea bag, which is more easily and conveniently accepted by global consumers. This strategic shift is represented by the upper left-hand corner in Fig. 6.

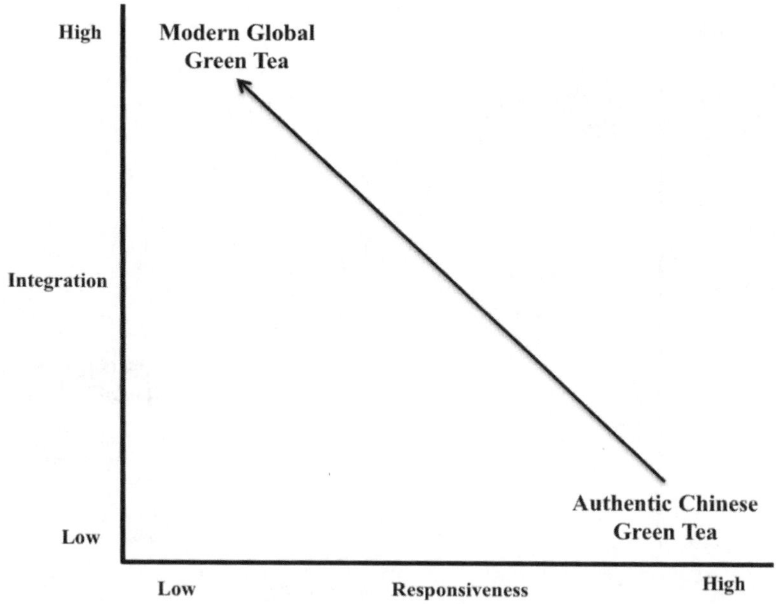

Fig. 5. Strategic positioning and strategy.

Therefore, Asian firms have taken a traditionally purely Asian product and altered it slightly to appeal to the masses. They essentially flattened their world through dynamic global strategies.

While the case of green tea does prove our point, there exists an even better and far more recognizable example than this. The product in point is the hamburger. Why make such a fuss over a piece of flattened beef wedged between two bread buns? Simply because the hamburger has gone through an amazing journey from its origins as a local product to becoming a global staple.

The hamburger's humble beginnings took place in the late 18th century, when sailors who visited the port of Hamburg in Germany were often tempted to eat the Hamburg-style steak, which was a hard slab of slated minced beef, often slightly smoked, mixed with onions and breadcrumbs. The sailors enjoyed not only the taste, but also the ease with which one could quickly consume the steak. Savvy Jewish immigrants quickly transferred the product to the New York City

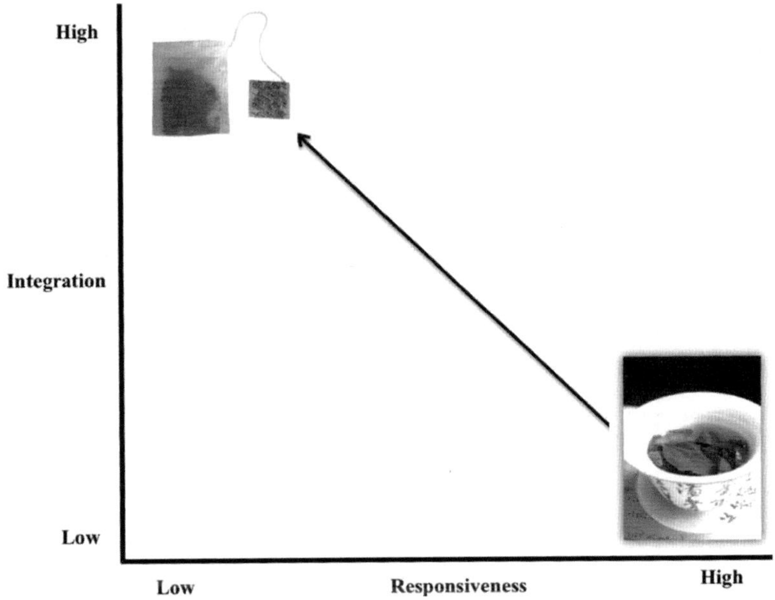

Fig. 6. Joint venture strategic shift.

Harbor in order to attract hungry German sailors, who would line up next to eating stands to grab a quick bite.[8]

While there continues to be much dispute in the US as to who exactly decided to place the meat between two pieces of bread or buns, and thus bestow upon the world the modern image of the hamburger, the hamburger became an instant success on the East Coast of America and its popularity quickly spread throughout the country. It was then that hamburger restaurants such as the famous White Castle, one of the earliest known hamburger chains, laid the path for the likes of the massively popular McDonald's and Burger King, to name but a few.

Thus, we can determine that while being sold in the port of Hamburg, Germany, the hamburger had a high level of local responsiveness as a tasty, filling yet durable meal which could be consumed quickly and easily. At this time, global integration was low as the

[8] Moon (2005).

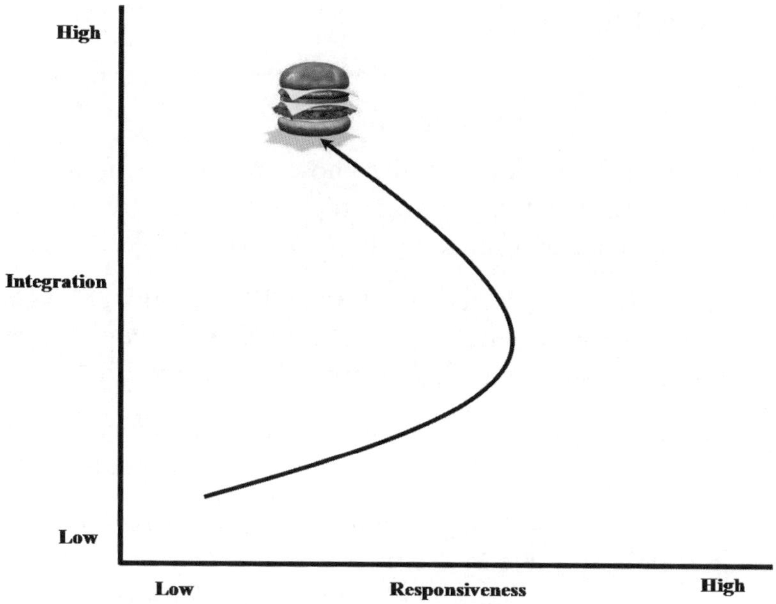

Fig. 7. Dynamic globalization of the hamburger.

product was only sold in Germany. However, the hamburger became a roaring success as it spread from Germany to America and then throughout the world via the global fast food chains. Thus, the hamburger's level of global integration moved from low to high, as the product was not much altered to specifically suit individual needs.

One might argue otherwise by pointing out the numerous localized versions of the hamburger. In Korea, the Bulgogi Burger (in which the patty is marinated with traditional Korean sauce) caters to Korean consumers; while in Japan, the Teriyaki Burger satisfies many Japanese customers. However, the hamburger is a more homogeneous than heterogenous product, despite some variations. This is evident from the numerous McDonald's chains that provide the standardized flagship products such as the Big Mac, Double Cheeseburger and McChicken Sandwich. From a dynamic perspective, the hamburger has been more globally integrative than locally responsive, as illustrated in Fig. 7.

Discussion Questions

1. How effective are various marketing tools in altering business environments? Discuss.
2. Which marketing tools, besides those mentioned in the above question, can effectively change the business environment? Do they always change it for the better? Why or why not?
3. Which particular characteristics of the CEE region make it receptive to standardized products? Could this strategy be simulated in other regions, such as Latin America? Why or why not?
4. Based on our discussions, which direction is better for a firm to go abroad — global integration or local responsiveness? Discuss.
5. How could kimchi change from being a domestic product to being a global product? Discuss.
6. Is the hamburger a global or transnational product? Discuss.
7. What is the most important lesson you have learned from the debate between standardization and differentiation? Discuss.

References

Journal Articles, Books and Periodicals

A.T. Kearney and *Foreign Policy*. (2006) "The Globalization Index 2006." *Foreign Policy* (November–December): 74–81.

A.T. Kearney and *Foreign Policy*. (2007) "The Globalization Index 2007." *Foreign Policy* (November–December): 68–76.

Ahn, H. (2001) "Applying the Balanced Scorecard concept: an experience report." *Long Range Planning* 34(4): 441–461.

Argyres, N., McGahan, A.M., Barney, J.B., Brandenburger, A. and Bachmann, J.W. (2002) "Retrospective: Michael Porter's *Competitive Strategy* [interview and commentaries]." *Academy of Management Executive* 16(2): 41–65.

Arnold, S., Chadraba, P. and Springer, R. (eds.) (2001) *Marketing Strategies for Central and Eastern Europe*. Aldershot: Ashgate.

Balmer, J.M.T., Fukukawa, K. and Gray, E.R. (2007) "The nature and management of ethical corporate identity: a commentary on corporate identity, corporate social responsibility and ethics." *Journal of Business Ethics* 76: 7–15.

Bartlett, C.A. and Ghoshal, S. (1989) "The emerging organization model." In: *Managing Across Borders: The Transnational Solution*. Boston: Harvard University Press, pp. 65–82.

Bartlett, C.A. and Ghoshal, S. (1992) "What is a global manager?" *Harvard Business Review* (August): 101–108.

Bartlett, C.A. and Ghoshal, S. (2000) "Going global: lessons from late movers." *Harvard Business Review* (March–April): 132–142.

Becker, G. (1976) *The Economic Approach to Human Behavior*. Chicago: University of Chicago Press.

Benedict, R. (1946) *The Chrysanthemum and the Sword*. Boston: Houghton Mifflin.

Bonaglia, F., Goldstein, A. and Mathews, J.A. (2007) "Accelerated internationalization by emerging markets' multinationals: the case of the white goods sector." *Journal of World Business* 42: 369–383.

Bourgeois, L.J. (1984) "Strategic management and determinism." *Academy of Management Review* 9(4): 586–596.

Brewer, P. (2002) "Putting strategy into the Balanced Scorecard." *Strategic Finance* 83(7): 44–52.

Butler, A., Letza, S.R. and Neale, B. (1997) "Linking the Balanced Scorecard to strategy." *Long Range Planning* 30(2): 242–253.

Cho, D.S. (1994) "A dynamic approach to international competitiveness: the case of Korea." *Journal of Far Eastern Business* 1(1): 17–36.

Cho, D.S. and Moon, H.C. (2000) *From Adam Smith to Michael Porter: Evolution of Competitiveness Theory.* Singapore: World Scientific Publishing.

Cho, D.S., Moon, H.C. and Kim, M.Y. (2008) "Characterizing international competitiveness in international business research: a MASI approach to national competitiveness." *Research in International Business and Finance* 22(2): 175–192.

Cho, D.S., Moon, H.C. and Kim, M.Y. (2009) "Does one size fit all? A dual double diamond approach to country-specific advantages." *Asian Business & Management* 8(1): 83–102.

Chomsky, N. (1976) "On the nature of language." In: Harnad, S.R., Steklis, H.D. and Lancaster, J. (eds.) *Origins and Evolution of Language and Speech. Annals of the New York Academy of Sciences* 280: 46–57.

Clausewitz, C.V. (1832, reprinted 1982) *On War.* Oxford: Penguin Group.

Cochran, P.L. and Wood, R.A. (1984) "Corporate social responsibility and financial performance." *Academy of Management Journal* 27(1): 42–56.

Contractor, F.J., Kundu, K.S. and Hsu, C.C. (2003) "A three-stage theory of international expansion: the link between multinationality and performance in the service sector." *Journal of International Business Studies* 34(1): 5–18.

Daniels, J.D. and Bracker, J. (1989) "Profit performance: do foreign operations make a difference?" *Management International Review* 29(1): 46–56.

DeRond, M. and Thietart, R.A. (2007) "Choice, chance and inevitability in strategy." *Strategic Management Journal* 28: 535–551.

Douglas, S.P. and Wind, Y. (1987) "The myth of globalization." *Columbia Journal of World Business* (Winter): 19–29.

Doz, Y., Santos, J. and Williamson, P. (2001) *From Global to Metanational.* Boston: Harvard Business School Press.

Drucker, P.F. (1969) *The Age of Discontinuity: Guidelines to Our Changing Society.* New York: Harper & Row.

Drucker, P.F. (1981) "Behind Japan's success." *Harvard Business Review* (January–February): 83–90.

Dunning, J.H. (1995) "Reappraising the eclectic paradigm in an age of alliance capitalism." *Journal of International Business Studies* 26(3): 461–491.

Ekelund, R.B. and Hebert, R.F. (1997) *A History of Economic Theory and Method.* Singapore: McGraw-Hill.

Eng, T.Y. (2007) "Relationship value of firms in alliance capitalism and the implications for FDI." *International Journal of Business Studies* 15(1): 43–68.

Fogel, K., Hawk, A., Morck, R. and Yeung, B. (2006) "Institutional obstacles to entrepreneurship." In: Casson, M., Yeung, B., Basu, A. and Wadeson, N. (eds.) *Oxford Handbook of Entrepreneurship.* Oxford: Oxford University Press, pp. 540–579.

Friedman, T.L. (2005) *The World Is Flat.* New York: Farrar, Straus and Giroux.

Fukuyama, F. (1992) *The End of History and the Last Man.* New York: Free Press.

Garvin, D.A. and Levesque, L.C. (2008) "The multi-unit enterprise." *Harvard Business Review* (June): 106–117.

Geringer, J.M., Beamish, P.W. and daCosta, R.C. (1989) "Diversification strategy and internationalization: implications for MNE performance." *Strategic Management Journal* 10(2): 109–119.

Ghemawat, P. (2007) "Why the world isn't flat." *Foreign Policy* (March/April): 54–60.

Ghemawat, P. and Hout, T. (2008) "Tomorrow's global giants: not the usual suspects." *Harvard Business Review* (November): 80–88.

Ghoshal, S. (1987) "Global strategy: an organizing framework." *Strategic Management Journal* 8: 425–440.

Grant, R.M. (1987) "Multinationality and performance among British manufacturing companies." *Journal of International Business Studies* 18(3): 79–89.

Greenwald, B. and Kahn, J. (2005) "All strategy is local." *Harvard Business Review* (September): 95–104.

Hambrick, D.C. and Fredrickson, J.W. (2005) "Are you sure you have a strategy?" *Academy of Management Executive* 19(4): 51–62.

Hamel, G. (1991) "Competition for competence and inter-partner learning within international strategic alliances." *Strategic Management Journal* 12: 83–103.

Hamel, G. and Prahalad, C.K. (1985) "Do you really have a global strategy?" *Harvard Business Review* (July–August): 139–148.

Hamel, G. and Prahalad, C.K. (1994) *Competing for the Future.* Boston: Harvard Business School Press.

Harvie, C. and Lee, B.C. (2002) "The study of small and medium sized enterprises in East Asia." In: Harvie, C. and Lee, B.C. (eds.) *Globalisation and SMEs in East Asia.* Studies of Small and Medium Sized Enterprises in East Asia, Vol. 1. Cheltenham: Edward Elgar, pp. 1–9.

Harzing, A.W.K. (2000) "An empirical test and extension of the Bartlett and Ghoshal typology of multinational companies." *Journal of International Business Studies* 31(1): 101–120.

Herbold, R.J. (2002) "Inside Microsoft: balancing creativity and discipline." *Harvard Business Review* (January): 143–178.

Hrebiniak, L.G. and Joyce, W.F. (1985) "Organizational adaptation: strategic choice and environmental determinism." *Administrative Science Quarterly* 30: 336–349.

Huntington, S.P. (1996) *The Clash of Civilizations and the Remaking of World Order.* New York: Simon & Schuster.

Ichijo, K. and Kohlbacher, F. (2007) "Global knowledge creation — the Toyota way." *International Journal of Automotive Technology and Management* 7(2/3): 116–134.

Institute for Industrial Policy Studies. (2007) IPS National Competitiveness Research Report. Seoul: Institute for Industrial Policy Studies.

Isenberg, D.J. (2008) "The global entrepreneur." *Harvard Business Review* (December): 107–111.

Jeurissen, R. (2004) "Institutional conditions of corporate citizenship." *Journal of Business Ethics* 53: 87–96.

Kaplan, R.S. and Norton, D.P. (2006) *Alignment.* Boston: Harvard Business School Press.

Kaplan, R.S. and Norton, D.P. (2007a) "Using the Balanced Scorecard as a strategic management system." *Harvard Business Review* (July–August): 150–161 [reprint of 1996].

Kaplan, R.S. and Norton, D.P. (2007b) *The Strategy-Focused Organization.* Boston: Harvard Business School Press.

Kedia, B.L. and Mukherji, A. (1999) "Global managers: developing a mindset for global competitiveness." *Journal of World Business* 34(3): 230–251.

Khanna, T. and Palepu, K.G. (2006) "Emerging giants: building world-class companies in developing countries." *Harvard Business Review* (October): 60–69.

Kim, M.Y. and Moon, H.C. (2006) "The global expansion strategy of Hyundai Motor: a dynamic diversification-coordination (DDC) approach." *Journal of Strategic Management* 9(2): 31–55.

Kim, W.C., Hwang, P. and Burgers, W.P. (1989) "Global diversification strategy and corporate profit performance." *Strategic Management Journal* 10: 45–57.

Kim, W.C. and Mauborgne, R. (2005) "Blue Ocean strategy: from theory to practice." *California Management Review* 47(3 [Spring]): 105–121.

Kirby, D. and Watson, A. (2003) *Small Firms and Economic Development in Developed and Transition Economies: A Reader.* Aldershot: Ashgate.

Kogut, B. (1985) "Designing global strategies: comparative and competitive value-added chains." *Sloan Management Review* (Summer): 15–28.

Kotler, P. (1986) "The prosumer movement: a new challenge for marketers." *Advances in Consumer Research* 13(1): 510–513.

Kuhn, T.S. (1962) *The Structure of Scientific Revolution.* Chicago: Chicago University Press.

Levitt, T. (1983) "The globalization of markets." *Harvard Business Review* (May/June): 92–102.

Luostarinen, R. and Gabrielsson, M. (2004) "Finnish perspectives of international entrepreneurship." In: Dana, L.P. (ed.) *Handbook of Research on International Entrepreneurship.* Cheltenham: Edward Elgar, pp. 383–403.

Machiavelli, N. (1532, reprinted 2003) *The Prince.* New York: Penguin Books.

Mathews, J.A. (2002) *Dragon Multinational: A New Model for Global Growth.* New York: Oxford University Press.

Moon, H.C. (1993) "The dynamics of Porter's three generics in international business strategy." In: Rugman, A.M. and Verbeke, A. (eds.) *Global Competition: Beyond the Three Generics.* Research in Global Strategic Management, Vol. 4. London: Emerald Group Publishing, pp. 51–64.

Moon, H.C. (1994) "A revised framework of global strategy: extending the coordination-configuration framework." *The International Executive* 36(September/October): 557–574.

Moon, H.C. (2005) "The new organization of global firms: from transnational solution to dynamic globalization." *International Journal of Performability Engineering* 1(2 [October]): 131–143.

Moon, H.C. (2007) "Outward foreign direct investment by enterprises from the Republic of Korea." In: *Global Players from Emerging Markets: Strengthen Enterprise Competitiveness through Outward Investment.* New York and Geneva: UNCTAD, pp. 91–106.

Moon, H.C. and Hur, Y.K. (2008) "Dynamics of how to sell what to whom: from three to eight generic strategies." Presented at the 7th Annual International Business and Economy Conference (IBEC) 2008, Kabuki Hotel, San Francisco, USA, January 10–13, 2008.

Moon, H.C. and Kim, M.Y. (2008) "A new framework for global expansion: a dynamic diversification-coordination (DDC) model." *Management Decision* 46(1): 131–151.

Moon, H.C. and Peery, N. (1995) "Competitiveness of product, firm, industry and nation in a global business." *Competitiveness Review* 5(1): 37–43.

Moon, H.C. and Roehl, T.W. (2001) "Unconventional foreign direct investment and the imbalance theory." *International Business Review* 10: 197–215.

Moon, H.C., Rugman, A.M. and Verbeke, A. (1995) "The generalized double diamond approach to international competitiveness." In: Rugman, A., Van Den Broek, J. and Verbeke, A. (eds.) *Beyond the Diamond.* Research in Global Strategic Management, Vol. 5. Greenwich, CT: JAI Press, pp. 97–114.

Moon, H.C., Rugman, A.M. and Verbeke, A. (1998) "A generalized double diamond approach to the global competitiveness of Korea and Singapore." *International Business Review* 7: 135–150.

Mooraj, S., Oyon, D. and Hostettler, D. (1999) "The Balanced Scorecard: a necessary good or an unnecessary evil?" *European Management Journal* 17(5): 481–491.

Morrison, A.J. (1990) *Strategies in Global Industries: How U.S. Businesses Compete.* Westpoint, CT: Quorum Books.

Nonaka, I. (2007) "The knowledge creating company." *Harvard Business Review* (November–December): 162–171 [reprint of 1991].

Nonaka, I. and Takeuchi, H. (1995) *The Knowledge Creating Company.* Oxford: Oxford University Press.

Nonaka, I., Toyama, R. and Hirata, T. (2008) *Managing Flow: A Process Theory of the Knowledge-Based Firm.* New York: Palgrave Macmillan.

Nørreklit, H. (2000) "The balance on the Balanced Scorecard — a critical analysis of some of its assumptions." *Management Accounting Research* 11(1): 65–88.

Ohmae, K. (1989) "The global logic of strategic alliances." *Harvard Business Review* (March–April): 143–154.

Oviatt, B.M. and McDougall, P.P. (1994) "Toward a theory of international new ventures." *Journal of International Business Studies* 25(1): 45–64.

Perlmutter, H. (1969) "The tortuous evolution of the multinational enterprise." *The Columbia Journal of World Business* 4(1): 9–18.

Porter, M.E. (1980) *Competitive Strategy: Techniques for Analyzing Industries and Companies.* New York: Free Press.

Porter, M.E. (1985) *Competitive Advantage: Creating and Sustaining Superior Performance.* New York: Free Press.

Porter, M.E. (1986) *Competition in Global Industries.* Boston: Harvard Business School Press.

Porter, M.E. (1990) *The Competitive Advantage of Nations.* New York: Free Press.

Porter, M.E. (1996) "What is strategy?" *Harvard Business Review* (November–December): 61–78.

Porter, M.E. (2001) "Strategy and the Internet." *Harvard Business Review* (March): 63–78.

Porter, M.E. (2008) "The five competitive forces that shape strategy." *Harvard Business Review* (January): 79–93.

Porter, M.E. and Kramer, M.R. (1999) "Philanthropy's new agenda: creating value." *Harvard Business Review* (November–December): 121–130.

Porter, M.E. and Kramer, M.R. (2006) "Strategy and society." *Harvard Business Review* (December): 78–92.

Prahalad, C.K. and Doz, Y.L. (1987) *The Multinational Mission: Balancing Local Demands and Global Vision.* New York: Free Press.

Prahalad, C.K. and Hamel, G. (1990) "The core competence of the corporation." *Harvard Business Review* (July–August): 55–70.

Prahalad, C.K. and Krishnan, M.S. (2008) *The New Age of Innovation: Driving Cocreated Value Through Global Networks.* New York: McGraw-Hill.

Prahalad, C.K. and Ramaswamy, V. (2000) "Co-opting customer competence." *Harvard Business Review* (January–February): 79–87.

Rangan, S. and Adner, R. (2001) "Profit and the Internet: seven misconceptions." *MIT Sloan Management Review* (Summer): 44–53.

Rehder, R.R. (1979) "Japanese management: an American challenge." *Human Resource Management* (Winter): 21–27.

Reich, B.R. (1990) "Who is us?" *Harvard Business Review* (January–February): 53–64.

Ridderstrale, K. and Nordstrom, J. (1999) *Funky Business.* Stockholm: BookHouse Publishing.

Robertson, R. (1995) "Globalization: time-space and homogeneity-heterogeneity." In: Featherstone, M., Lash, S. and Rolan, R. (eds.) *Global Modernities.* London: Sage, pp. 23–44.

Rugman, A.M. (2000) *The End of Globalization.* London: Random House and New York: AMACOM/McGraw-Hill.

Rugman, A.M. and D'Cruz, J.R. (1993) "The double diamond model of international competitiveness: the Canadian experience." *Management International Review* 2: 17–39.

Rugman, A.M. and Verbeke, A. (2004) "A perspective on regional and global strategies of multinational enterprises." *Journal of International Business Studies* 35(1): 3–18.

Saffo, P. (2007) "Six rules for effective forecasting." *Harvard Business Review* (July–August): 122–131.

Schuh, A. (2000) "Global standardization as a success formula for marketing in Central Eastern Europe?" *Journal of World Business* 35(2): 133–149.

Springer, R. and Czinkota, M.R. (1999) "Marketing's contribution to the transformation of Central and Eastern Europe." *Thunderbird International Business Review* 41(1): 310–326.

Sun, W. and Qin, Z. (1996) *The Essentials of War: The Masterpiece of a Strategist in Ancient China.* Beijing: New World Press.

Thurow, L.C. (1992) *Head to Head: The Coming Economic Battle Among Japan, Europe, and America.* New York: Warner Books.

Tichy, N.M. (1992) "Global development." In: Pucik, V., Tichy, N.M. and Bartlett, C.K. (eds.) *Globalizing Management: Creating and Leading the Competitive Organization.* New York: John Wiley & Sons, Inc., pp. 206–224.

Toffler, A. (1980) *The Third Wave.* New York: Bantam Books.

UNCTAD. (1995) World Investment Report 1995: Transnational Corporations and Competitiveness. New York and Geneva: United Nations.

UNCTAD. (2002) World Investment Report 2002: Transnational Corporations and Export Competitiveness. New York and Geneva: United Nations.

UNCTAD. (2007) World Investment Report 2007: Transnational Corporations, Extractive Industries and Development. New York and Geneva: United Nations.

UNCTAD. (2008) World Investment Report 2008: Transnational Corporations and the Infrastructure Challenge. New York and Geneva: United Nations.

Varadarajan, P.R., Clark, T. and Pride, W.M. (1992) "Controlling the uncontrollable: managing your market environment." *Sloan Management Review* 33(2): 39–47.

Vernon, R. (1966) "International trade and international investment in the product life cycle." *Quarterly Journal of Economics* 81(2): 190–207.

Vernon, R. (1971) *Sovereignty at Bay: The Multinational Spread of U.S. Enterprises.* New York: Basic Books.

Walton, S. (1992) *Sam Walton: Made in America.* New York: Bantam Books.

Weber, M. (1930, reprinted 2002) *The Protestant Ethic and the Spirit of Capitalism* (trans. Baehr, P. and Wells, C.G.). London: Penguin Books.

Yip, G. (1989) "Global strategy ... in a world of nations?" *MIT Sloan Management Review* 31 (1 [Fall]): 29–45.

Yip, G. (2000) "Global strategy in the Internet era." *Business Strategy Review* 11(4): 1–14.

Online Resources

Air China. http://www.airchina.com/ (accessed August 24, 2009).

Amore Pacific. http://www.amorepacific.com/ (accessed February 25, 2009).

Apple Asia. http://www.apple.com/asia/ (accessed February 25, 2009).

appliance DESIGN. (2002) "Arcelik aquires Arctic of Romania." September 5. http://www.appliancedesign.com/Articles/Breaking_News/2c78cf1d40a38010VgnVCM100000f932a8c0____/ (accessed August 24, 2009).

Arçelik. http://www.arcelik.com.tr/english/ (accessed February 27, 2009).

Balanced Scorecard Institute. http://www.balancedscorecard.org/ (accessed February 27, 2009).

BBC. (2001) "Warren Buffett: 'I told you so.'" March 13. http://news.bbc.co.uk/2/hi/business/1217716.stm/ (accessed February 13, 2009).

BBC. (2007) "Toyota 'world's largest carmaker.'" April 24. http://news.bbc.co.uk/2/hi/business/6586679.stm/ (accessed March 4, 2009).

Blizzard Entertainment. http://www.blizzard.com/ (accessed February 25, 2009).

Blue Ocean Strategy. http://www.blueoceanstrategy.com/ (accessed February 25, 2009).

Business Trends Asia. (2007) "Hyundai-Kia 5th largest automaker." July 2. http://www.businesstrendsasia.com/index.php?cat=1:3:54&art=1348/ (accessed August 24, 2009).

BusinessWeek. (2003) "The Samsung way." June 16. http://www.businessweek.com/magazine/content/03_24/b3837001_mz001.htm/ (accessed February 25, 2009).

BusinessWeek. (2008) "Beyond outsourcing to worldsourcing." May 29. http://www.businessweek.com/technology/content/may2008/tc20080529_101827.htm/ (accessed February 27, 2009).

Center for Management Research. (2006) "Tesco's globalization strategies and its success in South Korea." http://www.icmrindia.org/casestudies/catalogue/BusinessStrategy/TescoGlobalizationStrategiesanditsSuccessinSouthKorea.htm/ (accessed March 2, 2009).

DHC. http://www.dhccare.com/ (accessed August 24, 2009).

Dr. Lee's TeaForHealth. http://www.teaforhealth.com/ (accessed February 27, 2009).

Etude. http://www.etudehouse.com/ (accessed February 25, 2009).

Euromonitor International. (2004) "Coffee brews a future in China." September 13. http://www.euromonitor.com/Coffee_brews_a_future_in_China/ (accessed August 24, 2009).

Giordano. http://www.giordano.com.hk/ (accessed February 25, 2009).

Giordano online shopping website. http://hk.e-giordano.com/ (accessed August 24, 2009).

Hong Kong Trader. (2001) "Clothing retailer presses ahead with global expansion." May 1. http://www.hktrader.net/200105/200102/200102s4.htm/ (accessed February 25, 2009).

Hyundai Motor Company. http://worldwide.hyundai.com/ (accessed February 27, 2009).

International Herald Tribune. (2008) "Interconnected we prosper." June 25. http://www.iht.com/articles/2008/06/25/opinion/edamelio.php/ (accessed February 27, 2009).

Isehan. http://www.isehan.info/ (accessed February 25, 2009).

Jiangsu Longliqi Group. http://longliqi.fuzing.com/ (accessed February 25, 2009).

Kanebo. http://www.sensai-cosmetics.com/ (accessed February 25, 2009).

Knowledge@Wharton. (2006) "Michael Porter asks, and answers: why do good managers set bad strategies?" November 1. http://www.knowledge.wharton.upenn.edu/article.cfm?articleid=159/ (accessed August 24, 2009).

Kose. http://www.kose.co.jp/ (accessed February 25, 2009).

Kwintessential. "Cross cultural business blunders." http://www.kwintessential.co.uk/cultural-services/articles/crosscultural-blunders.html/ (accessed February 25, 2009).

Lenovo. http://www.lenovo.com/ (accessed February 27, 2009).

Links999 — Technology and Information Directory. http://www.links999.net/ (accessed August 24, 2009).

Management and Accounting Web. "What is strategy?" http://maaw.info/ArticleSummaries/ArtSumPorter96.htm/ (accessed February 25, 2009).

McDonald's. http://www.mcdonalds.com/ (accessed February 27, 2009).

Mitsubishi Corporation. http://www.mitsubishicorp.com/ (accessed August 24, 2009).

Mitsubishi Corporation: INNOVATION 2007 management plan. http://www.mitsubishicorp.com/jp/en/ir/library/earnings/pdf/200710e_00d.pdf/ (accessed August 24, 2009).

MOPAS (Ministry of Public Administration and Security), South Korea. http://www.mopas.go.kr/ (accessed February 27, 2009).

Nokia Asia Pacific. http://www.nokia-asia.com/ (accessed February 25, 2009).

Organization of Motor Vehicle Manufacturers. (2007) "World ranking of manufacturers." http://www.oica.net/category/production-statistics/ (accessed March 4, 2009).

Palladium Group. http://www.thepalladiumgroup.com/ (accessed February 27, 2009).

Renault. http://www.renault.com/ (accessed February 25, 2009).

Runckel, C. (2005) "Gamers going for the gold in Asia." http://www.business-in-asia.com/electronic_arts_games_asia.htm/ (accessed February 25, 2009).

Sa, E.Y. (2008) "Stanford MBA to learn from Hyundai Motor." Empas online news (October 15). http://news.empas.com/show.tsp/cp_mk/20081005n07974/ (accessed January 10, 2009).

Samsung. http://www.samsung.com/ (accessed February 25, 2009).

Seattle Post-Intelligencer. (2005) "Starbucks adjusts its formula in China." June 16. http://seattlepi.nwsource.com/business/228728_sbuxchina16.html/ (accessed February 25, 2009).

Sharp. http://www.sharp-world.com/ (accessed February 25, 2009).

Shiseido. http://www.shiseido.com/ (accessed February 25, 2009).

Singtel. http://www.singtel.com/ (accessed February 25, 2009).

Sinopec. http://english.sinopec.com/ (accessed August 24, 2009).

Smith, M.K. (2003) "Michael Polanyi and tacit knowledge." Reproduced from *the encyclopedia of informal education.* http://www.infed.org/thinkers/polanyi.htm/ (accessed February 21, 2009).

South Atlantic Fishery Management Council. http://www.safmc.net/ (accessed August 24, 2009).

Stradley, L. (2004) "History and legends of hamburgers." http://www.whatscookingamerica.net/History/HamburgerHistory.htm/ (accessed March 1, 2009).

Tata Tea. http://www.tatatea.com/ (accessed February 27, 2009).

Temasek Holdings. http://www.temasekholdings.com.sg/ (accessed February 25, 2009).

The Bank of Tokyo-Mitsubishi UFJ. http://www.bk.mufg.jp/english/ (accessed February 27, 2009).

The Chosun Ilbo. (2001) "Moon Kook-hyun, CEO of Yuhan-Kimberly." January 19. http://english.chosun.com/w21data/html/news/200101/200101190405.html/ (accessed February 25, 2009).

The Economist. (2007a) "The forbidden latte." July 17. http://www.economist.com/business/displaystory.cfm?story_id=E1_JQJRSSG/ (accessed February 25, 2009).

The Economist. (2007b) "Revving up." October 11. http://www.economist.com/specialreports/displaystory.cfm?story_id=E1_JJNRNVJ/ (accessed February 25, 2009).

The Economist. (2007c) "A wobble on the road to the top." November 8. http://www.economist.com/business/displaystory.cfm?story_id=10097827/ (accessed February 25, 2009).

The Economist. (2008a) "Wal-Mart: always low prices." February 21. http://www.economist.com/business/displaystory.cfm?story_id=10727908/ (accessed August 24, 2009).

The Economist. (2008b) "Asian invasion." June 26. http://www.economist.com/business/displaystory.cfm?story_id=11632829/ (accessed February 25, 2009).

The Economist. (2008c) "Charge!" May 8. http://www.economist.com/finance/displaystory.cfm?story_id=13136627/ (accessed February 25, 2009).

The Hindu Business Line. (2006a) "'Blue ocean' strategy helps HCL Tech bag DSG deal." January 20. http://www.thehindubusinessline.com/2006/01/20/stories/2006012001880600.htm/ (accessed February 25, 2009).

The Hindu Business Line. (2006b) "We are trying to dominate the multi-service space." July 2. http://www.thehindubusinessline.com/iw/2006/07/02/stories/2006070202420700.htm/ (accessed February 25, 2009).

The Korea Herald. (2004) "Time to talk to Yuhan-Kimberly." September 21. http://www.koreaherald.co.kr/archives/result_contents.asp/ (accessed August 24, 2009).

The Mac Observer. http://www.macobserver.com/ (accessed February 25, 2009).

The New York Times. (2002) "Renault rolls the dice on two auto projects abroad." August 29. http://www.nytimes.com/2002/08/29/business/renault-rolls-the-dice-on-two-auto-projects-abroad.html?scp=1&sq=Renault+rolls+the+dice+on+two+auto+projects+abroad&st=nyt/ (accessed August 24, 2009).

The New York Times. (2004) "Infighting left Sony behind." April 19. http://www.nytimes.com/2005/09/15/technology/15sony.html?scp=1&sq=Infighting%20left%20sony%20behind&st=Search/ (accessed February 25, 2009).

The New York Times. (2005a) "Starbucks aims to alter China's taste in caffeine." May 21. http://www.nytimes.com/2005/05/21/business/worldbusiness/21coffee.html?scp=1&sq=Starbucks%20Aims%20to%20Alter%20China%27s%20Taste%20in%20Caffeine&st=cse/ (accessed February 25, 2009).

The New York Times. (2005b) "Not to be outdone — the new urban spa." August 11. http://www.nytimes.com/2005/08/11/fashion/thursdaystyles/11skin.html?_r=1&scp=1&sq=Not%20to%20be%20outdone%20-%20the%20new%20urban%20spa&st=cse/ (accessed February 27, 2009).

The New York Times. (2006a) "Wal-Mart selling stores and leaving South Korea." May 23. http://www.nytimes.com/2006/05/23/business/worldbusiness/23shop.html?scp=1&sq=Wal%20Mart%20selling%20stores%20and%20leaving%20south%20korea&st=Search/ (accessed August 24, 2009).

The New York Times. (2006b) "Wal-Mart's overseas push can be lost in translation." August 2. http://www.nytimes.com/2006/08/02/business/worldbusiness/02iht-walmart.2363495.html?_r=1&scp=1&sq=Wal-mart's%20overseas%20push%20can%20be%20lost%20in%20translation&st=cse/ (accessed August 24, 2009).

The New York Times. (2006c) "Online game, made in U.S., seizes the globe." September 5. http://www.nytimes.com/2006/09/05/technology/05wow.html?_r=1&scp=1&sq=Online%20Game%20Seizes%20the%20Globe&st=cse/ (accessed February 25, 2009).

The New York Times. (2006d) "A gamble on LCD TV's meant survival for Sharp." March 22. http://www.nytimes.com/2006/03/22/technology/22sharp.html?scp=1&sq=A%20Gamble%20on%20LCD%20TVs&st=Search/ (accessed February 25, 2009).

The New York Times. (2007) "Bits." December 17. http://bits.blogs.nytimes.com/?scp=1-spot&sq=Bits&st/ (accessed February 25, 2009).

The New York Times. (2008a) "My son the blogger — an M.D. trades medicine for Apple rumors." July 21. http://www.nytimes.com/2008/07/21/technology/21blogger.html?scp=1&sq=My%20Son%20the%20Blogger&st=cse/ (accessed February 25, 2009).

The New York Times. (2008b) "Sony sets a new course to bolster electronics." June 27. http://www.nytimes.com/2008/06/27/technology/27sony.html?scp=2&sq=Sony%20Sets%20a%20New%20Course%20to%20Bolster%20Electronics&st=Search/ (accessed February 25, 2009).

Toffler, A. and Fisher, L.M. (2006) "Alvin Toffler: the thought leader interview." *strategy+business* (Winter). http://www.strategy-business.com/press/16635507/06408/ (accessed February 21, 2009).

Toyota. http://www.toyota.co.jp/en/ (accessed February 25, 2009).

Toyota Supplier. http://www.toyotasupplier.com/ (accessed February 25, 2009).

Wal-Mart. http://www.walmart.com/ (accessed August 24, 2009).

Wired. (2002) "The civil war inside Sony." February 11. http://www.wired.com/wired/archive/11.02/sony_pr.html/ (accessed February 25, 2009).

Wizard Robotics. http://www.wizardrobotics.com/ (accessed February 27, 2009).

World Advertising Research Center. (2009) "Nokia is top digital brand in Asia." April 7. http://www.warc.com/News/TopNews.asp?ID=24911/ (accessed August 24, 2009).

World Economic Forum. (2007) "The Global Competitiveness Report 2007–2008." http://www.weforum.org/en/initiatives/gcp/Global%20Competitiveness%20Report/PastReports/index.htm/ (accessed February 27, 2009).

Yuhan-Kimberly. http://www.yuhan-kimberly.co.kr/ (accessed February 25, 2009).

Zhejiang Tea Import and Export Company. http://www.chinagreentea.com/ (accessed February 27, 2009).

Index